Urban Disaster Resilienc

Accelerating urbanization worldwide means more urban-centered disasters. Floods, earthquakes, storms and conflicts affecting densely populated areas produce significant losses in lives, livelihoods and the built environment, especially in comparison to rural areas. Poor urban dwellers, almost always the most vulnerable, too often bear the brunt. Aid agencies and urban professionals have been slowly adapting to these new conditions, but older models and practices hinder the most effective engagements.

Drawing directly from the experiences of urban disasters in the Philippines, Chile, India, Thailand, Iraq, Haiti and Nepal, among other countries, *Urban Disaster Resilience* brings to light new collaborations and techniques for addressing the challenges of urban disasters in the coming years. Chapters range from country-specific case studies to more synthetic frameworks in order to promote innovative thinking and practical solutions.

Edited by David Sanderson, Jerold S. Kayden and Julia Leis, this book is a crucial read for humanitarian and disaster specialists, urban planners and designers, architects, landscape architects, housing and economic development professionals, and students interested in the subject, whether based in non-governmental organizations, local, state or national governments, international agencies, private firms, or the academy.

David Sanderson is the Inaugural Judith Neilson Chair of Architecture at the University of New South Wales (UNSW), Australia. He has held senior posts in both NGO and academic sectors, and has carried out work for a number of NGOs and donor organizations. In recent years he has led post-disaster reviews in Haiti, Pakistan, Bangladesh, India, the Philippines and Nepal.

Jerold S. Kayden is the Frank Backus Williams Professor of Urban Planning and Design at the Harvard University Graduate School of Design. He has consulted for the World Bank, USAID and UNDP, worldwide, and served as principal investigator of the Harvard-Netherlands Project on Climate Change, Water, Land Development, and Adaptation. He is an affiliated faculty member of the Harvard Humanitarian Initiative (HHI).

Julia Leis is a humanitarian relief and development worker. She has completed assignments in the Philippines, Gaza, Burkina Faso and Thailand. She holds a Master of Arts from The Fletcher School of Law and Diplomacy at Tufts University and a degree in Foreign Service from Georgetown University.

"*Urban Disaster Resilience* could not have been more timely. Following global processes in 2015, including the newly adopted Sustainable Development Goals, and the World Humanitarian Summit and Habitat III in 2016, this book has successfully captured a broad understanding of what needs to happen for resilience to be achieved. It will be an important introduction and reference to the subject and should be recommended reading for students of architecture, development and humanitarian studies, as well as policy makers and practitioners alike."

Jemilah Mahmood, Under Secretary General, IFRC (Partnerships)

"This is a unique and timely volume of innovations and insights into the theory and practice of building urban resilience. Drawing on international experience, and illustrated throughout with case examples, its authors argue the value of informality and of engaging civil society when planning for the challenges of humanitarian crisis. An excellent resource book for teaching, for research and for practice."

Nabeel Hamdi, Emeritus Professor, Oxford Brookes University

"*Urban Disaster Resilience* is a must read for those trying to catalyze resilience building in humanitarian and development assistance. It warns that humanitarian assistance is not only failing to meet the needs of an increasingly urban planet, but that its lack of a sense of space and place makes it ill equipped to do so without dramatic change."

Nancy Kete, Managing Director, The Rockefeller Foundation

Urban Disaster Resilience

New Dimensions from International Practice in the Built Environment

Edited by David Sanderson,
Jerold S. Kayden and Julia Leis

NEW YORK AND LONDON

First published 2016
by Routledge
711 Third Avenue, New York, NY 10017

and by Routledge
2 Park Square, Milton Park, Abingdon, Oxon OX14 4RN

Routledge is an imprint of the Taylor & Francis Group, an informa business

Library of Congress Cataloging in Publication Data
Names: Sanderson, David (Professor of disaster resilience), editor. | Kayden, Jerold S., editor. | Leis, Julia, editor.Title: Urban disaster resilience : new dimensions from international practice in the built environment / edited by David Sanderson, Jerold S. Kayden and Julia Leis.Description: New York, NY : Routledge, 2016.Identifiers: LCCN 2015038758| ISBN 9781138849624 (hardcover) | ISBN 9781138849631 (pbk.) | ISBN 9781315725420 (ebook)Subjects: LCSH: City planning. | Disasters. | Disaster relief. | Risk management. | Sustainable urban development.Classification: LCC HT166 .U7129 2016 | DDC 307.1/216--dc23LC record available at http://lccn.loc.gov/2015038758

ISBN: 978-1138-84962-4 (hbk)
ISBN: 978-1138-84963-1 (pbk)
ISBN: 978-1315-72542-0 (ebk)

Typeset in Galliard and Gill
by Saxon Graphics Ltd, Derby

Contents

Figures

Figures

Plates

Contributors

Book editors

David Sanderson is the inaugural Judith Neilson Chair of Architecture and Design at the University of New South Wales (UNSW), Australia. He has held senior posts in both NGO and academic sectors and is a member of several NGO boards and committees, including the Norwegian Refugee Council (NRC) and the Humanitarian Innovation Fund (HIF). Sanderson has published a number of articles and papers concerning urban livelihoods, shelter and disaster risk reduction. He has carried out a number of assignments for NGOs and donors across the world, and in recent years has led post-disaster reviews in Haiti, Pakistan, Bangladesh, India, the Philippines and Nepal. He was trained in architecture and holds a PhD in urban livelihoods and vulnerability. Between 2013 and 2014 Sanderson was a Visiting Professor at Harvard University's Graduate School of Design.

Jerold S. Kayden is the Frank Backus Williams Professor of Urban Planning and Design at the Harvard University Graduate School of Design, where he served as co-chair of the Urban Planning and Design Department. An urban planner and lawyer, he has advised governments, NGOs and private developers worldwide on land, housing, real estate, infrastructure and environmental issues. Kayden has been consultant to the World Bank, the International Finance Corporation, the United States Agency for International Development and the United Nations Development Programme, among others. From 1992 to 1994, he was Senior Advisor for Land Reform and Privatization to the government of Ukraine on behalf of USAID/PADCO. He recently served as principal investigator for a multi-year Netherlands-funded Harvard-Netherlands project on climate change, water, land development and adaptation. He is an affiliated faculty member of the Harvard Humanitarian Initiative (HHI).

Julia Leis is an international humanitarian relief and development worker. She has completed assignments in the Philippines, Gaza, Burkina Faso and Thailand. Her research centers on urban disaster risk reduction, information and communications technology (ICT) in emergencies and development, and sustainable agriculture. She holds a Master of Arts from The Fletcher School of Law and Diplomacy at Tufts University and a Bachelor of Science in Foreign Service from Georgetown University.

Chapter authors

Pablo Allard is Dean of the Faculty of Architecture and Arts, Universidad Del Desarrollo in Concepción and Santiago, Chile. He is currently principal partner at Urbanica architecture and urban design, director at Patagonia Sur dedicated to conservation and sustainable development in Chilean Patagonia and director at Nueva Via consultants focusing on the development of transportation infrastructure projects. Allard was a founding member of the *'Do-Tank'* Elemental, and participated in the post 2010 Chile earthquake recovery as National Urban Reconstruction Coordinator at the Ministry of Housing and Urban Development. Alongside his academic and professional work, he is a columnist for the newspaper *La Tercera* and has served as board member of the National Council for Culture and the Arts and member of the Presidential Commission for Urban Mobility and the Presidential Commission for the New Urban Development Policy.

Avar Almukhtar is a practicing Iraqi architect from Kurdistan. He has been involved in a variety of projects at different scales in Kurdistan, including regional planning, master planning and architectural design for housing complexes and local architecture and urban design projects. Almukhtar holds a bachelor degree in Architecture from Erbil, Iraq and an MA in Urban Design from Oxford Brookes University in the United Kingdom. He is currently pursuing a PhD in Urban Design at Oxford Brookes University, exploring the concept of place-identity in historic cities in Iraq and the Middle East.

María Ignacia Arrasate is engaged in the design and implementation of sustainable affordable housing projects and urban planning for post-disaster recovery in Chile. She began her career in the construction sector as an architect. She holds a professional degree in architecture from the Pontifical Catholic University of Chile, as well as a Masters in advanced architectural design from Columbia University. She recently graduated from the Master in Design Studies program at Harvard's Graduate School of Design, with a concentration in risk and resilience, and is a research associate at Harvard's Zofnass Program for Sustainable Infrastructure focusing on promoting sustainable practices and improving resilience conditions across Latin America.

Mihir Bhatt leads the independent All India Disaster Mitigation Institute (AIDMI) recognized as a Centre of Excellence by the UN Office for South-South Cooperation. AIDMI has worked across 35 cities and 49 districts in nine states of India as well as seven countries in Asia Pacific on reducing disaster and climate change risk since 1995. Bhatt is a member of several government and civil society committees and task forces in India and abroad. Educated at MIT (USA), he has received the Russell Train WWF Fellowship, Ashoka Fellowship, and Eisenhower Fellowship. He is a Senior Fellow of the Harvard Humanitarian Initiative and FXB Center for Health and Human Rights and advisor to the Climate and Development Knowledge Network.

Camillo Boano is an architect, urbanist and educator. He is Senior Lecturer at The Bartlett Development Planning Unit, University College London (UCL), where he directs the MSc in Building and Urban Design in Development. He is also co-director of the UCL Urban Laboratory. Boano has over 20 years of experience in research, design consultancies and development work in South America, the Middle East, Eastern Europe and South East Asia. His research interests revolve around encounters between critical theory and radical philosophy with urban and architectural design processes where collective agency and politics encounter urban narratives and aesthetics, especially those emerging in informal, disaster-related and contested urbanisms.

Georgia Butina Watson is Professor, Research Tutor and Research Director of Urban Design at Oxford Brookes University, Oxford, UK. Her professional background is in architectural theory and history, urban planning and urban design. Her academic and practice-based expertise includes research and consultancy work in urban regeneration, urban morphology, place-making, place-identity, community development and sustainable and resilient cities. She has an extensive portfolio of community and regeneration projects in the UK and overseas and has published a number of research papers and books, including *Identity by Design* and *Designing Sustainable Cities in the Developing World.*

John de Boer is a Senior Policy Adviser with the United Nations University's Centre for Policy Research. He specializes in research that identifies and responds to the multiple dimensions of vulnerability in urban contexts. He has published widely on issues related to urban violence, urban disaster, conflict and organized crime. De Boer has worked for Canada's International Development Research Centre as well as the Canadian International Development Agency, where he was Team Leader for Governance on the Afghanistan and Pakistan Task Force. De Boer has been a Postdoctoral Fellow at Stanford University and a lecturer at the University of California, Berkeley. He holds a PhD in Area Studies from the University of Tokyo.

Joanna Friedman is a humanitarian professional specializing in cash- and market-based interventions, livelihoods and economic recovery. She has worked for non-governmental organizations and UN agencies in Haiti, Sudan, Central African Republic and Democratic Republic of Congo, among others. She was a Fulbright Scholar in Senegal, holds a Master of International Affairs degree from the School of International and Public Affairs at Columbia University and has a Bachelor of Arts degree from Tufts University. She is currently a Cash and Protection Advisor at the headquarters of the United Nations High Commissioner for Refugees.

Alison Killing is an architect and urban designer based in Rotterdam, the Netherlands, where she runs her own design studio, Killing Architects. She holds an MA in Development Practice and has worked for the past five years on the subject of how cities might be better rebuilt after disaster, as part of the (re)constructing the city project. She is a TED Fellow.

Ronak Patel is an Assistant Professor of Medicine at Stanford University and an emergency physician. Patel's research focuses primarily on the challenges and opportunities presented by rapid urbanization for humanitarian crises, vulnerable populations and their health. His research focuses on exposing risks and developing tools and interventions to mitigate and address these risks. His recent work includes projects on micro-insurance for disasters, slum upgrading, urban violence, social cohesion and resilience, and vulnerability mapping in urban slums.

Marianne F. Potvin is a PhD candidate in urban planning at Harvard University, where she studies the linkages between humanitarian action, urbanization and the shifting patterns of forced migration. She is a licensed architect and has carried out several humanitarian assignments with the International Committee of the Red Cross, ACTED and other NGOs in Iraq, Afghanistan and Chad.

Theo Schilderman is a Dutch architect with over 40 years of experience in low-income housing and post-disaster reconstruction. He is involved in research, writing, lecturing and management of projects and programs in the South as well as the North. He has worked for COOPIBO, IHS, Practical Action and BSHF in the past, and is now a consultant. He has written numerous articles and was the editor, with Michal Lyons (2010) of *Building Back Better*, and with El Parker (2014) of *Still Standing?*

Pamela Sitko has been working in disaster, development and conflict settings since 2005. Her experience spans across over 20 countries in areas such as capacity building, disaster simulation training, humanitarian deployments and media work for agencies including the Canadian Consortium of Humanitarian Agencies, Habitat for Humanity International, IFRC, Plan International, the World Food Programme and World Vision International. Sitko is completing a PhD in urban disaster resilience from the Urban Planning and Design department at Oxford Brookes University in the UK. Currently, she is working as World Vision International's Global Urban Disaster Management Advisor.

David Smith is a PhD candidate at the Faculty of Architecture and Fine Art at the Norwegian University of Science and Technology (NTNU). His research investigates marketplaces' impacts on urban resilience after disasters. Qualified as an architect, Smith graduated from Oxford Brookes University with a Masters in Development and Emergency Practice. His thesis was shortlisted for the Royal Institute of British Architects President's Award for Research in 2012.

Victoria Stodart is a specialist in housing, land and property (HLP) rights with a particular focus on post-disaster situations. She spent a year in the Philippines for the Typhoon Haiyan response where she juggled her roles as HLP advisor and National Coordinator for the Shelter Cluster (co-led by IFRC). She holds a Masters degree in Development and Emergency Practice from Oxford Brookes University. Stodart is also a qualified lawyer and spent ten years working in the private sector in the UK and Asia Pacific. She joined IFRC in January 2012 to work primarily on addressing regulatory barriers to the provision of emergency and transitional shelter after naturally triggered disasters.

Foreword

This book results from a three-day conference, 'Design for Urban Disaster,' held at Harvard University in May 2014. The conference was hosted by Harvard's South Asia Institute and co-sponsored by Habitat for Humanity, the Harvard Graduate School of Design, the Harvard Humanitarian Initiative, the International Federation of Red Cross and Red Crescent Societies, and Oxford Brookes University.

Some 140 people participated in the conference, including individuals from aid agencies, NGOs, foundations, think tanks, donor organizations and consultancies, academic institutions, and design and planning firms. It was convened to explore the growing challenge of naturally triggered disasters and conflict in urban areas and to identify effective approaches to address these challenges. Over 30 papers were presented, from which 12 invited submissions were subsequently developed into the chapters that form the body of this book.

The conference took place at a time when engaging in urban disaster for many is still something relatively new: the 2010 Haiti earthquake, which badly affected that nation's capital, Port-au-Prince, was for many aid agencies in particular a wakeup call, because the urban context requires different skills, strategies, techniques and understandings as compared to disaster affecting rural areas from which many such organizations have honed their skills. Conversely, many urban professionals, such as planners and architects, are often left out of conversations with aid agencies concerning urban disaster response. This conference sought to bring these two worlds together.

As this book's title suggests, the intention here is to explore 'urban' and 'disaster' within the emerging framework of 'resilience,' which concerns itself with measures taken by different actors before and after a rapid onset event such as an earthquake, flood or typhoon. 'New dimensions' relates to larger themes, such as space, time and power identified within the Introduction, as well as new dimensions emerging from the case examples from over 20 countries examined by the chapter authors.

This book appears at a time when thinking in urban disaster resilience is rapidly evolving. While the ideas and approaches presented here may be fresh for now, we fully expect that they will be replaced by fresher ideas, perhaps sooner than later. That is not to say that you should not read this book. It is our hope, and the test of this book, that the lessons within it contribute to better thinking, as well as actions, that improve our maturing response to the growing threat of urban disaster.

In the making of this book we have many thanks to offer. The chapter authors responded cheerfully and with alacrity to our many suggestions, rendering our lives as the book editors that much easier. The 2014 conference sponsors mentioned above set the stage for the book, and our editors at Routledge, especially Judith Newlin and Alanna Donaldson, kept us on track and schedule. We also thank Richard Bauer, Samuel Carter, Jo Da Silva, Reinhard Goethert, Nancy Kete, Ann Lee, Rahul Mehrotra, Andrew Natsios, Graham Saunders, Kip Scheidler, Peter Walker, Dewald Van Niekerk and Steve Weir for their various contributions. Finally, we want to thank Dr. Stephanie Kayden, a leading humanitarian physician based at the Brigham and Women's Hospital and Harvard University for making the initial connection between us that ultimately led to both conference and book.

David Sanderson, Jerold S. Kayden and Julia Leis
September 2015

Abbreviations

ABA	Area-based approach
ACF	Action Against Hunger
ADB	African Development Bank
AIDMI	All India Disaster Mitigation Institute
ALNAP	Active Learning Network for Accountability and Performance
BACIP	Building and Construction Improvement Program
BBC	British Broadcasting Corporation
BCP	Business continuity planning
BMA	Bangkok Metropolitan Authority
CaLP	Cash Learning Partnership
CAS	Complex adaptive systems
CBO	Community-based organization
CCIMS	Common Crisis Information Management System
CCCM	Camp coordination and camp nanagement
CODI	Community Organizations Development Institute
CESCR	UN Committee on Economic, Cultural and Social Rights
CRED	Centre for Research on the Epidemiology of Disasters
CRF	Calamity Relief Fund
DEC	Disasters Emergency Committee
DFID	Department for International Development
DMP	Disaster mitigation and preparedness
DRR	Disaster risk reduction
DRRM	Disaster Risk Reduction and Management
DWF	Development Workshop France
EMMA	Emergency Market Mapping and Analysis
FAO	Food and Agriculture Organization
HFA	Hyogo Framework for Action
HHI	Harvard Humanitarian Initiative
HICT	Humanitarian information and communication technologies
HIF	Humanitarian Innovation Fund
HLP	Housing, land and property rights
IASC	Inter-Agency Standing Committee
ICRC	International Committee of the Red Cross

IDMC	Internal Displacement Monitoring Centre
IDNDR	International Decade for Natural Disaster Reduction
IDP	Internally displaced person
IFRC	International Federation of Red Cross and Red Crescent Societies
IIASA	International Institute for Applied Systems Analysis
IPCC	Intergovernmental Panel on Climate Change
IPT	Territorial Planning Instruments
IRC	International Rescue Committee
IRDA	Insurance Regulatory and Development Authority
KDP	Kurdistan Democratic Party
KRG	Kurdistan Regional Government
LRRD	Linking relief, recovery and development
M4P	Making Markets Work for the Poor
MERS	Minimum Economic Recovery Standards
MINVU	Ministry of Housing and Urban Planning
MMS	Moment Magnitude Scale
NBZ	No build zone
NCCF	National Calamity Contingency Fund
NDMA	National Disaster Management Authority
NGO	Non-governmental organization
NIDM	National Institute of Disaster Management
NIUA	National Institute of Urban Affairs
NRC	Norwegian Refugee Council
NRRC	Nepal Risk Reduction Consortium
OCHA	United Nations Office for the Coordination of Humanitarian Affairs
ODI	Overseas Development Institute
OECD	Organisation for Economic Co-operation and Development
OFDA	Office of US Foreign Disaster Assistance
OHCHR	Office of the High Commissioner for Human Rights
PDNA	Post Disaster Needs Assessment
ROSCA	Rotating savings and credit association
SDG	Sustainability Development Goal
SHG	Self-help group
SSP	Satellite Sentinel Project
STS	Science, technology and societies studies
SWAD	Society for Women Action Development
UNDP	United Nations Development Programme
UNHCHR	United Nations High Commissioner for Human Rights
UNHCR	United Nations High Commissioner for Refugees
UNISDR	United Nations Office for Disaster Risk Reduction
UNODC	United Nations Office on Drugs and Crime
USAID	United States Agency for International Development
WASH	Water, sanitation and hygiene
WHS	World Humanitarian Summit

Introduction

Introduction

Urban disaster resilience

New dimensions from international practice in the built environment

David Sanderson

Introduction: a disaster strikes a city

Imagine the following scenario. A fast growing city of some 500,000 people located in the hills of a middle-income country experiences a large earthquake. Within less than a minute hundreds of buildings have collapsed, all power is disrupted and roads are rendered impassable. The earthquake triggers a landslide that sweeps away surrounding villages and damages a dam, which threatens to break. The city hall building, the place where those designated to manage a disaster response work, has collapsed. Within the first few minutes dazed survivors begin to realize what has happened; immediately, those who can help those who are trapped. Others who are injured hope for help.

By nightfall thousands of people are sleeping outside, in makeshift tents and whatever else is at hand. Local non-governmental organizations (NGOs), churches, mosques and temples are providing food and water. Some individuals and organizations are able to get a signal on mobile phones while others can pick up national radio, which is reporting that the national government is appealing for international assistance.

One week later, many international aid agencies have arrived and are setting up operations. The United Nations and others are calling meetings to coordinate immediate relief supplies. 'Cluster' meetings are held, mostly attended by international organizations, to share information and approaches. Local businesses are missing from these meetings. The city mayor is attempting to organize a response, but there is confusion concerning who knows what, and many government staff members were killed or otherwise affected by the disaster. National government representatives have arrived and say they are in charge. Much of the city is in ruins and people are still in tents, often in makeshift camps. For the 80,000 poorest people in the city who were living in slums and squatter settlements before, there is little help – they have heard that there may be help for property owners, but that is all.

Six months later, the recovery is patchy: in some places NGOs and government employees are working, while other places have been all but ignored. Commercial districts are all but fully recovered. Other areas are taking more time. Many individuals are still living in temporary settlements in tents, often located in the small number of public parks. A large new temporary settlement established ten kilometers out of the city still exists: it is not clear whether this will be shut down by government or allowed to continue.

Media reports on the first anniversary of the earthquake are critical of what has transpired; many say that too much aid has been wasted. They ask why in some areas the city had recovered, while in other areas (especially the poor neighborhoods) little has changed. Debris is still everywhere and too many buildings are still unsafe. One report warns of temporary camps becoming permanent ('creating new ghettos') while another points to the failure to implement building codes as the cause of the disaster in the first place. The national press bemoans the large and confusing number of organizations ('what are they all doing here?') while all agree that the government and aid agencies were unready for this disaster. As one aid official says, 'It was as if the disaster took us by surprise. But there was no surprise; it was always going to happen.'

This after-disaster scenario is all too familiar to many humanitarian professionals: there are many actors; the landscape is complicated; who should be in charge and who actually holds power is unclear or in conflict; assumptions about what people need and what they can actually do themselves may be inaccurate; long-term considerations may be forgone in the immediate rush to respond; and opportunities that urban areas inherently present for recovery may be ignored.

Honest problem identification is surely necessary, but not sufficient in improving our responses to disasters. Beyond diagnosis, what are the insights emerging from current practices engaged with urban disasters? This chapter seeks to frame this question, first by discussing urban resilience, and then by exploring three 'dimensions' from international practice, namely: physical space (with regard to settlements and planning); power (concerning using businesses, markets and cash for better post-disaster recovery); and time (relating here to the need to balance aid responses with the pace of urban change).

Taking a resilience perspective

Resilience is a current understanding employed by many aid agencies to frame the links between responses to chronic conditions (developmental challenges such as slum and squatter settlements) and acute events, such as rapid onset disasters. Previous understandings over the last 40 years or so include disaster mitigation and preparedness (DMP), linking relief, recovery and development (LRRD), livelihoods (in the developmental meaning championed by Chambers and Conway[1]) and more recently disaster risk reduction (DRR). Much therefore that has been known for a long time has been repackaged. We have known for instance that disasters are worse where vulnerability is more prominent, and that vulnerability is a consequence of societal issues such as weak governance, poverty, economic conditions and corruption.

Resilience as an aspirational paradigm, however, has elements of newness within it and may provide opportunities that previous paradigms may not have provided. While in recent years much energy has gone into arguing the finer nuances of a definition of resilience (many different definitions are currently 'on the market'), this level of discussion misses the point – a definition that serves to provide a good enough understanding across disciplines, cultures and political and practical persuasions is, indeed, good enough. The Rockefeller Foundation's 100 Resilient Cities program provides one such definition, stating that resilience is,

> the capacity of individuals, communities and systems to survive, adapt, and grow in the face of stress and shocks, and even transform when conditions require it. Building resilience is about making people, communities and systems better prepared to withstand catastrophic events – both natural and manmade – and able to bounce back more quickly and emerge stronger from these shocks and stresses.
>
> (Rockefeller Foundation, 2015)

Let us unpack some of the advantages to the concept. First, and most important, it is readily understandable by politicians as much as by practitioners, academics and others. *We get it.* Given that so many failings (and opportunities) for better disaster reduction lie with political decision-making – at every level, from community to nationally and beyond – anything that builds improved collaborations in this area (and a lingua franca in this instance cannot be bad) is welcomed.

Second, resilience is a positive word that builds in notions of what people and societies can do, supplanting the enervating focus of what has been done to them. This goes to the very heart of many failings in response to disasters: that people are helpless victims, while in fact affected people are mostly in the driving seat of recovery, given that the majority of those caught up in disaster receive little if any help from humanitarian response (IFRC, 2013). This mistake is evident in aid language: for example the commonly agreed Post Disaster Needs Assessment (PDNA), used among a range of aid agencies, does not include in its title the word 'capacities' alongside 'needs,' an aspect long recognized as essential to effective recovery (Anderson and Woodrow, 1989).

Third, resilience resonates differently in the urban sphere. With one of its strongest roots[2] emerging from engineering, the link of resilience to physical form should not be underestimated. This is important for urban action given that almost all humanitarian aid thinking derives from rural experience. This history has had significant consequences in terms of the assumptions and practices of international aid agencies. To take just one example, the provision of post-disaster single-story temporary houses in dense urban neighborhoods causes more problems than the solutions it seeks to provide (Sanderson et al., 2014). The 2010 Haiti earthquake, with its urban-centered damage, perhaps provided a turning point for many agencies that quickly discovered that the urban landscape is a different world than the rural one. Put simply, agencies were no longer working 'in the field,' but rather, 'in the neighborhood.'

Within Rockefeller's definition of resilience, three levels of engagement are identified: individuals, communities and systems. The first two, individuals and communities, have been long-held as the focus for humanitarian action and remain the focus, for example in the drive for improved downward accountability as recognized in the recently agreed Core Humanitarian Standard on Quality and Accountability, whose central focus is 'communities and people affected by crisis' (CHS, 2015). Communities, however, have been thought to be different in urban areas compared to rural ones, most notably concerning a perception of the relative lack of social capital in towns and cities, i.e. that urban dwellers are alienated and may not know their neighbors, etc. However for many urban communities, and especially those where their members rely on each other for mutual support, including for borrowing and lending money, this is not the case (Sitko, chapter 5). Furthermore in towns and cities communities can be extended beyond the geographical to include communities of practice, for instance those bound by similar economic or social activity, such as migrant workers or taxi drivers. Communities therefore are not just spatially bound but are often linked through activity.

The third level, systems, has particular resonance for towns and cities, but is discussed much less (if at all) in humanitarian action. A systems approach seeks to make sense of chaos, complexity and interdependent activities, and as such is well suited to working in the messy reality that is city life. The development of complex adaptive systems (CAS) lends particular value, as 'dynamic systems able to adapt in and evolve with a changing environment' (Chan, 2001). Given rapid urban growth, which for many lower-income vulnerable urban dwellers is chaotic and unplanned, interpreting aspects of daily living, such as shopping, work patterns and informal trade, healthcare and informal housing construction, through a CAS lens provides humanitarian practitioners with new approaches for interventions spanning post-disaster assessment (examples of this in current practice include the roll-out of the Emergency Market Mapping and Analysis – EMMA – Toolkit and the Rapid Assessment for Markets – RAM – tool) to pre-disaster preparedness planning, such as planning a sectoral health intervention based on knowledge of formal and informal healthcare.

Resilience is concerned about pre-disaster actions (at least) as much as it is about post-disaster response. As the second sentence from the Rockefeller definition of resilience states, 'Building resilience is about making people, communities and systems better prepared to withstand catastrophic events – both natural and manmade – and able to bounce back more quickly and emerge stronger from these shocks and stresses.' Pre-disaster risk reduction has always been the poor relation within the totality of humanitarian action: post-disaster relief is high profile and unlocks large sums of cash, whereas successful prevention measures go largely unnoticed. This has been long recognized as a problem, and efforts over several decades by a range of actors have sought to highlight this imbalance, with to date limited success.

A sobering example is provided by efforts over many years to prepare Nepal's Kathmandu Valley, home to some two and a half million people and one of the fastest urbanizing centers in South Asia, to the inevitability of earthquake. Initiatives included high-level programs such as the Nepal Risk Reduction Consortium (NRRC)[3] and innumerable efforts of a large number of international and national NGOs. The 7.8 Magnitude earthquake of 25 April 2015 in Gorkha District and subsequent earthquake of May 12 close to Mount Everest killed just under 9,000 people and injured over 22,000, with an estimated economic loss of around one-third of Gross Domestic Product (GDP) (Government of Nepal, 2015). Three of the 14 earthquake-affected districts were in the urban Kathmandu Valley. What then was the benefit of preparedness planning? Many of the governmental and humanitarian response mechanisms (such as Clusters and the Government's Central Disaster Relief Committee) were implemented quickly. However, too little had been put in place that could have reduced the scale of the disaster. Two years before the earthquake, in 2013, the former United Nations Resident Representative in Nepal, Robert Piper, wrote that 'no one is kicking the tires' of the 12 antiquated fire engines, and that, concerning the perilous state of many of Kathmandu's buildings, 'Underpaid, transient civil servants are responsible for certifying that new building projects are "to code", but they would have to get out from behind their desks to see that the designs they have certified on paper do not remotely match the actual construction' (Piper, 2013). Piper noted that the key problem is the lack of political interest within government to unite to address seriously the threat of disaster: 'the real game-changer will only come about when risk reduction measures align with governance reforms. And when "duty of care" enters the political lexicon of the country concerned' (Piper, 2013).

New dimensions from practice

Noting the complexity of urban disaster, and the need for the implementation of a resilience-based understanding of events before and after disaster, the remainder of this chapter discusses three dimensions: physical space, power and time.

Physical space – settlements, planning and humanitarian action

In humanitarian practice the phrase 'physical space' is seldom heard or used. In examining the practices of planners and designers in urban disaster situations, Killing and Boano (chapter 2) make the observations that the language and various approaches of humanitarian practitioners and those trained in physical/spatial studies – planners, architects and engineers – are very different. The same may be said with regard to tools used. Killing and Boano note that whereas planners may use maps and diagrams to collect and present information, many of those within aid agencies may prefer spreadsheets or 'Word' documents. The very tools that urban planners and designers use in town and city planning may not be the default tools used by agencies tasked with engaging in post-disaster urban recovery. This also touches on a wider issue, also observed by Killing and Boano, which is the frequent omission of urban design – and urban designers – as part of humanitarian urban practice. Urban design is for instance not recognized within the humanitarian Cluster system, whereas shelter is.

Recognizing these deficiencies, and the growing need to respond to urban disasters with appropriate urban tools, there are positive signs of the emergence of better practice. For some time the United States Agency for International Development's Office of US Foreign Disaster Assistance (USAID/OFDA) has promoted the idea of shelter *and settlements*, i.e. that in considering post-disaster shelter interventions (in rural and urban areas) it is also necessary to consider the wider spatial needs of 'settlement-based assistance' (USAID/OFDA, 2013). This is also echoed elsewhere, for example in the IFRC's Shelter and Settlements Division (IFRC, 2015).

A more recent iteration of this is to be found in the (re-)emergence of area-based approaches (ABAs) in the humanitarian lexicon. The idea of an ABA is simple: that interventions are defined by the physical location of need. One defining factor of an ABA from USAID (2011, cited in Parker and Maynard, 2015) is that they 'focus on communities in defined spatial contexts.' This may seem at one level an obvious approach – what after all would be the alternative? Humanitarian response is not, however, organized in this way. The Cluster system for example is based essentially on grouping organizations according to the goods they deliver, such as Water, Sanitation and Hygiene (WASH), Protection, Camp Management and Shelter (which does not include the term Settlements, despite the cluster being co-led by the IFRC). There is no cluster for cities, city government or planning and design.

ABAs present opportunities for agencies to work in urban areas in ways that are 'geographically targeted; multi-sectoral (and adopt a) participatory approach' (Parker and Maynard, 2015, 3). As Stodart writes in chapter 6 about post-disaster housing following Typhoon Haiyan that struck the Philippines in 2013, a settlements perspective 'involves the consideration of other aspects of community life beyond shelter and how these aspects all fit together physically and functionally.' ABAs can embrace developmental approaches to urban disaster recovery, including multi-sectoral efforts with better coordination between actors, exploiting synergies, rather than competing for space and attention. They can foster participatory efforts which are of course the mainstream language of development, but a term that can easily become lost in the wrong-headed assumption that speed is what matters. Humanitarian literature and evidence points to better, stronger and more sustainable outcomes when participation is used in interventions: it may also be something of a surprise that this is not better understood.

Urban humanitarian practice needs to find the right language to use. As well as remembering words like participation and settlement, it needs to discard some of the misleading language from wider (rurally derived) humanitarian practice. For instance and as noted earlier, working in a dense, historic neighborhood is not 'field work,' and the word shelter implies a single-story, stand-alone temporary building. Yet living in this way is not an urban form affordable to most (except for those with no other choice but to live in informal settlements, discussed below): large and increasing numbers of people rent and live in multi-story buildings.

In this regard, the practice of adopting urban words to reflect the urban humanitarian landscape is increasing, if slowly. ACAPS's *Rapid Humanitarian Assessments in Urban Settings* Technical Brief (2015) uses an urban language that includes density, diversity, fluidity, mobility, complexity and industry as key characteristics of urban space.[4] Agencies are also innovating more with forms of 'sheltering' options that go beyond transitional shelter, in no small part due to the (at times painful) lessons learned from the 2010 Haiti earthquake response (Clermont et al., 2011). One example concerns the Norwegian Refugee Council's (NRC) approaches in Jordan wherein the chronic housing shortage for Syrian refugees is being addressed by funding the completion of unfinished properties in exchange for leases for refugees. And while not perfect (favorable rents for refugees are for a fixed term), such an approach invests in urban infrastructure rather than wasting it on temporary shelters, while providing greater security for vulnerable and fragile refugees (NRC, 2014).

Right now, however, an unresolved challenge concerns humanitarian responses to those living in informal settlements. If UN-Habitat is right, the 950 million or so informal urban dwellers (those living with an insecure form of tenure) will swell over the next 20 years to 2 billion. While considerable recent work has been undertaken in the relatively new area of housing, land and property rights (HLP), fragile tenure and how to help those living 'illegally' presents huge challenges. This ranges from agencies getting government permissions to work in 'illegal' settlements to determining meaningful interventions in places that were chronically poor before a disaster.

Finally, in terms of spatial interventions, post-disaster urban recovery models always prioritize keeping affected populations in their original locations, in order to preserve social capital, jobs and historic ties (Jha, 2009). But what do you do if you are a poor renter living in a tenement or a slum? Emerging lessons from the 2010 Haiti earthquake may offer fresh thinking, and in particular opportunities for low-income urban dwellers. Canaan, on the outskirts of Port-au-Prince, largely uninhabited before the earthquake, is now home to upwards of some 200,000 dwellers and is Haiti's third largest settlement (US News, 2015). Despite the informal status of the area[5] the UN calculates that some US$100 million of people's own money has been invested into homes, shops, streets and infrastructure there (UN-Habitat, 2013). Such investment appears to be unlocking an urban spirit. As one NGO working in Canaan observed,

> One thing that was striking is that a lot of the youth and of the population … aspire to establish and build up their own business ... You can really feel that entrepreneurial spirit, so we feel that there's a lot that can be done to support this spirit, to support burgeoning entrepreneurs into developing their business and carrying the economy in the area.
>
> (US News, 2015)

Such observations in an aid agency-managed recovery program would be heralded as emblematic of great success, yet the expansion of Canaan (which contradicts 'received wisdom' that forming new urban settlements after disaster is a bad idea) reflects a form of urban growth that has been prevalent outside of disasters for decades, i.e. where people themselves take control, often in the face of government opposition (Hamdi, 1989). Current practice therefore needs to learn from this if it has any chance of responding to urban need at an appropriate scale.

Power – whose disaster is it?

The PDNA issued by the government of Nepal following the 2015 earthquakes states that the recovery 'has to be developed and implemented in a way that is uniquely Nepali' (2015: 16). While there is hope that this will happen (the government of Nepal has kept a strong control on recovery efforts), the lessons of many post-disaster recovery operations elsewhere have been that local systems of management and decision-making have lacked the power to self-determine, and risk being overwhelmed by an influx of external support. In urban areas this can be especially damaging where politics and power are especially concentrated. A perspective on how aid exercises power post-disaster is helpful. Mitchell (2014) identifies four primary approaches (called the 'Four C's' model) for humanitarian response that are currently in operation: comprehensive (where the aid system assumes there is no local capacity, e.g. after the Haiti earthquake); constrained (where operations are limited, for instance due to conflict; an example would be the Syria crisis); collaborative (where agencies 'fill in the gaps' not provided by government; an example would be the 2010–2011 Pakistan floods); and consultative (where agencies provide support to strong local governance; the 2010 Chile earthquake, written about by Allard and Arrasate in chapter 3, provides an example here).

Mitchell notes that roughly 50 percent of aid spending to date has gone to the comprehensive, with less than 5 percent on consultative. It could be argued that this reflects the rural roots of aid – for comprehensive, 'nothing is there.' When this is applied to urban areas – home to skills, resources, commerce, competition and culture – the results are wasted aid and frustrated local capacities (Haiti provides an example of this, where many agencies brought in goods and services, such as healthcare that were locally available, thus, unwittingly, undermining the local economy). Applying the Four C's model therefore, an appropriate response for aid practitioners in cities and towns would be to adopt collaborative and consultative approaches, such as providing support, building skills and investing in actions that use existing resources.

These assumptions tie into the larger question of 'whose disaster is it?' Traditionally, as with the comprehensive model, aid actors may (wrongly) assume they are in charge. When this happens outcomes can be problematic. As with the Nepali PDNA aim quoted above, it is essential that aid responses fit into existing governance systems, no matter how weak they may be (noting that this may be a quite different discussion concerning conflict, for example currently in Syria). If not, then setting up 'parallel structures' may have the unintended effect of weakening local governance.

In cities and towns power is held at different levels by ranges of actors. Formal governance systems usually comprise a national government with various layers of local government, including different forms of city governments (who are often in opposition to national government). Power is also held by the private sector, including businesses ranging from multinationals to small business. Power may also be held by gangs and organized crime.

And degrees of power are held by those who may organize into groups to act collectively, or indeed individually (given the increasing power of social media). In traditional humanitarian action (perhaps here also given its rural roots) some actors are thought to be central – people and government – while others, namely businesses, are rarely considered as operational partners.

In urban areas, to ignore the private sector is to ignore a lifeblood of the city. Traditional humanitarian aid can learn from the private sector in urban recovery. A notable example is provided by the reconstruction of Port-au-Prince's Marché Hyppolite (the Iron Market), an emblematic and vibrant commercial area that was destroyed in the 2010 earthquake. The Iron Market was reopened on the first anniversary of the earthquake, with assistance from Haiti's large cellphone provider Digicel which was quite an achievement given the well-publicized perception of a slow response by aid agencies in Port-au-Prince at the time.

The intervention was not only about civic pride, but also about the re-creation of employment and boosting markets. In research into the Iron Market, Smith (chapter 10) concludes,

> The reconstruction of the Iron Market by Digicel demonstrates that a private sector company can be a powerful actor in reconstruction, strengthening the economy and impacting working environments. Increasing collaboration between the private sector, humanitarian organizations and governments in order to scale up and better tackle the urban post-disaster recovery offers opportunities for more effective responses for the next urban disaster.

Smith also records a statement by an Iron Market vendor: 'When you build a market, I like that. You build jobs. I lost my job when it burnt.' This is the level at which much of current humanitarian aid aims: at empowerment, taken here to mean literally 'the transfer of power,' to people after a disaster.

Perhaps one of the biggest shifts in power in aid programming in recent years has been the use of cash transfers, i.e. in its simplest form, giving money to people.[6] This fundamentally means (when cash grants are unconditional) that people themselves get to decide how relief funds are spent, and as such this is a powerful shift.

Evidence that cash transfers can disperse power to individuals has been gathering. Cash programming following Typhoon Haiyan was widely used throughout the Philippines to good effect. Attesting to its usefulness one NGO country director stated in a review, 'cash has come of age; it's now the number one intervention besides food and water' (Sanderson and Delica Willison, 2014: 7). Cash is also helpful in chronic conflict situations; an evaluation of a cash transfer program operated in Lebanon by the NGO the International Rescue Committee (IRC) for some 88,000 Syrian refugees found increased school access, reduced child labor and no meaningful impact on prices (IRC, 2014). Cash is therefore something of a *no-brainer* when it comes to urban interventions. The caveat for successful cash programming is functioning markets, and evidence shows that following disasters, markets recover quickly, as early as the first day following a disaster (Clermont et al., 2011).

Time – acting fast after disaster versus the pace of urban change

If the most authoritative voice comes from those affected by disaster – an aspirational belief on which the whole humanitarian system is based – then practitioners have a duty to listen better. The element of time and the pace of recovery and of interventions are vital, but appear to be concerns that almost willfully ignore the evidence of what people actually want. 'Time to Listen: Hearing People on the Receiving End of International Aid,' an initiative led by the influential humanitarian thinker Mary Anderson, interviewed over 6,000 people caught up by disaster about their experiences of humanitarian aid. Of the many powerful insights, an overriding view was that 'very few people call for more aid; virtually everyone says they want "smarter" aid. Many feel that "too much" is given "too fast"' (Anderson et al., 2012: 2). The point is that, in the rush to help 'helpless victims,' too many agencies ignore the capacities, needs, wants, desires – and consequently dignity – of those caught up in disaster. In towns and cities in particular it might be observed that many urban dwellers may have a multitude of ways of surviving, often relying on diverse skills and abilities, that traditional rural-oriented aid responses have never had to take into account.

Humanitarian practitioners are driven to respond at speed for a variety of reasons, many of which are of course good (no one would argue against life-saving operations and the meeting of immediate basic needs). But, after that, the reasons may be less good: there is a huge pressure on agencies to spend quickly in tight timeframes, which is a problem stemming from donors who feel they need to report to their respective constituencies that the funds they are stewarding are being spent to get the job done, which often equates with 'quickly.' This can lead to bad decisions, such as the temptation to spend large amounts of aid on temporary, stop-gap interventions. Taking temporary shelter, in 2013 *New York Times* journalist Deborah Sontag reported that, following the Haiti earthquake, 'Of over US$7.5 billion spent, US$215 million has been allocated to safe, permanent housing ... at least US$1.2 billion has been eaten up by short-term solutions – tent camps, temporary shelters and cash grants that pay a year's rent' (Sontag, 2013). In urban areas in particular, due to the presence of markets and commerce (discussed below), there is the opportunity to adopt an approach of 'aid as investments,' wherein actions have an eye to long-term improvements far beyond short-term help.

A further, wider time-related consideration concerns how cities change, grow, evolve and decline. Cities are defined by constant change, not only with current rapid urbanization, but also in terms of shifting commerce (with different types of industry and business), changes in infrastructure, buildings and nature. As a way of analyzing and describing how cities change over time, morphology offers some insights: 'Morphology is used to understand the multi-scalar nature of physical infrastructure and natural ecosystems' (Kropf, 2005, see Sitko, chapter 5). Sitko (chapter 5) notes four morphological layers that are particularly relevant to urban resilience: a topographical layer (land and water, sometimes referred to as green and blue layers); a public layer (streets and public space); a plots layer (relating to land tenure); and a buildings and services layer (relating to the quality of living space). Time in relation to each layer may be different: the topographical layer of rivers and coasts may shift slowly, sometimes over centuries, while the public layer of historic forms and culturally important buildings will experience incremental change or, in some cases, wholesale replacement. Plots shift, change and grow and may be the subject of contested space, while buildings and services may include recently provided public infrastructure such as hospitals and services of mobile phone masts and wi-fi networks.

Time-related morphological layers can help locate actions by practitioners before and after disaster in context. Butina Watson (chapter 1) discusses how green layers in cities (such as parks) help provide 'redundancy,' 'latency' and 'room to move' in urban form. Green layers have also been used in urban form for centuries to provide fire breaks. Concerning public and topological layers, Butina Watson cites the example of London, which over two millennia 'has survived a number of disasters, including the 1666 Great Fire, various floods and sustained bombing during the Second World War.' She notes that, in 'each incident, the city "bounced back." After the Great Fire, the buildings were burnt down, but the Roman and Mediaeval streets, the city's infrastructure and many of its key buildings and facilities survived, the latter because of good quality materials.'

The identification of culture and its importance in urban life is also gaining attention from practitioners engaged in urban disaster. The 2014 IFRC *World Disasters Report* (Cannon and Schipper, 2014), a leading annual state-of-the-art publication in disasters with a yearly global theme, focused on culture and risk. The publication examines the interactions between culture and disaster risk reduction, and how culture is affected by disaster. Since 2014 the issue of culture and crises has been reaffirmed by damage to a number of important temples in the 2015 Nepal earthquake as well as the deliberate destruction by ISIS of Iraq's Nimrud city (Independent, 2015).

Concerning the importance of ancient routes and culture, Almukhtar's research of Erbil, the capital of Iraqi Kurdistan, uses the concept of 'place-identity' as the physical representation of space, i.e. 'a collection of images that can transmit, at a glance, a suggestive reminder of the historical urban forms the city has acquired all along its evolution' (Castello, 2006, cited in Almukhtar, chapter 8). Contrasting the history of Erbil with its recent history of conflict (and echoing Killing and Boano's call highlighted earlier to adopt urban-related tools and understandings), Almukhtar concludes that urban actors must understand, indeed acknowledge historical urban form as a measure of resilience:

> NGOs, government officials, urban designers, planners, architects, developers and investors who are rebuilding the city must be especially aware of the multiple identities that exist in order to avoid spatially redesigning out of existence identities at neighborhood, district, city and regional levels.

Strengthening urban resilience: the challenges

What then does urban disaster resilience mean for humanitarian practice? Returning to the scenario presented at the beginning of this chapter, things might have turned out differently ... and better. Taking a resilience perspective, the city could have been much better prepared, both in terms of reducing through pre-disaster actions the scale of the disaster, and afterwards being ready with effective relief and recovery. Tires would have been kicked more often, and the political will to prepare would have been there: lots of political will appears after a disaster, but, unless maintained, ebbs away. To keep the momentum, civil society and in particular NGOs can play a catalyzing role in advocating for better preparedness and all-round risk reduction, as exemplified in the Philippines where years of NGO campaigning led to the passing of the Philippine Disaster Risk Reduction and Management (DRRM) Act in 2010, which refocuses disaster management towards disaster risk reduction. Such political galvanizing is needed in post-earthquake Nepal where the development of a Disaster Management Act has been in process since 2007.

In terms of improved resilience in urban planning and building design, morphology points to playing the 'long game.' Open spaces can be considered also as safe spaces. Full enforcement of seismically appropriate building codes in all new building construction – in this fictitious city, as elsewhere, the codes already exist – would make all the difference. A regular 'naming and shaming' of illegally built and/or poorly maintained buildings would help. Public buildings such as schools and hospitals can be retrofitted to be strong enough to withstand collapse, a practice that has demonstrated benefits in a number of cities around the world.

Aid agencies need to retool their skills for the new urban disaster landscape. While some of this is starting to happen, the pace needs to quicken. An urban approach, among other things, means adopting and embracing the language and norms of the city. Echoing Mitchell's Four C's model, four 'urban C's' for aid responses to grapple with might be cash, commerce, competition and culture. While cash-based programming is rapidly in the ascendancy, more humanitarian engagement in commerce could provide better engagement with private sector organizations to deliver greater efficiencies (many agencies currently have a problem with for-profit entities, suspecting motives that might not coincide with humanitarian principles). As the experience in Haiti demonstrated, the reconstruction of the Iron Market provides a potential model for enacting a large and relatively quick recovery that aid agencies could learn from and help to replicate. Using local competition in the form of markets offers better approaches than the importing and delivery of externally procured goods. Understanding competition better might also lead to NGOs in particular doing less to damage existing service providers in their well-intentioned provision of free post-disaster goods and services that, pre-disaster, people paid for.

Concerning culture, cities and towns embody traditions and practices. Cultural practices in particular need to be understood better, especially when it comes to risk reduction measures. The IFRC's 2014 *World Disaster Report* describes how those living on the slopes of Bolivia's capital La Paz group-organize to make land less risky to live on. However, as the report notes, such settlements 'have overwhelmed urban planning ... (and) as a consequence, disasters have dramatically increased, with losses of life, houses and livelihoods, especially for the poor and lower-middle-class people living in hazardous places' (Cannon and Schipper, 2014: 71). In such places, building resilience involves the engagement of people and their cultures for making better choices, combined with laws and codes that protect them.

Embracing opportunities in urban actions also means embracing innovation. Innovation in humanitarian circles has steadily grown following a 2009 report by the humanitarian think-tank Active Learning Network for Accountability and Performance (ALNAP) that advocated innovation as a way to rethink humanitarian practice, given that many problems and solutions are known, but that practices are slow to change (Bessant et al., 2014). Since then a number of initiatives have sought to build and harness innovation within humanitarian practice, not least the 2016 World Humanitarian Summit, the first of its kind, of which 'transformation through innovation' was one of the four themes.

Urban resilience provides an obvious hook for directing innovation: cities and towns are packed with entrepreneurs, many of whom – especially in low-income settlements – are endlessly creative in urban survival. Cities have always provided the engine for innovative change, from industrialization to governance. Innovations might be incremental (much as building codes or land tenure has developed), or they might be positional, as in the use of smartphones for mobile banking. They might also be radical innovations: 'game-changers' that fundamentally shift how business is done.

For urban disaster resilience one or more unanticipated game-changers might be just around the corner. Given that the experience of many aid agencies to date has been to adapt rural approaches to the city, such game-changers might render such rural-to-urban conversion practices irrelevant. Candle makers did not invent the light bulb. Likewise, as Henry Ford famously quipped on inventing the mass-produced car, if he had asked people what they had wanted they would have said a faster horse. If humanitarian actors working in cities and towns are not to be members of the 'faster horse better candle brigade,' then they would do well to recognize and embrace the urban landscape: in short, to urbanize themselves.

Notes

1 See for example Chambers and Conway's influential paper 'Sustainable rural livelihoods: practical concepts for the 21st century' (1991) which influenced developmental thinking for well over a decade and much of which has been incorporated into current thinking on resilience.
2 Resilience also has meaning in, among other disciplines, psychology and ecology. See Alexander (2013).
3 The NRRC was initiated in 2009 by the government of Nepal, UN, the Red Cross Movement, the World Bank and Asian Development Bank
4 The Assessment Capacities Project (ACAPS) works to improve coordinated humanitarian needs assessments. See: www.acaps.org/en/pages/what-is-acaps.
5 The government has been working since January 2012 on the formalization of the area including regularization of status, but is stuck in complex issues of eminent domain, compensation claims, etc.
6 Noting that other forms and varying conditions of transfers exist, for example conditional and unconditional transfers; also vouchers in place of cash.

References

ACAPS (2015). *Rapid Humanitarian Assessments in Urban Settings.* Technical Brief, January.

Alexander, D. (2013). Resilience and disaster risk reduction: an etymological journey. *Nat. Hazards Earth Syst. Sci.* 13: 2707–2716.

Anderson, M. and Woodrow, P. (1989). *Rising from the Ashes: Development Strategies in Times of Disaster.* Boulder, Colorado: Westview Press.

Anderson, M., Brown, D. and Isabella, J. (2012). *Time to Listen: Hearing People on the Receiving End of International Aid.* Cambridge, Massachusetts: CDA Collaborative Learning Projects.

Bessant, J., Ramalingam, B., Rush, H., Marshall, N., Hoffman, K. and Gray, B. (2014). *Innovation Management, Innovation Ecosystems and Humanitarian Innovation: Literature Review for the Humanitarian Innovation Ecosystem Research Project.* London: DFID.

Cannon, T. and Schipper, L. (eds) (2014). *World Disasters Report: Focus on Culture and Risk.* Geneva: IFRC.

Castello, L. (2006). City and time and places: bridging the concept of place to urban conservation planning. *City & Time* 2: 59–69.

Chambers, R. and Conway, G. (1991). *Sustainable Rural Livelihoods: Practical Concepts for the 21st Century.* IDS Discussion Paper 296, Brighton.

Chan, S. (2001). *Complex Adaptive Systems.* ESD.83 Research Seminar in Engineering Systems, October 31.

CHS (2015). *The Standard.* Available at: www.corehumanitarianstandard.org/the-standard (accessed July 2015).

Clermont, C., Sanderson, D., Spraos, H. and Sharma, A. (2011). *Urban Disasters – Lessons from Haiti. Study of Member Agencies' Responses to the Earthquake in Port au Prince, Haiti: January 2010.* London: Disasters Emergency Committee (DEC).

Government of Nepal (2015). *Post-Disaster Needs Assessment.* Kathmandu: National Planning Commission.

Hamdi, N. (1989). *Housing Without Houses: Flexibility, Participation, Enablement.* New York: Van Nostrand Reinhold.

IFRC (2013). *World Disasters Report.* Promotional video. Available at: www.ifrc.org/publications-and-reports/world-disasters-report/world-disasters-report-2013/ (accessed July 2015).

IFRC (2015). *Shelter and Settlements: What We Do.* Available at: www.ifrc.org/what-we-do/disaster-management/responding/services-for-the-disaster-affected/shelter-and-settlement/ (accessed July 2015).

Independent (2015). *Isis Video Shows Complete Destruction of Ancient City of Nimrud in Iraq.* Available at: www.independent.co.uk/news/world/middle-east/isis-video-shows-complete-destruction-of-ancient-city-of-nimrud-in-iraq-10170469.html (accessed July 2015).

IRC (2014). *Emergency Economies: The Impact of Cash Assistance in Lebanon. An Impact Evaluation of the 2013–2014 Winter Cash Assistance Program for Syrian Refugees in Lebanon.* Lebanon: IRC.

Jha, A. (2009). *Handbook for Post-Disaster Housing and Community Reconstruction.* Washington, DC: World Bank.

Kropf, K. (2005). The handling characteristics of urban form. *Urban Design*, Winter (93): 17–18.

Mitchell, J. (2014). From best practice to best fit. *Montreaux* XIII, December.

NRC (2014). *Integrated Urban Shelter Programme Factsheet.* August.

Parker, E. and Maynard, V. (2015). *Humanitarian Response to Urban Crises: A Review of Area-Based Approaches.* IIED working paper, July.

Piper, R. (2013). A perfect storm of earthquake and poor governance could cripple Nepal. *The Guardian.* Available at: www.theguardian.com/commentisfree/2013/jan/12/perfect-storm-earthquake-cripple-nepal (accessed July 2015).

Rockefeller Foundation (2015). *Resilience.* Available at: www.rockefellerfoundation.org/our-work/topics/resilience/ (accessed July 2015).

Sanderson, D. and Delica Willison, Z. (2014). *Philippines Typhoon Haiyan Response Review.* London and Ottawa: DEC/HC.

Sanderson, D., Sharma, A., Kennedy, J. and Burnell, J. (2014). Lost in transition: principles, practice and lessons from Haiti for urban post-disaster shelter recovery programs. *Asian Journal of Environment and Disaster Management (AJEDM)* 6(2): 131–151.

Sontag, D. (2013). *Rebuilding in Haiti Lags After Billions in Post-Quake Aid.* Available at: www.nytimes.com/2012/12/24/world/americas/in-aiding-quake-battered-haiti-lofty-hopes-and-hard-truths.html (accessed July 2015).

UN-Habitat (2013). *Analysis for Government of Haiti.* UCLBP, October.

USAID/OFDA (2013). *USAID/OFDA Humanitarian Shelter and Settlements Principles.* Washington, DC: USAID.

US News (2015). *The Promised Land: 5 Years Later, Haitians Find Hope in Canaan.* Available at: www.usnews.com/news/articles/2015/01/12/5-years-later-haitians-find-hope-in-canaan-after-the-2010-earthquake (accessed July 2015).

Strengthening collaborations for urban disasters

A call to urban planners, designers and humanitarians

Jerold S. Kayden

This book poses challenges to two distinctly different groups of professionals. For humanitarians, who are all about disasters (and have the acronyms to prove it), awareness and engagement are not the issues. Instead, this book commends to them that, because future disasters will be lodged increasingly in an urban context, existing models of disaster response tied to rural conditions will not suffice, new paradigms such as resilience may engender superior responses, and enduring partnerships with a wider range of professionals, including urban planners and designers, will be essential.

For urban planners and designers, the challenge is to infiltrate and mainstream considerations of disasters into and across their daily remit, in effect unsiloing disaster planning from a subspecialty to a piece of everyday planning and design. To be sure, this journey has already begun. In high-risk regions, there has always been a cadre of planning and design disaster specialists. Today, in the face of climate change and a well-publicized string of deeply destructive disasters, more planning and design professionals are thinking for the first and second times about adaptation of the built environment and the introduction of approaches that build resilience. This wedge needs to be expanded and deepened. Mainstreaming consideration of disasters requires changes in laws, institutions, professional practices and cultures, and preparatory education if urban planners and designers are going to contribute at the level demanded by the new world disaster order. It also demands a true collaboration between urban planners and designers and humanitarians that starts pre-disaster and continues through the episode and well beyond.

What has to happen to make this happen? For starters, the study of disasters must become part of the required curricula of planning and design schools. That is currently not the case, as any review of planning or design program catalog will reveal. Core courses need to incorporate the multiple manifestations and effects of disasters as part of the contextual physical environment in which planning and design occur, so that insertions of built form into that environment axiomatically take disasters into account. Elective courses at intermediate and advanced levels can supplement this learning, but curriculum accreditation criteria specified by government agencies and professional licensing bodies must make sure that no planning or design student educated anywhere in the world graduates without a genuine exposure to the anticipated range of disaster issues and technical responses.

Second, urban planners and designers need to insinuate disaster planning into planning for everything. The typical physical planning exercise involves the 'what, where, why, who, how and when' of buildings, infrastructure and open spaces that constitute the built environment. The goal of physical planning is to create a material vessel in which individuals and societies live, work, and play productively, equitably and sustainably. Housing, industry, markets, schools, hospitals, government buildings, bus and rail stations, community facilities and parks, served by an infrastructure of roads, rail lines, waterways, pedestrian paths, power grids, water and sewer lines and more, constitute the cities and towns within which most individuals now live.

Planners and designers deal with opportunities and constraints. They look at existing conditions and discover strengths, weaknesses, opportunities and threats (SWOT). Disasters are a threat that must, like any other threat, be part of the planning analysis. When decisions are routinely made with regard to laws controlling (or attempting to control) private formal and informal development and capital spending for public projects of infrastructure and government facilities, the risk and impact of disasters must be measured and addressed.

Third, paradigms for approaching disasters through planning and design must change, or change more. The Dutch have gone through an attitudinal shift over the past 20 or so years. After experiencing the horror of almost 2,000 deaths and massive physical destruction from the North Sea Floods of 1953, the Dutch decided to engineer their way to near certain safety. Protecting against events that may only occur once in thousands of years became the mantra and mission. And the Dutch, with much of their country at or below sea level, initiated and completed a multi-decade engineering project, the Delta Works, of dams, dykes and storm surge barriers that gave them that protection and apparent certainty. The rest of the country hardly changed, as if life behind the barriers could go on protected and unconcerned from what was happening in the North Sea.

Climate change has brought about a sea change (as it were) in the Dutch approach. With multiple points of water entry from north and south, higher base sea levels from which water during storms surges, and greater glacial melt and rain flooding rivers, the idea is not to fight the water, but to live with it. Suddenly the idea of building outside the dyke, an apostasy for the Dutch, becomes possible. The 'Room for the Rivers' project in the Delta region makes peace with a flooding river by enlarging the flood zone, moving some houses, and allowing permeable green surfaces to do their thing. 'Water plazas' in Rotterdam serve dual purposes of public spaces and places for water to collect during high water moments. 'Water is our enemy' transitions to 'Water is our friend.' That may sound silly to some, especially when vulnerable poor populations struggle to survive day to day, but the idea that, no matter what, it becomes impossible to engineer one's way out of the problem, is compelling.

The latest paradigm is resilience, building on a proud lineage of sustainability and adaptation. UN-Habitat provides a starter definition for what resilience is, referring 'to the ability of human settlements to withstand and to recover quickly from any plausible hazards.' It continues,

> Resilience against crises not only refers to reducing risk and damage from disasters (i.e loss of lives and assets), but also the ability to quickly bounce back to a stable state. While typical risk reduction measures tend to focus on a specific hazard, leaving out risks and vulnerabilities due to other types of perils, the resilience approach adopts a multiple hazards approach, considering resilience against all types of plausible hazards.
> (UN-Habitat, 2012)

The United Nations International Strategy for Disaster Reduction (UNISDR), among many others, offers a useful checklist for thinking about what resilience may require (UNISDR, 2015).

The Rockefeller Foundation, under the steady hand of Judith Rodin, has made resilience one of its key pillars. Moving the concept from conferences to the field, it has funded the newly invented position of 'Chief Resilience Officers' in 100 cities around the world. This heady initiative seeks to jump-start the practice of resilience in cities. The challenge is to make sure that such an effort itself does not become siloed, that cities embrace the lessons of a resilience-based approach across departments, and that urban planning and design departments make resilience a meaningful consideration as they go about preparing new plans and revising existing ones. If the point of the Chief Resilience Officer project itself is to be resilient, it must survive the expiration of the Rockefeller pilot.

Finally, humanitarians and urban planners and designers need to truly learn what the other does in order to truly engage with each other in improving disaster response. Coming mostly from different histories, educational backgrounds, technical training, cultural affinities and ethoses, institutional bases, funding sources, clients, crises and fondness for acronyms, they are alarmingly unaware of the base knowledge, expertise, technical skills and paradigms of the other. Of course humanitarians are concerned, eponymously, with humans, especially vulnerable ones under extreme conditions of distress from natural and man-made disasters. Urban planners and designers are focused on the built environment, even if they are not called builditarians. They are hardly emergency responders, rarely faced with an emergency need to churn out a plan, even if clients are demanding at times.

These different foci may lead to two ships passing in the night, but at the end of that night, when it comes to disasters, they are both interested in the same thing. Planners and designers, at least the best of them, never think about the built environment as an end in and of itself, but as a means to an end. The built environment is the physical vessel in which people live, work and play. Planners and designers believe that they can improve the outcomes of people by making that physical vessel more productive, equitable and sustainable. That puts them squarely in the camp of humanitarians. If lack of familiarity breeds lack of familiarity, it is time for urban planners and designers and humanitarians to learn what the other does. For urban planners and designers, it means examining in detail the approach of humanitarians and how they conceive of problems. For humanitarians, it means examining in detail standard, non-humanitarian urban planning and design. A new initiative – call it the Urban Planning, Design, and Humanitarian Institute (UPDHI) – would be a small start. By learning what the other does, without as well as with regard to disasters, each will begin to imagine changes to professional practices and initiation of new collaborations needed to make disasters more livable in the future. New specialties will emerge, to be sure, and we will be talking about 'humanitarian planners/designers' and 'planning/design humanitarians', but it is too early to think about boutique practices. For now, let a broad-based engagement prevail.

References

UN-Habitat (2012). *Resilience*. Available at: http://unhabitat.org/urban-themes/resilience/ (accessed November 28, 2015).

United Nations International Strategy for Disaster Reduction (UNISDR) (2015). *The Ten Essentials*. Available at: www.unisdr.org/campaign/resilientcities/home/toolkitblkitem/?id=1 (accessed November 28, 2015).

Part I

Urban planning, design and cities

Chapter 1

Designing resilient cities and neighborhoods

Georgia Butina Watson

Introduction

Many cities across the globe are offering a wealth of socio-economic and cultural opportunities that are an important factor in supporting the livelihood of much of the existing population as well as in attracting new residents. At the same time some cities and their regions are experiencing negative impacts of climate change, rapid urban growth, fragmented urban form, lack of proper infrastructure and the lack of social and governance structures (Zetter and Butina Watson, 2006).

Today some 3.6 billion people live in towns and cities and it is projected that by 2050 the total urban population is likely to increase to 6.3 billion, or nearly 70 percent of the global population (UN, 2012). This urban growth phenomenon puts a huge pressure on the existing and newly developing urban systems as cities are expanding faster than the planned provision of housing, urban infrastructure and many other facilities. As a result some urban areas have become very fragile and are unable to sustain an adequate quality of life. Many large urban systems also generate high levels of pollution which contribute negatively to climate change and as a result to an increased occurrence of disasters caused by hazards such as flooding.

Negative impacts and human sufferings are most obvious in poorer countries where resources are limited and where policy, planning and delivery mechanisms are weak or are still developing. Non-governmental organizations (NGOs) and humanitarian agencies struggle to meet all the demands, both in resource as well as in expertise terms. So, how can we plan and design cities and neighborhoods that can survive large negative impacts of disasters? What kind of future visions are needed and desirable to provide resilient solutions to offer safer and longer-lasting urban form and socio-economic and governance structures?

This chapter first discusses what is meant by the resilient city or resilient neighborhood and what are their key characteristics. The discussion is centered in contemporary planning and urban design concepts and is supported by examples of cities that have 'bounced back' quickly and successfully after a particular type of disaster. The second part of the chapter introduces the methodology developed as part of a research project, Retrofit 2050 (composed of multidisciplinary experts from six British universities: Cardiff, Cambridge, Reading, Oxford Brookes, Salford and Durham), which includes 'urban futures' visioning, pathways and roadmaps, and backcasting, that could assist urban planners, designers and other professionals to create more resilient cities. Backcasting is a method for creating 'futures' visions, then looking back to the present to see how these 'futures' visions may be achieved by developing strategies and by setting specific targets and milestones from the present forward. The last part of the chapter proposes some general and specific principles and a methodology that could be of value to urban professionals, governments, civil societies and NGOs when designing or retrofitting cities and neighborhoods, to enable cities to achieve a higher degree of resilience and cope more successfully with adverse natural and human adversities.

Defining resilient cities

There are many definitions of what a resilient city is. One definition most commonly used is that resilience is 'the capacity of urban systems to accommodate change over time and to withstand and rebound from disruptive challenges' (Coaffee, 2013). Miletti defines resilience as the ability of local areas 'to withstand an extreme natural event without suffering devastating losses, damage, diminished productivity or quality of life and without a large amount of assistance from outside the community' (Miletti, 1999, cited in Godschalk, 2003: 136). A resilient city is also a sustainable network of physical systems and human communities. Physical systems generally refer to both the natural environment and the constructed urban form components of the city (Butina Watson and Bentley, 2007). Natural systems mean geology, topography, water courses, fields, green spaces, and flora and fauna. Physical form components, or the 'urban morphology' of the city, consist of major infrastructure such as roads and streets, the system of urban open spaces, blocks and plots, buildings and the relevant associated pattern of uses across all different morphological scales (Moudon, 1997; Butina Watson and Bentley, 2007). They are the bones and the skeleton of the city (Rossi, 1986), its arteries and life veins. On the other hand, the communities that live in them are the vital 'brains' of the city where key decisions are made. Therefore, in addition to natural and physical form, resilient systems must also have resilient communities. Resilient cities need to be strong and flexible rather than brittle and fragile. If they are brittle and fragile, they can break and cause even bigger hazards and eventual disasters.

One key component in making cities more resilient is to examine their constituent parts. There are some recent concepts such as landscape urbanism (Waldheim, 2013) that can help in understanding the relationship between green and built form components. Green urban spaces are needed in the city for public use, but are also important for climatic and other reasons. Green spaces provide the elasticity for the city; they can also create areas after disasters to accommodate temporary resources, medical help and other facilities. De Sola Morales (1999) states that what is needed is a form of 'urban acupuncture'; a targeted urban intervention to allow urban systems to be readjusted and reorganized. Walker and Salt (2006) also talk about 'redundancy,' 'latency' and having 'room to move' as some of the key characteristics of urban resilience. They also state that resilience is composed of a number of characteristics that are closely linked to the ideas of good urban form principles. They suggest that important resilient attributes include diversity, modularity, tight feedbacks, innovation and overlap in governance, ecosystem services, social capital and allowing for variability. Modularity is particularly important as it enables neighborhoods to have different characteristics, allowing for different response, so that in critical situations not all systems fail. In terms of social composition, Lister (2007) states that it is important to have small, clearly defined neighborhoods, with strong identity, that correspond to social and governance structures. Such communities can regroup quickly and respond faster to emergency situations; in a sense, they tend to have stronger social capital.

Among other attributes commonly cited in urban design work are the qualities of permeability, variety of forms and functions, legibility and vitality, known as the 'responsive environments' principles (Bentley et al., 1985; Butina Watson, 2014) as well as Lynch's concepts of legibility and good city form (Lynch, 1960, 1981). Permeability is important as it defines accessibility to resources, people and facilities. Both Jacobs (1961) and Moudon (1989) suggest the design of small urban blocks of mixed use that allow easy connection. Legibility is important as it provides a sense of orientation, critical in any disaster-affected areas. Vitality refers to the availability of water, energy and other resources. Moudon also suggests that these qualities connect resilience with urbanism as they explain the spatial dimension of urban resilience. It is also important to note, however, that there are a number of dimensions or levels of resilience, and they are evolving and can be altered over time.

Allan et al. (2013) state that these attributes can help in analyzing places in terms of their potential for resilience; they can be the lens through which we see and understand how different components of urban form and socio-spatial components respond under pressure. This lens can also be applied at different scales of morphological levels from buildings to urban blocks to neighborhoods and city/region scales. Allan et al. also suggest that it is useful to study previous case studies, to see how different morphological structures, forms of governance and socio-spatial dimensions responded to a particular type of disaster.

Vale and Campanella (2005) claim that if we look at historical precedents most cities display a degree of resilience as they have withstood and have been adapted to many natural and human interventions. In urban design terms some observers also refer to such cities as being robust, or having the ability to accommodate different uses, people and other urban components over time. They have a good level of adaptability or, as some refer to it, 'future proofing.'

A good historic example is the city of London in the UK that is more than two millennia old. It has survived a number of disasters, including the 1666 Great Fire, various floods and sustained bombing during the Second World War. In each incident, the city 'bounced back.' After the Great Fire, the buildings were burnt down, but the Roman and Mediaeval streets, the city's infrastructure and many of its key buildings and facilities survived, the latter because of good quality materials. London also suffered many floods and through innovative engineering and management schemes it has protected its residents and its assets. By dredging the bottom of the River Thames and by installing the Thames Barrier, the water is successfully contained and tamed in the city's historic urban areas.

Particularly drastic was the bombing of London during the Second World War, with many buildings destroyed, demolished following extensive damage or burnt down. City parks and the underground railway tunnels provided shelter during the worst incidents of bombing, whilst front gardens became urban allotments, used to grow vegetables and feed its residents. Post-war large-scale reconstruction programs followed the original street layouts and over time London has acquired its present townscape and identity so much admired today. In parallel, voids left in the city after the bombing created new open spaces and memorial gardens (see Plate 1).

These transformations correspond to what urban morphologists refer to as 'the rules of the tissue' which suggests that roads, streets and other large infrastructure systems have the most permanence over time. The same applies to large open spaces such as parks, planted boulevards, river banks, canals and other green systems including the use of greenbelts as practiced in many UK cities. These systems are the life veins of the community through which water, energy, food, medical assistance and the overall mobility of people and goods are channeled. Of course, if not properly managed such systems can also become hazards in themselves as seen in some recent floods in Thailand, Vietnam and the UK (see Figure 1.1). Equally, greenbelts can attract illegal settlers, as seen in some parts of the UK, unless they are protected by strong policies and enforcement.

Figure 1.1 Floods in the UK
Photo: David Hedges

Even in such extreme cases of urban disasters we can see that urban areas respond differently to different kinds of shocks and hazards. Many, such as in Mexico City, bounce back to their relative normality after an earthquake, while others, such as Italy's ancient Pompeii following a volcanic eruption, do not. Sometimes post-disaster interventions can generate new opportunities, as in the case of the collapsed urban motorway in Seoul, South Korea. In response to the fracture of one of its motorway corridors, the local solution was to take advantage of the situation and turn the route into a linear urban green system which is used very much by its residents today (see Plate 2). Several cities also created their own solutions to the rigid structures of the urban motorways, by depressing or otherwise removing them and substituting a sequence of green open spaces, as in Boston, USA or Madrid, Spain, for example. On the other hand, the reuse of an abandoned rail track in New York, known as the High Line, into a popular green walkway has created a new and exciting opportunity, much admired across the world.

Disasters and resilience

With regard to disasters caused by natural phenomena, the type and nature of resilience of some urban places demonstrates that local areas can have the ability to withstand extreme natural events without suffering devastating losses, damage, diminished productivity or quality of life. Foster (1997) argues that cities and their neighborhoods need to be able to respond quickly and it is therefore necessary to design cities, or to retrofit them, to cope effectively with contingencies. Berkeley in California and Tulsa in Oklahoma are two US examples of urban innovation and risk reduction programs. Berkeley experienced earthquake and fire and invested resources in rebuilding its key infrastructure such as schools and other municipal buildings of strong materials to be able to sustain any future shocks. Through government loans, residential buildings were retrofitted to resist fire and earthquake shakes (Godschalk, 2003). Exposed to tornadoes, thunderstorms and flooding and in response to the naturally induced disasters, Tulsa created floodplains and drainage systems to channel the excess water. Similar initiatives were used in 2014 in the floods of some UK cities including Winchester and Oxford. Such floodplains can be turned into wetlands that can promote special flora and fauna and by planting willow trees along the river banks, they can slow down the rushing of water and naturally regulate the water flow and water levels. Coastal sandbanks are also being created around New York, USA and Conception in Chile to absorb the hurricane shocks.

Particularly innovative have been interventions in the aftermath of the 2011 earthquake in Christchurch, New Zealand. Immediately after the earthquake open space became 'pop-up' living rooms, kitchens, markets and communal gathering spaces, while people particularly gravitated to the city's damaged central business district (CBD) area, to its natural urban heart. There were also container facilities installed, to provide cafes, restaurants, health centers and other amenities that could replicate what was lost during the earthquake. An award winning competition entry (see Plate 3) following the earthquake illustrates how design ideas can help in healing the city. Voids left behind by demolished buildings have been connected into a large urban memorial park, stretching across the whole city, while locally there are pathways that connect individual neighborhoods. It is proposed that 'pop-up' kitchens and markets continue to function, in memory of the days when they were essential for human survival.

How then can resilient cities and neighborhoods be designed? What kind of scenarios can be employed within existing cities, and how can what is already there be retrofitted given scale and cost?

A methodology for designing resilient cities and neighborhoods

There are a number of initiatives currently underway aimed at achieving a greater degree of resilience. Many cities across the globe are putting forward 'horizon scanning visions' for 2030 and beyond to develop strategies to make cities more resilient and sustainable (Pearson et al., 2014). While there are many definitions of both concepts, the debates are particularly focused on climate change and the effects in human, environmental and resource terms. The issues of intergenerational equity are also being addressed when it comes to the future supply of food, water, energy and other resources. These concerns are now also debated by international and national governments: in the UK the 2008 Climate Change Act has led to a number of specific initiatives and target setting, including the 80 percent reduction of carbon emissions by 2050 (measured against the benchmark of 1990). Of course, we continue to witness a greater degree of natural hazards and the negative impacts of tsunamis, hurricanes, earthquakes, flooding and other disaster incidents affecting our cities and their regions. While different geographies and socio-political systems may determine what kind of natural hazards might affect them, it is useful to consider some generic principles that could guide specific interventions at city and neighborhood levels.

The next section of the chapter explains a methodology developed by a research initiative, Retrofit 2050. The project was set up to develop a methodology for retrofitting cities with an overall aim to explore scenarios for cities to deliver more sustainable and resilient futures. The project illustrates how it is possible to use different concepts to construct a new approach for forecasting urban transformations and for finding solutions for future cities and their neighborhoods. The project was structured into four stages: urban transition analysis; urban foresight analysis; urban options: modeling, visualization and pathway analysis; and synthesis, comparison and knowledge exchange.

The overall approach utilized a number of concepts. They included 'urban future visioning' scenarios, transition theory, disruptive innovation theory, roadmaps and pathways, and participatory forecasting and backcasting. The overall aim was to use the methodology to create 'urban futures' scenarios for delivering more resilient and sustainable cities. In addition to improving environmental aspects the project also focused on promoting transition that would create economic security, social inclusion and resilience of both physical form and social structures.

While much of the retrofit work today has focused at the level of buildings, it is now important to scale up the level of interventions, going into both the neighborhood as well as city levels. In order to do that it is necessary to develop an integrated (or co-evolutionary) perspective on medium- to long-term innovation as well as to simulate potential disruptive hazards and define transition pathways. It is also useful to establish 'what' is to be done to cities, as well as 'how' and 'who' should implement it.

The scale and nature of urban retrofitting requires an integrated approach which includes physical urban form, social and governance structure as well as technological innovations. Using transition theory can be useful in helping understand the complex and multidimensional aspect of urban transformation. A good example is the Fourth Dutch Environment Policy Plan (2001–2030), which incorporates a transition development plan to a more sustainable future. It is equally important to recognize that retrofitting can happen at different morphological levels, from building level and block and plot structures to neighborhood and city/region scales.

The methodology developed by the Retrofit 2050 project team started with the urban analysis of the state of UK cities and problem framing, followed by creating 'visions' of potential desirable futures. These visions are not fixed models but flexible potential scenarios that encourage participatory discussion about a kind of city people want to live in, both now and in the medium- to longer-term future. Visioning allows a shared set of expectations of the future(s) to be created; they are guiding visions. Once these visions are formulated and discussed, roadmaps and pathways to achieve them can be established. In this roadmapping process hypothetical shocks and disturbances can be introduced, with the impact of interventions analyzed. Roadmaps therefore are in a way measures designed to bring about desirable futures. Once the vision and pathways are formulated backcasting can also be used to look at various incidents and milestones that need to be achieved in order to arrive at a desirable future.

The initial Retrofit 2050 visions were based on the supposition that the future is uncertain and that wider sustainability issues are contested politically and socially, where different actors and groups compete for their interests. The challenge was therefore to propose a range of alternative futures, or prototype scenarios, to debate their acceptability and the level of preference or acceptance. Each vision incorporated different morphological levels – building, neighborhood and city/region. Initial prototype visions were derived from literature review, a national questionnaire survey involving recognized subject experts and a number of regional workshops with participation of key professional experts, NGOs, civil society representatives, government officials and professional bodies. There were originally five 'urban futures visions' proposed, but they were later reduced to three main prototypes. Each prototype was defined through urban form and socio-spatial attributes. A resilient city concept was an umbrella scenario under which other visions were incorporated.

Vision one: smart-networked city

In this scenario the city is utilizing the latest technology; it is a hub of highly connected information technology (IT) systems and globally networked society. IT and physical form are well integrated and there is real-time information to measure resource efficiency in terms of energy use and clean and efficient public transport. This is an open, outward-looking society, but the system is market led and is expensive. Such a networked city can provide good support for communication purposes, particularly in the aftermath of disasters. Social values are market-oriented and there is use of smart-grids of energy supply and use. Water usage is metered and most of the technological innovations are at infrastructure and building levels. Buildings incorporate the latest technology in terms of water recycling, solar panels and other innovations.

Vision two: compact city

There has been much literature stating the advantage of a compact city model. In such a system, urban form is reasonably dense, and there is a good concentration and variety of land use, infrastructure, buildings and services. Concentration in urban centers, at both city-wide and neighborhood levels, reduces pressure on the periphery. This idea is also well supported by the latest ideas on walkable neighborhoods that are based on locating mixed use developments within 400x400 meters walking distances, with easy access to shops, neighborhood markets and other facilities. Dense urban fabric supports public transport and energy supply. However, caution has to be taken how spatially such cities are organized. Too high density, as in Hong Kong for example, can be problematic in earthquake areas as there is little open space provision to allow quick recovery interventions. Therefore, a dense urban form has to have parks, gardens, tree-planted boulevards and wide main streets to allow easy access. Buildings can also be retrofitted with the latest technological innovations.

Vision three: self-reliant green city

In this vision, the city is seen as an integrated bio-region, where residents live in harmony with nature, also defined as co-dwelling with nature (Butina Watson and Bentley, 2007). Resources such as food and energy supply are local, where neighborhood heating plants and urban agriculture can thrive. This is an inward-looking society, based on cooperative actions and voluntary buy-in into the scheme and the way of life. Such a vision also implies reduced density, to allow 'green fingers,' pathways and patches to thrive in an urban context. At the building level there are rooftop gardens; at the neighborhood level there are small farm holdings and in some cases there could be shared ownership of urban allotments and other facilities. Such communities also use biomass, solar and thermal energy, wind farms, strict water management and water recycling, sustainable urban drainage systems (SUDS) and planting trees, particularly willow trees, to stabilize the river banks and slow down the flood water flow.

In addition to identifying the prototype visions, roadmaps were developed for each vision with targets and milestones set, and the implication for each retrofit intervention at different morphological scales to achieve as much as possible of the specified vision. Each of the visions was then interrupted by a certain type of disruption or shock, such as lack of water or energy, to see what new measures would be needed to accommodate and adapt to these disruptions. It was also important to establish the level of resilience of each vision, to see the impact of potential disruption on the city and its residents.

What also emerged from the workshops is that different futures visions can co-exist and can have different characteristics at different morphological levels and at different scales of development. For example, a smart-networked city or a compact city is better suited to a large scale of retrofit intervention. On the other hand, a self-reliant green city is better suited to a more localized neighborhood scale. This also corresponds to the earlier mentioned idea of modularity, where different systems respond differently to different types of shocks. It is also important to take into account what types of politics, governance and resources are needed to deliver such visions.

In order to test how these visions could be retrofitted and incorporated into the existing cities, the next stage of the projects applied the methodology to the Welsh city of Cardiff (see Figure 1.2). It was also important to test how different solutions would be accepted by different actors, what resources would be needed to deliver each vision and which governance structures and implementation mechanisms would be required. Collage ideas were used to illustrate the image character and concepts of each vision.

First, Cardiff's morphological structure, resilient city attributes and its socio-spatial dimensions were analyzed. Key actors were identified and invited to the local workshop sessions. The three visions – a smart-networked city, compact city and self-reliant green city – were adapted to fit into Cardiff's city profile (see Plate 4). These visions were linked to the city's longer-term strategy, already adopted for the city and the region as part of the normal planning decision-making process. Each vision was also considered at building, neighborhood and city/region scales and linked to strategies for urban growth. Potential threats to Cardiff were also identified, including floods, and water, energy and food shortages. Different visions were discussed by actors organized into three groups, composed of a mix of politicians, professionals, NGO representatives, traders, business organizations and local civil and activist groups.

The format of the workshops was similar to those run at the national level, but in the case of Cardiff the aim was to see how the generic visions discussed at the national workshops could fit into the local/regional context. In so doing, the project team was seeking answers to the following questions:

- What is to be retrofitted to achieve a greater degree of sustainability?
- Who are the key actors to be involved in this process?
- Why is change needed and desirable?
- How will it be implemented, and what resources/structures would be needed?

Each city vision was mapped against the present land use and urban form patterns and then correlated with the level of change required to achieve as many specific objectives, targets and milestones as possible, within each vision discussed. The low-level alteration required little intervention but at the high level there were a number of transformations needed to achieve the desired goals. Social values and institutions were also mapped out, to see how any retrofit would be delivered, and by whom, and if new organizations would be needed to deliver change. A variety of market-led and community organizations were identified to see how different scenarios would be delivered.

Figure 1.2 Panoramic view of Cardiff
Source: the author

For example, the ideas linked to the 'Smart-networked city' of Cardiff forecasted high economic growth, increased urban densities in the city center, new peripheral developments at the edge of the city, investment in infrastructure (smart-grid systems), distributed renewable energy supply, electric car usage, metered water monitoring and market-led recycling of waste. Particularly important in this scenario is a wired-up IT system connecting various services, but the natural environment is secondary to this form of urban retrofit/ growth. At the building level, there is much reliance on the retrofit of existing buildings using the latest energy-efficient building materials and cladding, whilst at the neighborhood and city levels, present systems of governance would continue. In terms of potential disasters, a good wired-up and connected communication system is seen as essential and useful, and it would utilize current civil and governance systems and networks.

In the 'Compact city' vision, urban land use, buildings and infrastructure are utilized to create a dense urban form that encourages a reduced usage of energy, water and other resources to optimize supply. Urban growth is of a moderate nature and retrofit is carried out through the densification of the existing morphology and the pattern of use. Concentration of mixed use and good IT network systems reduce the need for travel. There is also a good supply of green open space and some buildings may have planted green roofs. There is a potential for a good public transport system to connect various neighborhoods and to promote walking and cycling. District heat and power come from recycling of waste and from the latest technology for rain harvesting, use of sustainable urban drainage systems, solar energy supply and city/neighborhood power heating plants. Buildings are also retrofitted to conserve energy or generate new energy supply. There is also good potential for local governance at the neighborhood level while regional government, local authorities and social housing providers play an active role.

The 'Self-reliant green city' for Cardiff is a self-replenishing bio-region where people live in harmony with nature. The system relies on local resources, demand and supply are measured and the overarching idea is to live within limited resources. This vision implies lower economic growth and fall in urban densities while cooperative and collective social values underpin models of shared ownership, rise of urban agriculture and localized food supply. Green and blue systems are integrated, while the use of biomass, wind farms and micro-hydro plants at the local level provide energy. Some observers see this prototype as a medieval self-sufficient city. Green corridors and green fingers are a prominent part of the urban morphology. Building materials are recycled while buildings are insulated with straw, hemp and other natural materials. Water supply is integrated into the lower urban densities, urban centers are re-greened and there is good use of sustainable urban drainage systems (SUDS). This model also relies heavily on voluntary buy-in into the scheme and a distributed form of governance. Relevance to potential disasters is that such a city can provide useful local resources, have space to accommodate damage caused by disasters, and rely on a strong governance structure and communitarian spirit. In this scenario intergenerational equity is also of paramount importance.

As part of the workshop discussion, different ideas were rated, accepted or rejected, and potential pathways and roadmaps identified. Key targets were set and likely drivers of change were mapped into the pathways, correlating negative impacts of climate change and other potential impacts due to the types of shocks projected into the system, which had to be addressed in the scenario building schedule. Each scenario was also assessed through the participatory backcasting. The results of each group testing were compared, and then a more integrated approach to solving Cardiff's future was generated (see Figure 1.3).

The final conclusion of the workshop was that an integrated system of all three visions is needed. There is no one single solution, which leads us to the earlier concept of modularity. In the case of Cardiff, the city would benefit from some densification of its center while maintaining its green fingers and patches, such as parks and shores. The city also needs to integrate mixed uses at both the city center and neighborhood levels. Measures could be introduced to reduce the need for individual car travel and the city/region should invest in an efficient public transport system, IT and other forms of innovative infrastructure. Much can be achieved through the retrofit of buildings and some small-scale urban agriculture could be beneficial. If implemented, Cardiff would become a more resilient city as it would be able to absorb shocks and bounce back faster from potential negative impacts. In this way, the city and its region could ensure better and more secure intergenerational and intragenerational equity.

In a similar way, a competition entry for New Zealand's capital city Christchurch (see Plate 3) proposing a recovery plan after the 2010 earthquake illustrates how existing urban fabric can be retrofitted to create a more resilient urban future. This is to be achieved through a linear urban park that connects different neighborhoods and would allow residents to seek refuge in any future earthquake events. The park itself is wide enough to accommodate a variety of temporary shelters and other facilities and it is connected to city-wide access to water, electricity and other resources.

The pathways to achieving greater resilience are providing guiding directions giving indication to the policy changes required to deliver a more resilient and sustainable city, the resources needed and political will. It also requires multidisciplinary experts to work together as well as community and civic groups to engage fully in the delivery of a more resilient future city (Butina Watson, 2013). It also requires that regular checks and audits be carried out to monitor how particular milestones are met. The overall conclusion of the testing is that the approach to designing resilient cities and neighborhoods is an integrated system.

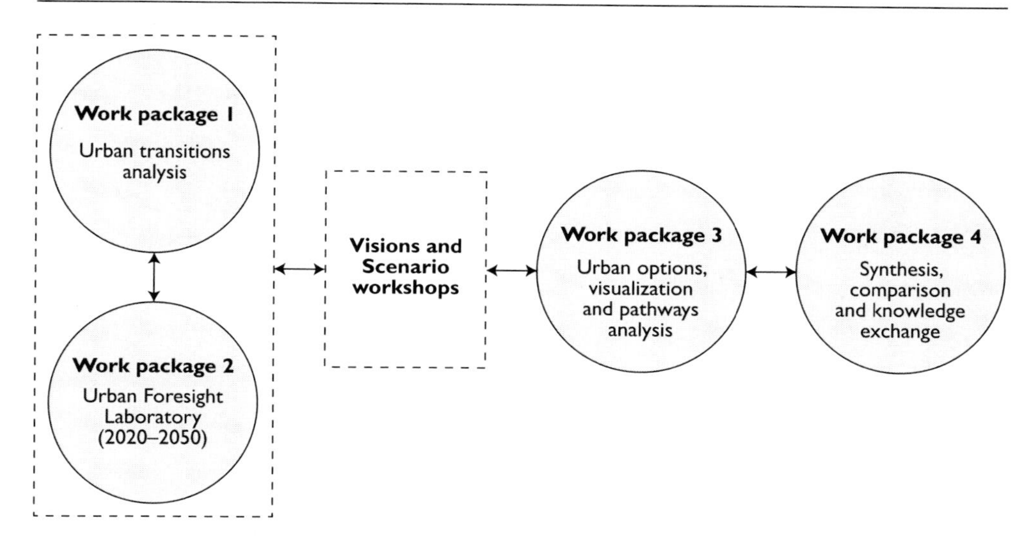

Figure 1.3 Steps of Retrofit 2050 program
Source: redrawn by the author (from Dixon et al., 2014)

A generic methodology for designing resilient cities and their neighborhoods

Key findings from the Retrofit 2050 project and other literature and projects discussed in this chapter suggest that a generic methodology could be useful when designing other types of resilient cities and neighborhoods.

First, a city-wide audit should be carried out, using the key attributes of resilience, at different morphological levels (see Figure 1.4).

By analyzing the levels and dimensions of the overall spatial structure, a picture of how a particular place has evolved over time can be formed, indicating what has changed and what is permanent. This could include the overall natural system/environment, the city morphology and its infrastructure and the characteristics of urban neighborhoods established, including streets, blocks, plots and buildings defined with their characteristic pattern of use as well as urban qualities such as permeability, variety, legibility, distinctiveness and vitality. In addition, this evaluation could also include the economic performance of the city, social/humanitarian issues and politics and governance.

Second, different city/neighborhood futures visions should be proposed and tested through collaborative workshop discussions involving all key players. These are best articulated at city and neighborhood levels, but they should also include a wider environment as well as individual buildings.

Third, pathways, roadmaps and participatory backcasting should be introduced to see how different visions would perform over time. Milestones and targets can be identified as well as shocks and potential disasters mapped onto different scenarios. Measures for resolving critical situations, resources and organizations needed to deliver a particular type of vision, and political/governance structures required to deliver a particular type of a resilient city, need to be specified.

	Empowerment	Roots	Transculturally	Co-dwelling with nature
City-wide Landform/ Linkage	Adaptability Permeability Legibility Vitality Flexibility Infrastructure	Identity Memory	Modularity	Flexibility Adaptability Green Network Access to water, food, power
Blocks/Streets Plots/ Buildings/Open spaces	Variety Vitality Adaptability	Traditional typologies	A variety of building types	Flexibility Adaptability Green buildings/ uses
Components/ Details	Identity Richness Variety	Materials and details	Identity	Energy efficiency

Figure 1.4 A matrix of resilience/morphological levels
Source: the author

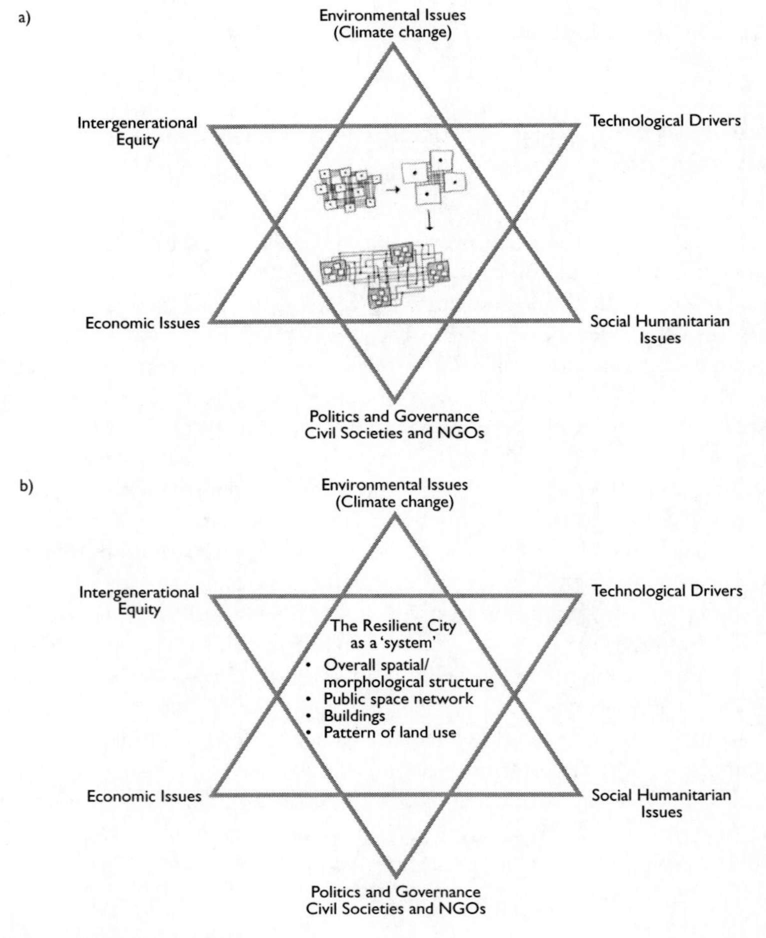

Figure 1.5 The resilient city as a system
Source: adapted from Roberts et al. (2009)

The research also identified that transition to more sustainable futures and resilient city structures cannot be achieved in a traditional way, because cities and their futures are complex and uncertain. An integrated system is needed that brings together different and multidisciplinary bodies of knowledge and understanding of different dimensions of resilience, through the attributes analysis of resilience at different scales of urban form (see Figure 1.5). Identification is also needed of the economic drivers of change and the political/governance structures to deliver such complex solutions.

Conclusion

This chapter suggests that we can learn much about instilling resilience in our built environments by studying cities that have experienced negative impacts of disasters, understanding the performance-related aspects of urban form, and seeing how different morphologies and typologies survive particular types of shocks. Resilience attributes and urban form analysis are very useful in understanding how cities are structured today, including what their key characteristics are and their forms of governance. This is already evident from 'future proofing' interventions such as 'greening' Detroit and making a self-reliant green city of Christchurch where aspects of modularity and urban memory are being used to heal the city and its people.

In a world of uncertain futures, with an increase in the type, frequency and levels of disaster, it is important to create the right platform for debate and intervention that can save many future lives and minimize the negative impacts of disasters. An 'Urban futures vision' approach is a very useful method for exploring how best to deal with negative events. As this approach involves key actors in the decision-making system, potential agreements or disagreements can be resolved earlier and can generate structures and delivery mechanisms for dealing with future disasters. Finally, it is vital to plan and design cities and neighborhoods by taking into account multiple aspects of urban life, from environmental and physical form to socio-spatial, technological, economic and political/governance dimensions to achieve more resilient urban futures. At the end of the day, good planning leads to resilience when needed and better lives daily.

References

Allan, P., Bryant, M., Wirsching, C., Garcia, D. and Rodriguez, M.T. (2013). The influence of urban morphology on the resilience of cities following an earthquake. *Journal of Urban Design* 18(2): 242–262.

Bentley, I., Alcock, A., Murrain, P., McGlynn S. and Smith, G.P. (1985). *Responsive Environments.* Oxford: Architectural Press.

Butina Watson, G. (2013). The art of place-making. In Krause, L. (ed.) *Sustaining Cities – Urban Policies, Practices and Perceptions.* New Brunswick, NJ: Rutgers University Press.

Butina Watson, G. (2014). Urban design and the retrofit agenda. In Dixon, T., Eames, M., Lannon, S. and Hunt, M. *Urban Retrofitting for Sustainability: Mapping the Transition to 2050.* Abingdon: Earthscan/Routledge.

Butina Watson, G. and Bentley, I. (2007). *Identity by Design.* Oxford: Architectural Press.

Coaffee, J. (2013). Towards next-generation urban resilience in planning practice: from securitization to integrated place making. *Planning Practice and Research* 28(3): 323–339.

De Sola Morales, M. (1999). Designing cities. *Quaderni di Lotus* 23: 80–83.

Dixon, T., Eames, M., Lannon, S. and Hunt, M. (2014). *Urban Retrofitting for Sustainability: Mapping the Transition to 2050.* Abingdon: Earthscan/Routledge.

Foster, H.D. (1997). *The Ozymandias Principles: Thirty-one Strategies for Surviving Change*. Victoria, Canada: UBC Press.
Godschalk, D. (2003). Urban hazard mitigation: creating resilient cities. *Natural Hazards Review* 47(3): 136–143.
Jacobs, J. (1961). *The Death and Life of Great American Cities*. New York: Random House.
Lister, N.M. (2007). Sustainable large parks: ecological design or designer ecology? In Cherniak, J. and Hargreaves, G. (eds) *Large Parks*. New York: Princeton Architectural Press.
Lynch, K. (1960). *The Image of the City*. Cambridge, MA: MIT Press.
Lynch, K. (1981). *The Good City Form*. Cambridge, MA: MIT Press.
Miletti, D. (ed.) (1999). *Disasters by Design: A Reassessment of Natural Hazards in the United States*. Washington, DC: Joseph Henry Press, pp. 32–33.
Moudon, A.V. (1989). *Built for Change; Neighborhood Architecture in San Francisco*. Cambridge, MA: MIT Press.
Moudon, A.V. (1997). Urban morphology as an emerging interdisciplinary field. *Urban Morphology* 1: 3–10.
Pearson, L.J., Newton, P.W. and Roberts, P. (eds) (2014). *Resilient Sustainable Cities*. Abingdon: Routledge.
Roberts, P.W., Raztez, J. and George, C. (2009). *Environment and the City*. Abingdon: Earthscan/Routledge.
Rossi, A. (1986). *The Architecture of the City*. Cambridge, MA: MIT Press.
UN (2012). *World Urbanization Prospects: The 2011 Revision*. New York: UN.
Vale, L.J. and Campanella, T.J. (2005). *The Resilient City: How Modern Cities Recover from Disaster*. Oxford: Oxford University Press.
Waldheim, C. (2013). Notes toward a history of agrarian urbanism. In Krause, L. (ed.) *Sustaining Cities – Urban Policies, Practices, and Perceptions*. Brunswick, NJ: Rutgers University Press.
Walker, B. and Salt, D. (2006). *Resilience Thinking*. Washington, DC: Island Press.
Zetter, R. and Butina Watson, G. (eds) (2006). *Designing Sustainable Cities in the Developing World*. Aldershot: Ashgate.

Chapter 2

Reconstructing the city

The potential gains of using urban planning and design practices in recovery and why they are so difficult to achieve

Alison Killing and Camillo Boano

Introduction

The fact that more than 50 percent of the world's population now lives in urban areas (UN, 2010) is frequently cited in order to summon a vision of the Zeitgeist and to get a grip on the shifting framework for human activity, humanitarian action being no exception. Around 1 billion of those urban dwellers are thought to live in slums, with this number projected to rise to 1.4 billion by 2020 (IFRC, 2010). This large-scale urban shift, bringing with it associated vulnerabilities, has heightened urban risk and already led to an increased incidence of urban disaster. From this, it has been posited that urban disaster risk reduction (DRR), response and reconstruction will dominate humanitarian efforts in the coming years (Zetter and Deikun, 2010).

But for all that agencies see the future as urban, they also see cities as presenting a confounding series of challenges which they are not yet fully equipped to meet. Aid agencies' experience to date is largely rooted in a rural context, and this is often cited as the source to which these difficulties are traced back. That general claim, however, demands a deeper dive which reveals a disengagement between relevant professions and practices in the urban arena. Urban planning and design is at best poorly understood by humanitarians and when relevant planning/design approaches have been identified, professional cultural conflicts between urban planners, designers and humanitarians make their adoption by humanitarian agencies less likely.

The challenges of urban areas

Humanitarian agencies' experience in disaster response over the past few decades has been heavily biased towards rural areas. A number of recent analyses have highlighted essential differences between rural and urban emergencies, leading to questions about humanitarian agencies' capacity to respond appropriately to disasters in urban areas (Zetter and Deikun, 2010; Sanderson et al., 2012). In an examination of the capabilities of the agencies themselves, the Inter-Agency Standing Committee (IASC) notes the lack of technical surge capacity due to the lack of suitably qualified staff (IASC, 2010). Turning its attention to the urban context, the IASC's 'Strategy for Meeting Humanitarian Challenges in Urban Areas' notes a number of key differences between rural and urban contexts, essentially reducible to the higher concentrations of people and resources in urban areas and the resulting complexity of their interactions, combined with a scarcity of land (IASC, 2010).

To be sure, urban population densities are often high in comparison to rural areas, increasing the likelihood that large numbers of people will be affected by a disaster, with a correspondingly high demand for assistance (IFRC, 2010). In Pakistan, following the October 2005 earthquake it was noted that 36 people may be housed on an urban plot in a multi-story accommodation, where the same size piece of land in a rural area would be home to only seven or eight, living in single-story dwellings (Quzai, 2010). High population densities are likely to be associated with greater building heights and greater proximity of buildings and this has serious implications for the number of individuals killed or injured due to building collapse, the greatest cause of death in an earthquake (Cosgrave, 2008). Sanitation is also much more problematic in urban areas than in rural ones (O'Donnell et al., 2009), since large numbers of people produce correspondingly large amounts of waste, while greater densities increase the ease with which disease can spread (Clermont et al., 2011).

Density of population also tends to mean scarcity of land to accommodate human activity (O'Donnell et al., 2009). This can be exacerbated post-disaster with land destroyed (typically in earthquakes) through landslides, or occupation by the rubble from collapsed buildings. There are ensuing difficulties in accessing land for temporary shelter, owing to the need for land to be freed from rubble as well as complex patterns of tenure (IASC, 2010). Formal access to land and the need for titles constitute a much greater issue in urban areas than rural ones (Schilderman, 2010).

Haiti after the 2010 earthquake suffered badly from this melange. A sizeable amount of land was lost due to the earthquake as the sides of Port-au-Prince's many ravines, and the hillside terraces on which many houses were built (see Plate 5) collapsed and space was needed for the 8 million cubic meters of rubble burying parts of the capital some two years later (Reitman, 2011) (see Figure 2.1). Only 5 percent of the country's land was registered pre-earthquake (Shelter Centre, 2010a) and 'land tenure and occupancy arrangements were often informal and poorly documented' (International Crisis Group, 2011: 17), making it difficult to find land on which to settle people and to implement a fair restitution policy.

Figure 2.1 Bulldozer clearing rubble from the marketplace in Campeche, Port-au-Prince
Source: Alison Killing

In addition, the 'urban landscape requires more collective vision – [with its] smaller spaces, services have to be shared' (Quzai, 2010: 132), an observation which co-exists unhappily with the often poorer social cohesion of urban areas. While communities in rural areas tend to be relatively homogeneous, usually with strong traditions of self-help (Schilderman, 2010), cities are much more heterogeneous and may lack the strong social capital necessary to solve certain problems, particularly those which must be tackled communally. For humanitarian actors, this can cause problems: 'it may be difficult to organise a humanitarian intervention at neighborhood scale where there is a weak tradition of investing in shared infrastructure and/or public goods' (Shelter Centre, 2010b). Post-disaster, in a situation where the majority of work done in responding to a humanitarian emergency is carried out by the affected population themselves (Sphere Project, 2011), the absence of a collective spirit can be problematic.

While local diversity can also be a strength, offering a wide range of skills available within the population from which civil society organizations can draw for help contributing to a faster recovery (IASC, 2010), this local capacity is often overlooked due to aid workers' sense of urgency in an emergency response (Rencoret, 2010). The concentration of economic resources can also lead to larger losses. Where people's livelihoods are rooted in a market economy and concentrated in secondary and tertiary industries there is a greater chance of severe disruption following a natural disaster. Strong connections between a city and its peri-urban and rural hinterland mean that areas perhaps physically unaffected by the primary disaster will nonetheless suffer from damage to the city's economy and the resulting disruption of services and supplies.

Damage to the physical environment entails disruption to other aspects of urban life (Boano and Hunter, 2011). The economy, as well as the social and political life of urban areas, is closely bound up with the physical environment in which it takes place. The density of population and resources, their strong interconnection and the resulting complexity of urban areas means that activities required for post-disaster recovery are correspondingly complex. 'Effective recovery requires the coordination of initiatives to support livelihoods/ employment, shelter/housing, and urban services, such as water and sanitation systems, power, communications and transport' (O'Donnell et al., 2009: 10). Several of these elements comprise networks which extend across an entire city and beyond and are necessarily considered and acted upon at the level of the city or region. Where humanitarian agencies find themselves working in urban areas they may of necessity find themselves working with, and to the benefit of, a wider group of people than they might typically work with (as they negotiate the route and construct a sewer, for example). This contrasts sharply with the standard model for the provision of humanitarian aid, based as it is on assistance to individuals and individual households, with a focus on those perceived to be most vulnerable (Crawford et al., 2010).

Humanitarian approaches to urban planning and design

Within the humanitarian literature several commentators have called for a larger-scale approach to complement existing assistance methods, with such approaches referred to variously as settlement planning, urban planning and spatial planning (Kennedy et al., 2008; Crawford et al., 2010; Shelter Centre, 2010a). Urban planning is taken in this chapter to be a field whose 'broad objective is to guide the development of the city for a specified time period and to promote the land-use pattern which most efficiently fulfils the objectives of the government' (UN, 1998: 10). The actual plans may take a variety of forms and involve projects at a variety of scales. Within this range of approaches, it is important to note that much of the practice of the discipline, both historically and today, is concerned with physical planning and with guiding the physical form of the built environment.

Recommendations for the use of urban planning on the part of humanitarian actors are generally not advanced in these terms. Instead, reference to urban planning tends to signify the existence of issues which cannot be tackled at the level of the individual and which therefore sit awkwardly with more traditional approaches to emergency shelter. Kennedy et al. (2008) in their paper on the shelter response in Sri Lanka and Aceh following the Indian Ocean tsunami of 2004 specifically recommend that spatial planning should be incorporated into the reconstruction. They suggest that the settlements there require a series of measures to be taken to reduce their vulnerability to further risk, including the construction of evacuation routes, locating shelters and infrastructure to reduce exposure to wind and water flows, to channel surface runoff following heavy rain and to provide fire breaks between buildings.

To date there have been limited, and often somewhat halting, attempts to integrate urban design and urban planning approaches into agencies' work; the tensions are especially apparent where attempts have been made to reconcile these approaches with the formal structures of humanitarian assistance. Urban planning makes an appearance in the 2010 publication *Shelter After Disaster* as that publication deals with the makeup of the shelter sector coordination body, which formulates and then oversees the implementation of a common shelter strategy (Shelter Centre, 2010a). Urban planning is included as one of the technical working groups of the shelter sector, which, together with risk mapping, GIS data, land registration and structural engineering, may help inform the shelter strategy, but are clearly subordinated to it. Later, with reference to program implementation, 'infrastructure and settlement planning support' is included as one of the '18 assistance methods' for helping to achieve durable shelter for populations affected by disaster (Shelter Centre, 2010a: 98). Examples of this include rebuilding of infrastructure such as roads and bridges, or for energy supply, the provision of community buildings, or the management of rubble clearance. But there is little guidance given on how these measures might be integrated into the humanitarian response. The authors also fail to go beyond the specific tasks which may be required, to give more general guidance on how a community-level intervention might fit into the typical organization of a humanitarian response. Despite the calls for integration and the fact that many of the tasks listed affect more than one sector of the humanitarian response, responsibility for urban planning is seen to be split amongst those sectors which deal with the built environment, with tasks related to spatial planning variously subordinated to the shelter cluster, water, sanitation and hygiene (WASH), telecommunications, schools or health, presumably to be coordinated via inter-sectoral meetings, rather than being pursued as a genuinely cross-sectoral activity.

A second tendency in humanitarian agencies' thinking about urban planning and design is also revealing: that the favoured expression for referring to these approaches is 'settlement planning.' Within the humanitarian literature, the word 'settlement' is often used to convey a series of meanings. It has two dictionary definitions: the first is a concrete noun and refers to the settlement as a physical, tangible thing, i.e. the town, village, or city; the second is an abstract noun which means 'the act of settling.' In the humanitarian world the two versions of the term have a typically narrower definition, redefined with a displaced population in mind, one that has been displaced from its original home by a significant distance. When 'settlement' is used in the concrete sense, it has often been found together with the descriptor 'transitional,' attached to the idea of a settlement camp.

Figure 2.2 Transitional shelter in Baillergeau, Port-au-Prince
Source: Alison Killing

'Settlement' is also regularly conflated with the term 'shelter,' mainly with reference to the series of 'shelter options' to assist an affected population – a mix of tenure arrangements, such as owner occupation or renting and building types such as apartments, individual houses, shared evacuation centers. The list of 'shelter options' also typically includes 'transitional settlement,' the one reference in this list to settlement as a concrete physical thing and not in the abstract sense (see Figure 2.2). It sits slightly uncomfortably among the other 'shelter options' however, mainly because of its scale – because it is in fact made up from a collection of all the other shelter options, oriented towards individual families.

Lessons from slum upgrading

In *The Placemaker's Guide to Building Community*, Hamdi (2010: 37) describes a slum upgrade which he worked on:

> the first interventions were typical of most upgrading projects: improve sanitation, manage solid waste efficiently and profitably, ensure security of tenure, reduce the risk of fire, improve most and expand some of the houses, ensure access for small vehicles and for pedestrians.

Further problems identified in the area included malnutrition, unemployment and a lack of pre-natal care. Where this scenario deals with chronic poverty which has not been subjected to the sudden disruption of a disaster, the list of needs is comparable to a reconstruction project, particularly as it relates to the poorest and most vulnerable parts of the city.

Later in the text, Hamdi describes an early stage in the slum upgrading process, where people have discussed and prioritized their needs and must now work out the physical form of the buildings and outdoor spaces that would best meet these requirements. The first step was to work with the residents to negotiate the standards and rules which would guide the development of this small neighborhood. Restrictions on plot boundaries were agreed, the amount of the plot which could be covered by building, the distance by which the front of the building must be set back from the road, the uses of ground floors facing onto the streets, building heights and the positions of windows to avoid overlooking, and other physical planning features. Further discussions produced agreements on tree planting in the streets, bulk purchasing of materials and on how waste could be collected and disposed of (Hamdi, 2010). While this work was clearly developmental, rather than taking place as part of an emergency response, it addresses a similar community to that which a humanitarian agency might find itself working with post-disaster and lists many of the challenges of working in urban areas, as well as offering potential approaches to resolving them. Of course, the need for action on a compressed timetable and the extreme conditions of a disaster aftermath would affect the rhythm and substance of participation and discussion, but the structure of discussion could be quite similar.

Beyond improvements in sanitation, access and reduced fire risk, a crucial part of these slum upgrades is establishing security of tenure, whereby the poor are brought into the formal land market (UN, 1998), with the parcels of land they live on, their boundaries and ownership recognized by the state. This may be achieved in a number of ways. Land sharing and land readjustment are commonly described methods of regularization. Land sharing involves the land owner and occupants reaching an agreement whereby the land owner develops the most economically attractive part of the site and the occupants acquire leasehold over the rest. The occupants base their right to the land on their possession of it, but plots must often be readjusted (typically with the land being pooled and then redivided) to accommodate both the owner's new buildings and the new, common infrastructure. The reduced space has often necessitated building higher, something which has often proved unpopular with slum dwellers. Land sharing and land readjustment are often complex and time consuming processes, due to the large number of stakeholders and the need to reach consensus.

Hamdi (2010) describes the typical *informal* process by which many poorer people arrive at secure housing, i.e. move onto/invade land owned by others, incrementally build, then put in infrastructure, and then after some time, obtain some form of tenure. This is contrasted with the *formal* way in which a wealthier household might acquire housing in the formal market, which is the same process, but in reverse. Attempts to house low-income groups through the formal process have generally failed, as being unaffordable for the poor (UN, 1998). Hamdi concurs: 'when a progressive or incremental process is denied to the poor, the burden of investment all at once and the repayment of loans, often pushes people back to the insecurity and vulnerability from which they came' (2010: 120). Although the context of this example is developmental, in a post-disaster situation 'the resources and capacities available usually mean that damaged buildings cannot be replaced like for like' (Shelter Centre, 2010a: xvi). The need to work with lower-income groups and pursue reconstruction approaches that are affordable to them makes an incremental approach especially valuable.

In its need to establish permission to use land before construction can begin and the general model of top-down centralized delivery, reconstruction in a humanitarian emergency more closely approximates the model of formal housing. Following an emergency and in a situation where outside assistance is relied upon, the poor are pushed towards a model of development comparable to that of the formal housing market. Instead there is a need to adopt models based more on an informal, incremental approach.

The role of urban planning and design

Outside of an aid and development context, Hamdi's slum upgrade and the land regularization processes that run alongside would probably be described as urban planning processes. In fact, urban planning did have a place in attempting to provide housing for low-income groups in developing countries in the 1960s and 1970s mostly as part of the large-scale provision of serviced sites, sometimes with ready-built houses, an approach referred to as 'sites and services.' This approach was eventually discredited due to its high cost and failure to reach target groups, with the houses often being appropriated by less poor groups or falling into the hands of speculators. In addition, spatial planning was, in the words of the UN, 'most often regarded as essentially static in nature' (UN, 1998: 9). It was unable to keep pace with the speed of change in cities and so policy moved on from 'delivering' to 'enabling' with self-build and slum upgrades involving participatory approaches such as community action planning (Wamsler, 2006).

There is, however, still a need for urban planning, if in a more modern and flexible form, as a way to reconcile the spatial form of the city with its economic and social development. 'Strategic urban planning recognises that urban issues cannot be addressed in isolation, but considers the citywide relations and linkages between different interventions and looks at the city as a system with interlinked components' (UN-Habitat, 2010a: 6). The broad objective of spatial plans 'is to guide the development of the city for a specified time period and to promote the land-use pattern which most efficiently fulfils the objectives of the government' (UN, 1998: 10).

Master plans, the kind of planning product that Wamsler referred to in describing the 'centralist, social planning' (2006) and which had caused so many to reject urban planning outright, operate on the basis of spatially fixed top-down determined geographies, with change taking place slowly. Moreover, they often fail to take into account the impact of the economy on the need for different types and amounts of spaces (UN, 1998). Structural, or strategic, plans are far more flexible, identifying critical issues and then setting priorities for investment, thereby providing a framework for decision-making at a smaller scale, that of a neighborhood, for example. According to UN-Habitat (2009): 'Citywide strategic planning aims to establish a structure of principles (policy and regulations) and a strategic action plan inside which different interventions can be carried out to reach the city's development goals.' Using this type of urban planning, participation and 'decentralisation are possible within a central strategic framework' (Lyons, 2009).

The need for strategies at a city-wide scale is starting to be recognized. Community action planning is limited to the level of the neighborhood, but Hamdi points out the need to work, in addition, at what he refers to as an 'urban' rather than a 'project' scale (2010). Where the projects referred to are neighborhood plans, the implication is of the need to work at a larger city scale. This can be seen as an acknowledgment of the need to coordinate what happens at community levels with a larger scale and a reciprocal recognition of the impact of higher-level policies, dealing with spatial planning or the economy for example, on smaller-scale community interventions. The neighborhood-scale projects need to be linked to the larger, city scale, in the same way that the neighborhood-wide rules that residents develop for the construction of their individual houses will link into and be governed by the relatively larger neighborhood scale. As Schurch puts it, 'intervention at one scale requires consideration of the context of the others' (1999: 17).

Urban design as specific practice, and what it has to offer humanitarian response

The process of urban design, the distinctly design-oriented piece as part of physical planning or as a stand-alone concept and practice, is comparable to Hamdi's slum upgrade in the scale addressed and in the development of rules around height, density and other shape and bulk rules to guide individual interventions. It is not necessarily participatory, nor is it tied to a specific sort of neighborhood in the way that community action planning and slum upgrading are. As a young field, which emerged only in the 1960s, it is often poorly understood, a problem that can also be partly ascribed to its interdisciplinary nature. It brings together aspects of 'both architecture and planning, but extends beyond the remit of either of these disciplines' (Moudon, 2003).

In addition to architecture and planning, urban design combines elements of urban geography, sociology and economics. The scale at which issues are addressed is seen as a defining factor – a scale larger than that of a single building (Schurch, 1999) – which is evocative, if simplistic. Urban design builds on the skills of the architect in its morphological connection and its concern with design at the scale of several buildings. Among other factors, Schurch describes urban design's remit as encompassing density, the mix of uses in an area (residential, commercial, industrial, public, for example), public realm and human scale, for example, how far an average person could reasonably be expected to walk to reach a certain destination, which has a bearing on distribution of services and on the size of the street grid.

As such it is useful as a bridge between the disciplines it draws on, taking the written strategies and abstracted diagrams, used in urban planning to accompany its drawn plans and providing the detailed information necessary for architecture and smaller-scale interventions to be realized, in keeping with wider economic, social and spatial planning aims. In providing detailed, localized rules for density, mixed use and the organization of the public realm it can mediate between the demands of individual built interventions and wider community and societal needs.

For humanitarians faced with the need to reconstruct an urban area and struggling with a context in which the buildings, infrastructure and public spaces which make up the urban environment are tightly packed, urban design provides a set of tools to mediate competing claims on limited space. Working at a scale larger than that of individual interventions means that it can take a role in coordinating them. Where there have been calls to work at the level of the community, rather than only targeting individuals, urban design provides a way in which this can be done by the sectors involved in the built environment. Where there is a need to create closer links to development, it introduces a process familiar to development practitioners at a relatively early point in a response to a disaster, providing an easy way to engage with these actors. In the development of neighborhood plans it is impossible to realize everything at once. Interventions must be realized over a period of time and this means that priorities must be set, which, in turn, must relate to the economic and social priorities of the neighborhood and city. In this way urban design is able to address issues beyond the purely physical. As a result it is possible therefore to posit four main roles for urban design:

1 Coordination: the ability to represent and understand information spatially and graphically can be useful in coordinating small-scale spatial interventions, preventing both gaps and overlapping, disjointed interventions.

2 Linkages: between long-term, large-scale strategies and short-term, small-scale interventions. Urban design's link to planning means that it is able to take a long-term, strategic view, while also providing enough detail to guide smaller-scale interventions in the short term. It defines a spatial and volumetric framework within which a humanitarian program of, for example, shelter, can take place.
3 Synthesis: offering a spatial response to a variety of economic, social and political needs, convening a discussion around competing demands for the same space and providing the tools to resolve them.
4 Communication: using tools related to urban design, detailed maps in particular, to effectively communicate proposals and keep an accurate record of proposals and interventions that can survive the rapid staff turnover common to humanitarian deployments.

Tensions between urban design and humanitarian response

If urban design has so much to offer, why have aid agencies yet to adopt relevant tools from it? The answer comes down to a complex mix of factors: while both humanitarians and urban designers see the need for, and value highly, each other's skills, deep professional and cultural differences can prevent their working together effectively. These include conflicting organizational methods and ways of working, very different views on how to achieve equity, the principles underpinning humanitarian action which preclude involvement in many of the processes around land use, and different ways of conceiving of the city.

When the humanitarian cluster system was first implemented in 2005,[1] one of the problems it was intended to solve was the need for better coordination within and between responders. A number of the clusters formed are particularly relevant to the physical reconstruction of the city, with shelter perhaps being the most obvious. Other clusters – water, sanitation and hygiene (WASH), livelihoods, protection (especially as it relates to land and housing rights) and camp coordination and camp management (CCCM) – also have important roles to play. In some cases significant gains have been made in coordination since the introduction of this system and it is recognized that while in some cases it is helpful to separate sectors, in others this results in difficulties. The need for clusters dealing with 'cross-cutting issues,' such as gender, age, environment and HIV and AIDS, as well as the multi-sectoral early recovery cluster is an implicit recognition of the problems of dividing a humanitarian response into discrete sectors and the need for a more holistic and developmental approach once immediate life-saving measures have been taken.

The cluster system contrasts with the approach of urban designers. Urban design is a synthetic field which favours looking at a multitude of factors together in order to arrive at a solution which satisfies all of them. The aim in urban design is to bring these issues together and develop a guiding concept which can allow them to be more than the sum of their parts, something which becomes possible when working at a larger scale. This perhaps constitutes a key difference between urban design and humanitarian approaches based on the cluster system which typically seeks to do no more than coordinate. This more modest vision is in some senses limiting, but is also in many ways more appropriate to humanitarian agencies' principles and conceptions of equity. The limited funding of the clusters and the wish of many humanitarian agencies to retain greater independence also serves to limit the clusters' role.

The issue of impartiality is not a purely philosophical issue and has important practical ramifications related to the safety of humanitarian workers and agencies' access to those in need. Worker security and access to the needy are fundamentally based on humanitarians' impartiality (Ashdown, 2011), though this is often a greater issue in a conflict scenario that a naturally induced disaster. Nevertheless, concerns have been raised around the extension of what Stoddard refers to as the 'humanitarian footprint' (2008: 10), as agencies remain operational for longer periods post-disaster and take on a wide range of tasks, many of which are the legitimate job of government. This has led some commentators to suggest that humanitarian action should stop after the relief stage (Crawford et al., 2014), although this brings practical problems of its own, particularly with regard to the continuity of transition to recovery and development. The humanitarian aim to put people back where they were before the disaster, albeit with reduced vulnerability (Shelter Centre, 2010a), inevitably draws humanitarian action into activities beyond emergency relief. While Christoplos argues that the transitions between phases of an emergency are the responsibility of government and are not the concern of humanitarians themselves (2006), this does not answer the question of how to proceed when government is unable to direct humanitarian action, nor does it answer the question whether self-imposed visions of what a humanitarian does should remain controlling.

In addition to problems of equity, work at a scale larger than that of an individual poses questions of legitimacy. The humanitarian approach to equity and impartiality, focusing purely on need and discounting loss beyond need appears to be a barrier to reconstruction and wider recovery. 'Founded on egalitarian mandates, which insist upon viewing all emergencies at the level of the individual or individual household, [humanitarian agencies] have often proved unequal to the task of supporting the reconstruction of urban areas' (Crawford and Kennedy, 2011: 9). This raises the question of what scale is appropriate for humanitarian actors to work at and their legitimacy in doing so. Working in urban planning and with urban design 'is not neutral, since the decisions required regarding property rights, land-use planning and access to natural resources are by nature part of political processes at national and local levels' (Christoplos, 2006: 51) and therefore must be subject to democratic oversight.

Enlarging the scale of humanitarian response

This is not to argue that humanitarian agencies should refrain from engaging in these processes – in fact it is argued that they need to. Rather, they may need to take a more developmental approach. 'Shelter has frequently been addressed in a narrow perspective, without sufficient concern for the functionality of the communities being rebuilt and created' (Christoplos, 2006: 14). There is a need to move beyond the view which conflates the city with a physical collection of residential buildings. O'Donnell et al. suggest that 'successful recovery is ultimately about rebuilding settlements' (2009: 22), which, if interpreted broadly to mean supporting the recovery of the range of physical, economic and social processes that combine to make up an urban area, would suggest that work may also be needed to replace the other buildings of the city, as a means to supporting local government, health and medical care and education.

It is helpful to look back at what humanitarian agencies wish to achieve in working in emergency shelter. The Sphere Project notes that, 'beyond survival, shelter is necessary to provide security, personal safety and protection from the climate and to promote resistance to ill health and disease. It is also important for human dignity, to sustain family and community life' (2011: 244). The right to housing, which is based on a range of international legal instruments, sees this definition extended further (UNHCHR, 1991). It encompasses much which extends beyond the basic habitability of an individual dwelling:

> the availability of services, facilities, materials and infrastructure; affordability, habitability, accessibility, location and cultural appropriateness; sustainable access to natural and common resources; safe drinking water; energy for cooking, heating and lighting; sanitation and washing facilities; means of food storage; refuse disposal; site drainage; and emergency services.
>
> (Sphere Project, 2011: 243)

A key observation is that a number of aspects of the right to housing can only be addressed through interventions at a scale larger than that of the individual house and household. These interventions may be provided as a service to a community, or require coordination among multiple stakeholders, and consideration at a larger scale may be necessary due to competing demands for limited space. Examples of interventions include infrastructure, refuse disposal, site drainage and services and facilities. In urban areas, where livelihoods, health and security are linked more closely to the wider built environment, can the justification for investing in shelter not then be extended to rebuilding the wider city?

Where shelter, livelihoods and health are so intimately connected, it may be effective in some cases to focus on non-residential parts of the built environment which provide room for other aspects of people's lives: rebuilding a shop for example, as a way of helping to re-establish someone's livelihood, so that they can pay to rent an apartment, or reconstruct their house. In another area it may be appropriate to focus on sanitation so that existing dwellings can be clean and healthy. Assisting people in achieving durable shelter solutions then may become more about addressing issues which are tangential to the dwelling itself, i.e. a wider process of 'sheltering.'

It is at this point, however, that differing conceptions of equity come into play. Building a sewer through a neighborhood will benefit everyone in that area (see Plate 6), not only the most vulnerable (although the neighborhood a humanitarian agency works in is likely to be selected precisely because it is home to large numbers of 'vulnerable' individuals). It is in dealing with the economy, typically through programs that address people's livelihoods that the tensions in different views of equity are exposed, as questions of social good are set against those of private profit. Of course building a sewer is costly and is intrinsically 'developmental' in nature; however, this points to the need for agencies to coordinate efforts and budgets more wisely and to consider long-term interventions, not only relief measures.

There is already some support for this kind of approach from agencies and assistance to restore livelihoods alongside shelter broadly matches the stated priorities for the affected population themselves. Clermont et al., in their review of the UK Disasters Emergency Committee's (DEC)[2] member agencies' response to the Haiti earthquake, describe an agency survey which found that people considered livelihoods, education and shelter to be their most important concerns, in that order (Clermont et al., 2011). Following the Bhuj earthquake in India, low-income groups made cumulatively large investments in their own recovery, with a rough 50/50 split between recovering livelihoods and rebuilding houses (O'Donnell et al., 2009). With cash-assistance programs, money has frequently been diverted to livelihoods and away from housing, with buildings being completed later, or in stages, although if this leads to decreased vulnerability and strengthened livelihood assets it is not necessarily an issue (Schilderman, 2010). 'It might be an argument for agencies to offer people a broader package of support with some flexibility for individual households to determine the sequence of spending on their priorities' (Schilderman, 2010: 37) so as to best meet their own recovery needs as defined by them.

The most obvious way in which reconstruction of the wider physical environment might support livelihoods is through re-providing the sites of employment. At the level of support to an individual this may mean the rebuilding of a shop, office or studio owned by the individual earning his or her livelihood within it. This would obviously do much to support the individual owner's livelihood, but would also form part of rebuilding that community. Small businesses provide a service to their customers, may generate a small amount of employment and also support other businesses in the city and in surrounding areas through their trade transactions. There were instances of shopkeepers in Haiti after the earthquake asking for assistance in rebuilding their damaged shops (and not only for the reconstruction of houses); however, it was not possible to accommodate this within the relevant agency's program. Agencies need to consider including this sort of intervention as part of their legitimate support to an individual if the notion of people-centered responses is genuinely held to be true. Wider support to petty traders should perhaps also be more widely adopted, not only through employing people for the delivery of assistance in the relief phase, as the NGO Christian Aid did with street food vendors in Haiti (Clermont et al., 2011), but also in recovery operations. This could take the form of technical assistance for the repair of buildings, or cash grants for replacing equipment and stock.

Humanitarian agencies' support to livelihoods has typically followed the pattern of provision of objects to individuals and for a long time credence has been given to the idea that direct support to own-account production (where people produce food and other goods for their own use) or to self-employed 'entrepreneurs' is the most equitable way to provide assistance. While this assumption has long been questioned in development circles and, indeed, is disparagingly referred to as the 'yeoman farmer fallacy,' it has yet to be discredited among humanitarians, at least to the same extent as it has been in development circles (Christoplos, 2006). Particularly in urban areas, where 'local livelihoods are reliant on the local labour market and local economic dynamism' (O'Donnell et al., 2009: 18), there may be a case for support to medium and large enterprises to help replace lost employment opportunities (Christoplos, 2006).

These direct and indirect forms of support to individuals' shelter will almost certainly need to be supported by direct and indirect forms of shelter and reconstruction support at a larger scale. Examples of direct support at a larger scale are those built environment interventions which need to be coordinated with the wider community, across a series of households, for example, installing drains along a street. A larger-scale indirect measure might be rebuilding the main market of the city, helping to re-establish this as a service for people to obtain the goods they need, but also as a site of employment supporting livelihoods. These indirect, larger-scale interventions can help support smaller-scale measures, but it can be much more difficult to measure their impact, a factor important for accountability to mention nothing of funding.

Assistance provided indirectly at a larger scale may be both efficient and even vital to the recovery of urban areas, but it poses awkward dilemmas for humanitarians. Indirect support to employment and livelihoods by helping recover the losses of medium and large enterprises may be effective in helping to reinstate the livelihoods of a community, but on the surface at least, this appears to contradict the humanitarian commitment to impartiality and targeting the most vulnerable (Sphere Project, 2011). Humanitarians are told to focus on need and not loss. There is some evidence, however, that 'losses that reduce economic activity ... may have the greatest impact on the poor' (Sphere Project, 2011: 67), both through the loss of individual jobs, but also in the damage to the city's tax base and resulting damage to service provision. Lyons et al. (2010) highlight the need to connect interventions to regional planning and regional economies. If it is accepted that a broader development approach to reconstruction is required this may also provoke a reassessment of the principles governing relief, recovery and reconstruction, and lead to the adoption of standards derived from development practice. In development, 'issues of sustainability, public finance of basic social services, alignment with national policies and congruence with local norms all enter the equation' (Christoplos, 2006: 67). It could also lead to a greater engagement with urban planning and design.

There is a squeamishness on the part of humanitarians to engage with this issue, which is understandable given the overriding humanitarian focus on need. There is for many (though not all) agencies a continuing reluctance to support the recovery of the private sector, which 'appears to be primarily due to a pre-existing belief that such support is not "equitable"' (Christoplos, 2006: 68). These doubts need to be tested in relation to the lessons which emerged from three countries and regions which have undergone some of the largest relief-recovery-development operations from the mid-1990s on – Bosnia-Herzegovina, Kosovo and East Timor – all three of which continue to suffer from very high unemployment and regular public finance crises.

In shelter, the equivalent of this support to medium and large businesses would be support to landlords who have lost rental properties to help them quickly rehouse former tenants who may have lost their homes. A case can probably be made for this sort of assistance in terms of avoiding relocations and the breakup of communities. Precedents exist of low-cost loans being made to construction companies to rebuild blocks of flats (O'Donnell et al., 2009). In Haiti cash grants were provided to the occupants of houses designated as 'red' (severely damaged or destroyed) and 'yellow' (in need of repair), whether the occupants were owners or tenants. The rights of landlords and tenants also need to be balanced carefully, with UN-Habitat cautioning that landlords may feel threatened if assistance focuses purely on tenants (2010b).

Conceiving the city – how do we represent and analyze its data?

The final issue that makes it challenging for urban planners and designers to work effectively with humanitarians is their different ways of conceiving the city, the sorts of data they choose to look at to inform their analyses, the means by which this information is then broken down and analyzed and finally how it is communicated. Humanitarians have a clear preference for information presented in text and on spreadsheets, where urban planners and designers tend to work with images and spatial data, typically employing detailed maps of a given area.

One example from Haiti is illustrative. In one neighborhood data about the number of houses requiring rebuilding was not collected via a physical survey of the area in which the information would have been recorded as a detailed map of the area. Instead, with the houses having already been classified by the Haitian Ministry of Public Works as requiring demolition (red houses), repair (yellow houses) or being safe (green), the information about who required what sort of shelter assistance was collected by asking individual families what 'color' house they were living in and apportioning the corresponding level and type of assistance accordingly. With this information recorded as a list of names in a

Figure 2.3 Enumeration team in Simon Pele, Port-au-Prince
Source: Alison Killing

spreadsheet, the fact that families shared houses was overlooked and this led to duplication in the list; two families reporting that they lived in 'red' houses was assumed to be two individual 'red' houses, when in fact there may only have been one. It should be pointed out that urban planners and designers, with their maps, would have brought a different set of biases. By taking the physical characteristics of the local environment as the main lens for thinking about what should be done, individual vulnerability becomes less significant as a guiding factor and can itself lead to distortions.

Of course neither way of thinking about the city has the monopoly on 'right' answers. In fact the complexity of urban areas demands a correspondingly complex means of analysis. The typical analyses of both humanitarians and urban planners and designers have their strengths and in other ways are lacking; they should be seen as complementary and enriching of the other perspective, rather than necessarily contradictory. At the moment it is difficult for humanitarians to access and integrate these multiple perspectives even if they were so inclined to do so, because the relevant information and tools, and often the skills to make sense of them, are not easily available to humanitarian agencies.

Recent advancements in digital mapping and the ability to capture detailed aerial photographs of affected areas present new opportunities for agencies. However, as currently used, maps tend to be at an extremely large scale – showing the entire country for example, and used to represent spreadsheet data visually, rather than describe physical characteristics of place, such as where houses, roads and rivers are located. More detailed maps and aerial photographs may currently be used to describe the boundaries of an agency's area of intervention, but (at least up until now) have largely only been put to greater use in isolated cases.

For the purposes of coordinating the reconstruction of neighborhoods, many of the maps traditionally produced are not comprehensive and lack the necessary level of detail (see IASC, 2011a, 2011b). This practice of mapping needs to be extended, with more detailed maps, ideally able to describe land parcel boundaries, building outlines and open spaces. In this way, conflicting interventions can be avoided, and geographical gaps in the response can be identified and hopefully filled. UN-Habitat suggests that 'district plans should ensure coordination and compatibility between various community plans, particularly in terms of trans-community infrastructure such as roads, sewage and water supply' (2010b: 104).

For humanitarians, use of plans drawn at a larger, city scale could be limited to the role of providing oversight of the various reconstruction efforts across a city (although recent innovations from organizations such as OpenStreetMap and MapAction in producing maps derived from crowdsourced data provide hope for future increased resolution and accuracy of map quality).

Moving beyond coordination to take strategic decisions based on a city-wide strategic plan is a different matter. The job of setting the priorities in reconstruction belongs properly to national governments, perhaps assisted by international actors where capacity is lacking and when invited. Where these strategic spatial plans did not exist pre-disaster and where neither the government, nor agencies with the skill to potentially assist, have the capacity post-disaster, there will almost certainly be no strategic framework to refer to. While humanitarian agencies cannot take this task on, they may find themselves making de facto strategic decisions. Opting to rebuild a country's main port or repair the primary trunk roads from the capital may be valid decisions, justified in terms of enabling aid delivery, but they are also significant strategic, spatial planning decisions. They need to be seen as such.

Conclusion

While it may not be initially comfortable or always appropriate for humanitarians to work at very large scales, there are valid reasons to work at a scale somewhere between that of the individual dwelling and the city, even if it is also desirable for government to lead on neighborhood plans. Where direct support to individuals and individual households to achieve durable shelter solutions relies not only on the indirect support of livelihoods assistance, but also on the support of direct, larger-scale interventions such as infrastructure, an urban planning and design approach is required not only to coordinate action, but also to resolve competing demands for limited space and to set priorities. Urban planning and design's longer-term view can also accommodate many of the indirect means of providing support to shelter, such as livelihoods, through the priorities it sets – to rebuild the roads connecting a predominantly residential area to the market, or perhaps to rebuild the market itself. In responding and giving form to a wider set of priorities it can also link to larger, city- and regional-scale strategic plans, where these exist. In providing a method for drawing together these different scales of intervention and the numerous factors which contribute to the achievement of durable shelter solutions, the use of urban planning and design can potentially lead to a wider form of sheltering.

Even if urban planning and design has lots to offer for resolving some of the seemingly intractable challenges facing humanitarian agencies working in urban areas, it is unlikely that the many tensions that exist between humanitarian and urban planning and design approaches will be resolved in the near future. There appears to be a need for a move towards more developmental approaches in the recovery of the built environment as a consequence both of the long-term nature of any (re)construction project and of the

Figure 2.4 Construction site in downtown Port-au-Prince
Source: Alison Killing

complexity and close interconnections of spatial, social and economic factors in urban areas. The developmental nature of this approach brings some conflicts with humanitarian principles already, however, particularly with regard to impartiality and the humanitarian view of equity, which dictates that assistance be provided based on need alone. The realities of budget allocation, with funds split between sectors and between separate phases of a response and the fact that they must often be spent within a tight timeframe, mean that the introduction of development practices and principles in a humanitarian context and integration with and between relief and recovery remains difficult, even several decades after the need for links between these phases was first put forward.

It is important to take into account the stated concerns of humanitarian agencies about engaging in urban planning and design processes, not least if these apparently valuable approaches are to have a chance at being effectively adopted. Urban planning and design currently falls outside the mandate of any of the relevant clusters. Concerns have also been raised about the availability of staff with the appropriate skill sets, were agencies to commit to greater involvement in and of urban planning and design processes. While these objections need to be taken seriously, the urban planning and design approaches identified above seem to offer real answers to a set of problems that agencies have been struggling with for a number of years, making further investigation worthwhile. Going beyond the workings of the humanitarian system, there are also serious questions to be asked about how agency engagement in this sort of work integrates with the processes, both formal and informal, by which cities are built outside of emergencies.

Notes

1 As a result of the Humanitarian Reform Agenda in response to recurrent criticisms of humanitarian response.

2 A funding mechanism that provides funds to 15 of the largest international NGOs.

References

Ashdown, P. (2011). *Humanitarian Emergency Response Review*. London: DFID. Available at: www.dfid.gov.uk/Documents/publications1/HERR.pdf (accessed July 6, 2011).

Boano, C. and Hunter, W. (2011). *Architecture at Risk (?): The Ambivalent Nature of Post-Disaster Practice*. Oxford: Oxford Brookes University.

Christoplos, I. (2006). *Links Between Relief, Rehabilitation and Development in the Tsunami Response*. London: Tsunami Evaluation Coalition. Available at: http://ochanet.unocha.org/p/Documents/TEC_LRRD_Report.pdf (accessed July 17, 2011).

Clermont, C., Sanderson, D., Sharma, A. and Spraos, H. (2011). *Urban Disasters – Lessons From Haiti: Study of Member Agencies' Responses to the Earthquake in Port au Prince, Haiti, January 2010*. London: Disasters Emergency Committee. Available at: www.dec.org.uk/download/856/DEC-Haiti-urban-study.pdf (accessed April 1, 2011).

Cosgrave, J. (2008). *Responding to Earthquakes: Learning from Earthquake Relief and Recovery Operations*. London: ALNAP. Available at: www.alnap.org/pool/files/ALNAPLessons Earthquakes.pdf (accessed June 6, 2011).

Crawford, K. and Kennedy, J. (2011). *Whose City Is It Anyway? Limiting International Humanitarian Direct Action in Urban Disaster Response*. Unpublished paper.

Crawford, K., Kennedy, J. and Killing, A. (2014). Path-dependency culture in humanitarian decision-making: why it was hard to change direction in Haiti. *Humanitarian Exchange Magazine* 61. Available at: www.odihpn.org/humanitarian-exchange-magazine/issue-61/path-dependency-culture-in-humanitarian-decision-making-why-it-was-hard-to-change-direction-in-haiti.

Crawford, K., Suvatne, M., Kennedy, J. and Corsellis, T. (2010). Urban shelter and the limits of humanitarian action. *Forced Migration Review* 34: 27–28. Available at: www.fmreview.org (accessed July 7, 2011).

Hamdi, N. (2010). *The Placemaker's Guide to Building Community*. London: Earthscan.

IASC (2010). *Final Strategy for Meeting Humanitarian Challenges in Urban Areas*. Geneva: United Nations. Available at: www.citiesalliance.org/ca/sites/citiesalliance.org/files/CA_Images/IASC_Strategy_Meeting_Humanitarian_Challenges_in_Urban_Areas%5B1%5D.pdf (accessed April 7, 2011).

IASC (2011a). *WASH and Shelter Cluster Coordination Plan for Port au Prince* (not to scale). July 20. Port au Prince: United Nations. Available at: https://sites.google.com/site/shelterhaiti2010/information-management/map-room (accessed August 18, 2011).

IASC (2011b). *Agency T-Shelter Implementing Areas Around Fort National Priority Area* (not to scale). May 17. Port au Prince: United Nations. Available at: https://sites.google.com/site/shelterhaiti2010/information-management/map-room (accessed August 18, 2011).

IFRC (International Federation of Red Cross and Red Crescent Societies) (2010). *World Development Report 2010 Focus on Urban Risk*. Geneva: IFRC. Available at: www.ifrc.org/Global/Publications/disasters/WDR/WDR2010-full.pdf (accessed April 7, 2011).

International Crisis Group (2011). *Post-Quake Haiti: Security Depends on Resettlement and Development*. Policy Briefing, Latin America/Caribbean Briefing No. 25. Port-au-Prince/Brussels, June 28. Available at: www.crisisgroup.org/~/media/Files/latin-america/haiti/B25%20Post-quake%20Haiti%20-%20Security%20Depends%20on%20Resettlement%20and%20Development.pdf (accessed August 18, 2011).

Kennedy J., Ashmore, J., Babister, E. and Kelman I. (2008). The meaning of 'build back better': evidence from post-tsunami Aceh and Sri Lanka. *Journal of Contingencies and Crisis Management* 16(1): 24–36.

Lyons, M. (2009). Building back better: the large-scale impact of small-scale approaches to reconstruction. *World Development* 37(2): 385–398.

Lyons, M., Schilderman, T. and Boano, C. (eds) (2010). *Building Back Better. Delivering People-Centred Housing Reconstruction at Scale*. London: Practical Action Publishing.

Moudon, A.V. (2003). A Catholic approach to organising what urban designers should know. In Cuthbert, A. *Designing Cities: Critical Readings in Urban Design*. Oxford: Blackwell Publishers, pp. 362–386.

O'Donnell, I., Smart, K. with Ramalingam, B. (2009). *Responding to Urban Disasters: Learning From Previous Response and Recovery Operations*. London: ALNAP. Available at: www.alnap.org/pool/files/alnap-provention-lessons-urban.pdf (accessed April 7, 2011).

Quzai, U. (2010). Pakistan: implementing people-centered reconstruction in urban and rural areas. In Lyons, M., Schilderman, T. and Boano, C. (eds) *Building Back Better. Delivering People-Centred Housing Reconstruction at Scale*. London: Practical Action Publishing, pp. 113–134.

Reitman, J. (2011). How the world failed Haiti. *Rolling Stone*, August 4. Available at: www.rollingstone.com/politics/news/how-the-world-failed-haiti-20110804 (accessed August 18, 2011).

Rencoret, N., Stoddard, A., Haver, K., Taylor, G. and Harvey, P. (2010). *Haiti Earthquake Response; Context Analysis*. London: ALNAP. Available at: www.alnap.org/pool/files/haiti-context-analysis-final.pdf (accessed April 7, 2011).

Sanderson, D., Knox Clarke, P. and Campbell, L. (2012). *Responding to Urban Disasters: Learning From Previous Relief and Recovery Operations*. London: ALNAP. Available at: www.alnap.org/resource/7772.

Schilderman, T. (2010). Putting people at the centre of reconstruction. In Lyons, M., Schilderman, T. and Boano, C. (eds) *Building Back Better. Delivering People-Centred Housing Reconstruction at Scale*. London: Practical Action Publishing, pp. 7–38.

Schurch, T.W. (1999). Reconsidering urban design: thoughts about its definition and status as a field or profession. *Journal of Urban Design* 4(1): 5–28.

Shelter Centre (2010a). *Shelter After Disaster: Strategies for Transitional Settlement and Reconstruction*. Geneva: Shelter Centre.

Shelter Centre (2010b). *Urban Shelter Guidelines: Assistance in Urban Areas to Populations Affected by Humanitarian Crises*. Geneva: Shelter Centre.

Sphere Project, The (2011). *The Sphere Handbook 2011*. Geneva: The Sphere Project. Available at: www.sphereproject.org/component/option,com_docman/task,cat_view/gid,70/Itemid,203/lang,english/ (accessed June 8, 2011).

Stoddard, A. (2008). *International Humanitarian Financing: Review and Comparative Assessment of Instruments. A Study for the Good Humanitarian Donorship Initiative Commissioned by the Office of US Foreign Disaster Assistance*. London: Humanitarian Outcomes. Available at: www.humanitarianoutcomes.org/pdf/HumanitarianFinancingReview2008.pdf (accessed July 12, 2011).

UN (1998). *Urban Land Policies for the Uninitiated*. New York: United Nations. Available at: www.unescap.org/huset/land_policies/index.htm (accessed March 2, 2011).

UN (2010). *World Population Prospects, the 2010 Revision*. New York: United Nations. Available at: http://esa.un.org/unpd/wpp/Excel-Data/population.htm (accessed August 1, 2011).

UN-Habitat (2009). *Strategic Citywide Spatial Planning: A Situational Analysis of Metropolitan Port-au-Prince, Haiti*. Nairobi: UN-Habitat. Available at: www.gltn.net/index.php?option=com_docman&gid=250&task=doc_details&Itemid=24 (accessed April 1, 2011).

UN-Habitat (2010a). *Citywide Strategic Planning*. New York: United Nations. Available at: www.unhabitat.org/pmss/listItemDetails.aspx?publicationID=3020 (accessed April 19, 2011).

UN-Habitat (2010b). *Land and Natural Disasters: Guidance for Practitioners.* Nairobi: United Nations. Available at: www.unhabitat.org/pmss/listItemDetails.aspx?publicationID=2973 (accessed June 6, 2011).

UNHCHR (1991). *The Right to Adequate Housing (Article 11 (1). Covenant on Economic, Social and Cultural Rights), CESCR General Comment 4,* December 12. New York: United Nations. Available at: www.unhchr.ch/tbs/doc.nsf/0/469f4d91a9378221c12563ed0053547e?Opendocument (accessed July 20, 2011).

Wamsler, C. (2006). Mainstreaming risk reduction in urban planning and housing: a challenge for international aid organizations. *Disasters* 30(2): 151–177.

Zetter, R. and Deikun, G. (2010). Meeting humanitarian challenges in urban areas. *Forced Migration Review* 34: 5–8. Available at: www.fmreview.org (accessed July 7, 2011).

Chapter 3

Fables from the reconstruction

Lessons from Chile's recovery after the 2010 earthquake and tsunami

Pablo Allard and María Ignacia Arrasate

Introduction

The past decade has been particularly devastating for cities on the natural disaster front, leaving millions of people displaced, especially in low- and middle-income countries. Only in 2015, natural catastrophes claimed 23,000 lives, substantially more than the previous year's figure of 7,700, but below the annual average for the last 30 years (54,000). The year's most devastating natural catastrophe was the earthquake in Nepal, with 9,000 victims. Overall losses in 2015 totalled US$ 90bn, of which roughly US$ 27bn was insured.[1]

According to the UN, the magnitude of lives lost and physical damage is of course a consequence of the frequency and impact of naturally induced disasters, but locally generated environmental degradation and poor urban planning exacerbate the problem.[2] The apparent effects of climate change, such as extreme weather and sea level rise, have contributed to increased global awareness about how cities should prepare to confront these challenges and achieve successful recovery. The popularity of the concept of urban resilience on the planning agenda of many cities and worldwide campaigns led by international organizations such as the Rockefeller Foundation,[3] and the term's inclusion in the 2015–2030 Sustainable Development Goals (SDGs),[4] suggest how seriously jurisdictions worldwide are confronting the issue.

From a social perspective, the literature illustrates that poorer people around the world are more vulnerable to naturally induced disasters due to factors that include place and type of residence, building construction, social exclusion and location (Fothergill and Peek, 2004). This is especially relevant in lower-income countries where poor populations are highly vulnerable to displacement or relocation in the context of disaster recovery. This poses a special challenge to architects, planners and policymakers who seek to restore the lives of affected families and at the same time achieve safer standards of habitability for vulnerable populations.

In this context of physical and social vulnerability, both high- and low-income countries have grappled with recovery processes elaborating and implementing reconstruction plans in cities to recover from the massive destruction caused by natural disasters. Such recovery plans not only seek to address immediate reconstruction needs, but they often envision strategies for sustainable future development, coping with a variety of challenges, to provide a larger planning framework necessary for ongoing community development. In many low- and middle-income countries, especially in cities and towns with low human capital, which is usually accompanied by weak economies and institutions, the risk that a healthy balance among environmental, social and economic aspects will not be accomplished is high and the expectations of the affected communities are often left unfulfilled.

In Chile, the 8.8 Magnitude earthquake and resulting tsunami of February 27, 2010 led to the development of a recovery plan prepared by the government, driven by the premise 'Rebuild back better', which was composed of multiple programs and public policies, which all called for timely reconstruction and, more broadly, an opportunity to improve overall livability conditions of the ones recovering from the disaster. The national recovery plan considered a timeframe of four years and different lines of actions, including the reconstruction of affected health facilities, public education schools, road infrastructure, penitentiary complexes, police departments, cultural heritage buildings and housing. Different ministries, according to the sector involved, were the institutions in charge of the plan's implementation.

This chapter focuses on the analysis of the housing and urban recovery programs implemented by the government's Ministry of Housing and Urban Planning (MINVU). This includes learning from the damage and need assessment and an analysis of the principles that guided the recovery process, summarizing the complexities and challenges of the plan's implementation. Lessons learned are also presented. The analysis builds on the discussion of underlying tensions and dilemmas confronted by Chilean policymakers such as creating mechanisms to promote urban reconstruction, setting up the criteria to enable the reconstruction of coastal cities and ensuring heritage reconstruction in historic towns. The final aim of this analysis is to provide a set of recommendations to help other developing countries around the world to confront the challenges of post-disaster recovery.

The 2010 Chilean earthquake and tsunami

Chile is exposed to different types of natural events, such as earthquakes, tsunamis, volcanic eruptions, landslides and flooding. Some of these events throughout the history of the country have been extremely severe with catastrophic social and economic costs. The most powerful earthquake ever recorded occurred in the city of Valdivia, located in the south of Chile, in 1960, rating 9.5 on the Moment Magnitude Scale (MMS), triggering a tsunami with high levels of destruction. Other notable disasters are the 2008 eruption of the Chaitén volcano, which left the town of Chaitén, with a population of 5,000, partially buried by ashes and led to the complete evacuation of the city and future relocation. The 8.3 Magnitude earthquake in Tarapacá and the great fire of 2014 in Valparaíso destroyed neighborhoods and left thousands homeless.

The succession of post-disaster recovery processes that have taken place in Chilean settlements include the continuous improvement of building codes implemented for the first time after the 7.8 Magnitude earthquake in the town of Chillán in 1939 with more than 24,000 fatal victims.[5]

The advancements in this area were validated during the 8.8 Magnitude earthquake on the morning of February 27, 2010, known to many as the '27F' disaster. Many buildings that collapsed were built before the existence of the codes. Buildings subject to the new building codes and standards for infrastructure operability suffered much less damage and lives were also saved. However, the event revealed a deficiency in the emergency management protocols and early warning systems. Besides, the damage assessment pointed out that bigger damages and losses were caused by the tsunami in urban coastal areas, highlighting a lack of consideration of tsunami risk in the existing Chilean planning instruments (Franco and Siembieda, 2010).

The 27F earthquake ranks as the sixth-largest earthquake ever recorded by a seismograph. It was felt strongly in six Chilean regions, affecting about 75 percent of the country's population, equivalent to over 12 million people. Subsequent blackouts affected around 93 percent of the country. Over 500 people died with around 25 missing. The earthquake and tsunami partially devastated a broad range of urban settlements, comprising five cities of more than 100,000 inhabitants, 45 towns of over 5,000 inhabitants, and more than 900 villages and communities distributed across more than 600km of length, from coastal areas to rural settlements (MINVU, 2010). The total cost of the damage was estimated at US$30 billion, equivalent to 18 percent of Gross National Product, composed of US$21 billion in physical assets (including buildings, housing, roads, and schools) and US$9 billion in business and indirect losses.[6]

The extent and diversity of the damage across the Chilean territory highlighted the need to integrate disaster risk management into the recovery process focused on a more broad-based, sustainable future development. This was a particular challenge for governmental agencies and officers, since the earthquake happened two weeks before the elected president Sebastián Piñera moved into office as the first center-right administration in two decades. Therefore, the recovery process started with the complexity of a new administration. This, however, also served as an opportunity to incorporate important changes and adjustments in the government's development agenda to strengthen both the emergency response and recovery policies nationwide. Governors and secretaries were appointed considering post-disaster recovery as their main task, and a series of reforms and special programs were drafted to fund and coordinate the process. Among these were a Special Reconstruction Tax Reform and the creation of a network of seismographs (managed by the National Seismological Centre), implemented for the primary impact assessment when an earthquake event occurs. Redundancy was added to the telecommunication system to avoid the cessation of service in such an event, and a law was proposed[7] to reformulate the National Office of Emergency regarding emergency management response, disaster prevention and other procedures to better address future risks. The new law also incorporated a National Fund for Civil Protection to prepare people for risk events at the local and regional levels and to increase the responsiveness of public institutions and private entities. Finally, other regulatory updates included strategies addressing hazard and risk assessment, improvement of early warning systems, upgrades to building codes and other regulations, risk reduction policies integrated into land-use planning, and the development of regional and local capacity through decentralization.

In terms of housing damage the initial estimation indicated that more than 370,000 houses suffered damage of various kinds, from unusable units to repairable ones. However, these initial estimates did not necessarily correspond to the actual demand of victims who would require the government's help. In order to determine those households eligible for governmental help, Chile relied on its well-developed housing demand subsidy policies which prioritize funding for homeownership to the most vulnerable and poor. By using the application process for subsidies as the backbone of housing reconstruction, a few weeks after the earthquake the government was able to open a 'Victims Registry' and ask those households requiring government assistance to rebuild or repair their homes to apply for subsidies. A significant number of families enrolled in the registry, but with a limited amount of resources for reconstruction, the Chilean government prioritized the most vulnerable families to receive help. Several conditions and requirements were established to grant fair and ample access to reconstruction subsidies. In the case of homeowners, they needed to prove they owned only one affected property; for renters or the ones living with relatives, they needed to demonstrate such status at the time of the earthquake. The official reconstruction plan of MINVU was published within six months of the disaster and described subsidies to repair or rebuild 220,000 units of low- and middle-income housing with government assistance within four years. At the closing of the Victims Registry, the official number of beneficiaries eligible for assistance reached 222,418 housing units. This number rose to 240,657 units by May 2014 after an audit was performed by the new administration of President Michelle Bachelet that assumed office in March 2014 (Ministerio del Interior y Seguridad Publica, 2014). Pondering the magnitude of the disaster, the plan articulated by MINVU described more than US$3 billion in housing subsidies, urban infrastructure plans and projects for the affected communities.

The Chilean context

Of course, recovery not only refers to repairing or rebuilding homes, it also refers to the reconstruction of the social and urban tissue devastated by the earthquake and tsunami (Boano, 2011). In this holistic perspective, the reconstruction – and, in many cases, renewal – of towns and cities required a combination of both economic and social development with necessary infrastructural changes to promote the communities' competitiveness and resilience to face future disasters. Disasters involve losses and generate anxiety among the affected population, but they can also be considered an opportunity for change and improvement (Rahman and Kausel, 2012). In most situations reconstruction will require a combination of different policies to make critical decisions to achieve transformation. Three key aspects may help in understanding the context that supported the creation and implementation of the Chilean recovery plan after the earthquake.

First, both local and national governmental leadership are needed to manage these aspects of recovery. Cooperation between these two levels is essential because programs necessarily need local input and coordination to succeed (Siembieda, 2012). While Chile had been in the process of decentralizing decision-making responsibilities to regional authorities before the disaster occurred, the complexity of the challenge highlighted the urgency of participation and inclusion of all stakeholders in the recovery process. The 27F recovery partnership model utilized by the Chilean government considered a decentralized scheme with strong direction from the national-level ministries in relation with the design of the policies and programs for recovery, and relied on the efforts at the regional and municipal levels to implement those policies (Siembieda et al., 2012). As the regional and local governments improve their capacity to assess and prepare for the risks of earthquakes and tsunamis, they will be able to protect local economic growth and improve their ability to plan for the future. Furthermore, their improvements in capacity also help the national government meet its goals of economic reform, proactive social investments, transparent public sector management and stable consensual governance.

Second, recovery is a political process. In the case of the Chilean experience no analysis in social and policy terms can be done without acknowledging that Chile was already a government in transition when the earthquake struck, moving from 20 years of liberal governments, known as 'Concertación,' to a more conservative one (Siembieda et al., 2012). Acknowledging the high expectations about the new administration among citizens, from the very outset President Piñera decided to place the central government in the leading role assuming the responsibility to plan and foster recovery from the disaster, even committing to reach full recovery within the four-year presidential term (Useem et al., 2015). The central government took the lead in the reconstruction process, not by imposing top-down decisions, but as an intermediary between the different players involved in this process, linking the private sector with the affected families and articulating actions and policies. In a study of Chile's recovery process, Comerio (2013) notes that when compared to housing recovery programs in other countries, Chile's program stands out, combining both top-down strong government management and bottom-up citizens' participation.

Third, institutions and economic stability are important. Chile is a country with stable institutions and a prosperous economy, with strong ministries and regional agencies. Therefore, one of the first critical decisions taken by the government was to use the existing ministerial structure, with already established ministerial programs and budget lines for the recovery effort, stating that in times of crisis it is better to adapt and innovate within existing capacities rather than experiment and move into uncertain reforms and implementation. Each ministry managed recovery programs in their areas, with MINVU in charge of the reconstruction of cities and housing. Some critics of this strategy argued that the government missed an opportunity to create a new institution in order to give continuity to present and future disaster recovery efforts and to internalize the knowledge acquired by the 27F experience (Bresciani, 2012).

MINVU'S reconstruction plan

MINVU has a long tradition of improving housing conditions for low-income families and working to eliminate informal housing (Comerio, 2013). Therefore, the plan articulated an extensive array of tools and instruments strategically adjusted to the different conditions and contexts, adapting existing and proven instruments, such as subsidy programs, to the specific demands of the reconstruction. According to the existing organizational structure of the Ministry, the plan involved two major areas of work implemented in parallel: first, MINVU's housing reconstruction program, which was composed of different types of subsidies for housing reconstruction or repair in order to respond to the diversity of problems of the affected families; and second, MINVU's urban reconstruction program, which had the aim to integrate risk assessment with urban planning and to ensure a holistic view of the reconstruction through the elaboration of master plans that could foresee future development and preserve the identity of the affected areas.

MINVU's housing reconstruction program

The model implemented for housing reconstruction used existing programs and institutions, which had the benefit of staff on site and established procedures and budget lines. Nevertheless flexibility and innovation were required to adjust existing programs and to develop new programs within existing structures to meet disaster conditions. The model utilized was known among all stakeholders. The model articulated the efforts of the public and private sectors, as well as civil society, encouraging competition among the private sector and giving the affected families the freedom to choose among different options. The model also revived and strengthened local economies and industry, which were hit hard by the earthquake and needed to move together with the community's recovery.

In order to provide a definitive housing solution for families affected by the earthquake, the housing plan was structured on the basis of grouping problems into three categories: owners with non-repairable houses; owners with repairable houses; and non-owners, i.e. renters or co-dwellers.

For the implementation of the housing reconstruction program three different approaches were defined according to the level of participation of the stakeholders involved: a community-driven approach; a construction-driven approach; and a government-driven approach. The first one referred to self-build or self-repair, implying a high level of community involvement.

Problems / Approach	Repairable house land owner	Non repairable house land owner	Non land owner – co-dwellers and renters
Self led community level	Bank of materials (gift card for repairs)	Self construction with technical assistance	Acquisition subsidy (market houses)
State led government level	Social condominiums repair program (major damage)	Social condominiums for demolition & reconstruction	New developments
Third party led intermediary level	Repair subsidy	Prefabricated houses	Urban densification

New programs   Existing programs

Figure 3.1 Diversity of housing programs according to the type of damage and approach
Source: MINVU/table elaborated by the authors

The second involved reconstruction and repair of houses by construction companies and developers. The third approach included new developments for homeless co-dwellers and renters, and the reconstruction or repair of social housing condominiums with a high level of involvement from the government (Arrasate et al., 2012).

Considering the diversity of problems and approaches, the housing reconstruction program provided a diversity of solutions for the affected families (see Figure 3.1). Moreover, the aim of the program was to provide a variety of choices to allow beneficiaries the opportunity to choose the house that best met their characteristics and needs, in the understanding that housing is a family's greatest investment and that a housing subsidy is usually the largest government subsidy that they receive in their lifetimes (MINVU, 2010).

MINVU's urban reconstruction program

Reconstruction not only refers to repairing or rebuilding of homes, but also to the reconstruction of the social and urban tissue that was devastated by the earthquake and tsunami (Nigg, 1995). With this holistic perspective in mind, the urban reconstruction – and, in many cases, conversion – of towns and cities required both economic and social development with necessary infrastructural changes to promote the communities' competitiveness and resilience in facing future natural disasters. For this purpose, 150 master plans were developed to guide the reconstruction of different types of affected urban settlements (MINVU, 2013a).

The urban reconstruction program required private-public partnerships to develop 27 master plans in the main populated centers of the coastline located in the disaster area and subject to some degree of risk, and 123 master plans for major inland localities affected by the earthquake and requiring replacement or new infrastructure. This model of collaboration among public and private entities in the context of disaster recovery was a new precedent for Chilean urban planners. External consultants firms prepared the coastline master plans, guided by government officials, and the Ministry's urban planning department developed the inland master plans.

The master plans recognized the value of existing development and the particularities of each locality, in order to orient and propose reconstruction actions that enhanced already existing urban character and identity. The objective of these plans was to orient decision-making regarding the allocation of housing reconstruction/repair subsidies, to prioritize projects for reconstruction of infrastructure, to establish long-term investment criteria and planning for these cities, and to stimulate economic, social and environmental development incorporating instances of citizen participation and integrating those variables to raise the standard of livability.

In the case of coastal town master plans, the proposed criteria for reconstruction established land-use conditions in direct relation with the local Territorial Planning Instruments (IPT), construction codes and technical norms, allocation of subsidies for tsunami-resilient housing, and the prioritization of public investment for tsunami mitigation, combining structural and non-structural measures. Structural measures refer to physical construction to reduce or avoid possible impacts of hazards and non-structural measures relate to measures undertaken to increase public awareness, training and education.[8] The action plan and criteria for the reconstruction of coastal cities responded to the constitutional mandate of prioritizing the safety of citizens, as well as promoting public policies to ensure the rational, efficient and sustainable use of the coastal area compatible with the economic and social interests of the public and the private sector.

Principles of MINVU's reconstruction plan

A set of common principles for both housing and urban reconstruction programs acted as guidelines for the design of MINVU's reconstruction plan (MINVU, 2010). These included the following:

- Valuing existing communities by avoiding displacement. This refers to the importance of protecting pre-existing social networks and communities, strengthening their economy and focusing the efforts on the most vulnerable and needy families. Therefore, the reconstruction prioritized on-site reconstruction by taking place in the same locality and on the same land on which the disaster-hit families had lived.
- Rebuilding quickly and including citizens' participation. This appeals to the need to move as soon as possible from the emergency to permanent reconstruction and create instances for participation where affected families can choose and agree on those solutions that most fit their needs.
- Prioritizing the preservation of identity. The plan committed to the recovery of tangible and intangible heritage by establishing incentives and guidelines by which the communities themselves could decide how to reconstruct their urban image.
- Respecting attachment to the land. The plan acknowledged the strong attachment that communities have to their territory, particularly the coastal communities that live from, and respect, the sea. It prioritized the protection of people's lives by generating technical information and mitigation measures which would help communities to co-exist safely with natural hazards.
- Validating strategic and sustainable urban planning. Master plans should be the 'navigation charts' that allow communities, mayors and regional authorities to participate in the decision-making that will guide the future of their cities and towns.

- Responsible innovation and flexible structure. The diversity of problems posed by the disaster allowed for innovation and the exploration of new response capabilities and solutions for recovery.
- Guaranteeing the legality and formality of solutions. All subsidized construction needed the necessary building permits according to municipal requirements. Assisted self-construction was encouraged when it conformed to set standards. The normalization of property titles also contributed to eradicating informality, giving legal rights to the families inhabiting the land.

Challenges confronted

The following three specific cases illustrate some of the major challenges, successes and failures confronted during the implementation of MINVU's reconstruction program.

Urban reconstruction: Talca

MINVU implemented several housing programs for the reconstruction of houses on the same sites where the families always lived. These programs were especially successful in rural contexts and small towns and villages. For example, in the case of Cumpeo, a small town of 2,651 inhabitants in the Maule region and surrounding countryside, the program achieved high rates of completion in a short period of time, demonstrating the effectiveness of this type of housing recovery.

Of course, different tools and mechanisms would be necessary to address site-specific problems. While obvious, it was two years after the reconstruction plan started that special mechanisms were introduced. In the case of Talca, an inland medium size city of 220,000 people and the capital of the Maule region, where 30 percent of the housing stock was severely damaged, the higher prices of land in the city core imposed a serious constraint on urban recovery. New developments were constructed on the periphery of the city to house displaced renters. Some families preferred to sell their land plots for real estate development and move to other locations (Hong and Brain, 2012).

The Victims Registry for affected families indicated a high percentage of renters and co-dwellers, because in the large adobe[9] houses where damage was common, portions of houses had been rented out. In central Talca the Registry included 1,200 owning families and 1,800 renting families. Such information led the Ministry to develop special subsidies for increasing housing density in urban settings. The program created by the Ministry to add density was called the Urban Densification Program (see Plates 7 and 8), which provided a subsidy to builders to develop infill center city sites with proximity to shopping, healthcare and other services, in an attempt to counteract the rush to build on the periphery, and at the same time to rebuild the post-disaster landscape predominant in the city center (see Figures 3.2–3.4).

The goal of the program was to keep families in their neighborhoods, avoiding displacement, and to encourage higher-density development in central neighborhoods, through innovation in existing Chilean housing and urban policy mechanisms. The regeneration of these neighborhoods as a broad-based, ongoing process demonstrates that disaster-specific, planning tools and complementary public investments are required to achieve recovery. This fact indicates that better coordination between housing policy and urban policy, let alone between these two and disaster policy, is needed.

Moreover, the social complexity underlying recovery should be addressed by providing better information and participatory processes to include the perspective of affected communities in the redevelopment of their own neighborhoods. For example, for the families that lost their rental incomes or for the ones that depended on sharing arrangements of their children or elderly care, the provision of new houses would not be a full solution to their economic or social problems (Comerio, 2013).

Figure 3.2

Figure 3.3

Figures 3.2–3.4 Views of three urban infill condominium projects under construction in Las Heras neighborhood, Talca (October, 2012)
Source: photos by the authors

Coastal reconstruction: Dichato

To guarantee a comprehensive holistic approach to reconstruction and to ensure a resilient approach to inhabiting the coast, MINVU with the collaboration of a series of public and private entities prepared 27 master plans for the main urban centers located in the coastal area affected by the tsunami. Dichato, a small coastal town reliant on tourism located north of Concepción, Biobío region (see Figure 3.5), with around 4,000 residents[10] was severely damaged by the disaster, with 80 percent of the town destroyed. The aftermath of the earthquake and tsunami in Dichato presented a unique situation compared to other affected urban areas in terms of the scale of the destruction and the resulting scale of the needed aid. There were significant political, organizational, environmental, logistical and capacity issues. The reconstruction master plan of Dichato sought to promote resilience through zoning, the construction of mitigation infrastructure, a coastline park with contention walls, and updates to construction codes for tsunami flooding areas supported by housing subsidies. The plan involved different mechanisms of participation such as assemblies and meetings across communities. Between May and November 2010, the Dichato recovery planning process included 23 meetings, focus groups and workshop discussions. Between 10 and 400 people participated in these meetings (Cartes, 2010).

The Dichato reconstruction master plan was one of 18 master plans, known as PRBC18,[11] for coastal cities located in the Biobío Region. The regional government took a proactive role and led the development of all the region's master plans, creating a special local team consisting of urban planners and architects. This case was an unprecedented experience at a regional level, demonstrating that a regional platform with a level of autonomy from central government could respond adequately to a local problem, facilitating coordination,

Figure 3.5 Aerial view of Dichato town
Source: photo by the authors

monitoring and implementation of all decisions and projects, all essential conditions to realizing public investment initiatives.

The criteria utilized to inhabit the flooding area defined by the tsunami risk modeling studies conducted was a mixed strategy combining mitigation works to reduce the energy of the waves and avoid future damages (see Figures 3.6 and 3.7), zoning according to tsunami exposure conditions and constructing tsunami-resilient housing with special subsidies to cover the extra costs of construction (see Figure 3.8 and Plate 9). The purpose was to respect the attachment of coastal communities to the land without hindering reconstruction. For a middle-income country such as Chile this was especially relevant because if reconstruction in coastal areas were completely forbidden, communities would build back anyway, resulting in informality and low quality construction.

Besides the case of Dichato, several initiatives were undertaken by non-governmental organizations with government support such as Desafío Levantemos Chile, providing new boats for fishermen to restore their jobs, Harvard Recupera Chile, helping communities through livelihood-restoration and economic-development oriented projects (Ahlers, 2013), and Viva Dichato, a music festival with the aim of attracting people to reactivate tourism in the town. These initiatives were key to fostering the community's economic recovery and contributed to restoring livelihoods during the period of reconstruction.

Five years after the disaster, Dichato's reconstruction shows high levels of completion both in housing and urban projects accompanied by the social and economic recovery of the community. At least to these ends the recovery of this town should be considered a good example of Chilean recovery, validating strategic and sustainable urban planning and citizen participation during all stages of the process. Moreover, the strategy utilized in Dichato highlights the importance of strengthening local capacities, fostering partnerships among stakeholders and promoting decentralization to ensure the implementation of the plan.

Figure 3.6

Figures 3.6 and 3.7 Tsunami mitigation and generation of new public spaces in the coastal strip of Dichato
Source: photos by the authors

Figure 3.8 Tsunami-resilient housing designs in Dichato
Source: photo by the authors

Heritage reconstruction: Vichuquén

Chile's built heritage has always been at risk to natural catastrophes (Loustalot, 2013). Poorly maintained buildings, scarce funding, loss of technical knowledge and constructions of adobe without seismic resistant structural designs are among the causes which, when combined with a destructive event like an earthquake, produce a significant impact on these buildings. In the case of housing with historical value, preservation is especially difficult because there is no special Chilean funding available. Furthermore, in case of disaster, under current regulations, no special funds or policies exist to foster recovery and no institution is responsible for this task. Acknowledging these existing gaps, the reconstruction plan introduced a special heritage recovery program for historical valuable areas damaged by the earthquake.

The heritage recovery program defined 140 areas for preservation. The houses located in these areas were entitled to a subsidy with a higher amount to cover the extra costs of construction associated with these house typologies. More than 5,000 heritage preservation subsidies were delivered. New regulations, checklists and approval processes had to be adapted for heritage projects. In many cases the program considered the upgrade of the damaged adobe structures to mixed-structures, integrating new construction techniques, in order to guarantee future seismic resistance of new construction. The program had two objectives: first, that the affected families recover their houses; and second, that the affected settlements preserve their urban image and local identity (MINVU, 2013b).

Vichuquén is a small town located in the Maule region known nationally for its 400-year-old adobe buildings (see Figure 3.9 and Plate 10). After the earthquake many families

Figure 3.9 Traditional corridors in Vichuquén town
Source: photo by the authors

wanted to demolish their damaged homes and reconstruct as quickly as possible, but the mayor, a town native, argued that they should preserve their heritage. In this case, the first decision made by the local authority was key to preserving a coherent urban form. A public-private partnership, with collaboration of other institutions such as UNESCO and non-governmental organizations, supported the implementation of the overall process. These alliances were key not only to finance the higher costs of construction, but also to gather the knowledge needed to repair and reconstruct with adobe, a construction technique lost in many parts of Chile (see Figures 3.10 and 3.11). The techniques were learned from Peruvian craftsmen and generated new jobs for small local contractors.

The experience of Vichuquén shows that even with the constraints that characterize a post-disaster scenario it is possible to preserve both the built form of heritage areas and the

Figure 3.10

Figures 3.10 and 3.11 Recovery of adobe construction technique in Vichuquén
Source: photo by the authors

underlying building traditions. The experience reveals that inhabitants can participate not only in the decision-making process during the design of the new houses, but also during the construction phase itself, learning new skills for their own development. Vichuquén also demonstrates the considerable challenges of heritage reconstruction, including time constraints, high costs of construction and the need of case-by-case solutions. Other aspects should also be considered such as coordination with families during reconstruction when they may still live in the houses being rebuilt, along with the maintenance of livelihoods which may also be related to their homes.

Lessons learned

The three cases described above illustrate some of the challenges confronted in Chile's reconstruction process. From an analysis of the cases, seven lessons can be extracted in order to guide others that might confront similar challenges in the frame of post-disaster recovery. They are as follows:

1 *Achieve a balance between the speed of construction and community participation.* Disaster can be an opportunity to introduce better conditions than in the past. A disaster opens a brief window of opportunity for broader change. Decisions should be made early after a disaster and be clearly articulated and communicated to the affected populations as soon as possible. The more delayed the decision-making, the harder it is to facilitate changes. It is also important to remember that considerations that appear technical and economic may actually have major social consequences. Therefore, instances for promoting social consensus and meaningful participation from all sectors should be considered as part of the core of the recovery process even if the speed of construction is affected in this endeavor (Jha et al., 2010).
2 *Integrate in the decision-making process all the stakeholders involved and promote decentralization.* Participation of affected individuals, communities and different levels of government in the processes of decision-making is essential. It contributes to clarified expectations about the constraints of reconstruction and design conditions for housing. In Chile, from the first moment, the government assumed a key role and worked with energy to form a reconstruction plan with very ambitious targets. The government assumed a leadership role not as sole implementer but as an intermediary linking the private sector, civil society and the affected families. In this way recovery became a partnership between affected communities, government and multiple stakeholders. The way the partnerships were formed and carried out determined the path to recovery (Siembieda, 2012). The different reconstruction cases analyzed above support this claim, showing the importance of partnerships between public institutions, private entities and non-profit organizations to achieve a successful reconstruction implementation. The 27F disaster catalyzed the already ongoing Chilean process of decentralization in terms of investment and social and political power from the capital city and geographic center, Santiago, to the rest of the country. This changed the relationship between national and local governments, and more importantly, contributed to the empowerment of communities affected by the disaster (Comerio, 2013).
3 *Integrate housing and urban reconstruction programs to ensure a long-term vision for future development beyond immediate needs.* An integrated approach to housing and planning reconstruction should be adopted that addresses both short-term and long-

term needs, whereby houses are coordinated spatially and programmatically with access to services, public buildings and livelihood facilities (Da Silva et al., 2010). A holistic view of reconstruction interventions should take into account local resources, needs, perceptions, expectations, potentials and constraints. In so doing, the discussion is broadened from responses that take into consideration the needs of individuals and families to responses that consider the wider benefits to communities. An integrated approach refocuses the discussion from a single house or shelter to a process, thereby reintegrating housing reconstruction into the wider recovery context (Barakat, 2003). The master plans developed in the frame of the Chilean reconstruction fostered the ability of communities to influence post-disaster redevelopment processes through the use of various planning measures. In addition, planning instruments could also contribute to enhancing the integration of housing projects with the broader context considering a long-term vision for development as needed in the case of Talca.

4 *Avoid population displacement and prioritize reconstruction on the same site.* In the case of Chile, the reconstruction plan minimized displacement by prioritizing reconstruction on the sites where families always lived. The benefit of this approach is that the basic economy of an affected area remains the same, and the existing infrastructure investment is not lost. In this way social networks are maintained, ensuring a sustainable long-term recovery for the affected communities. If, on the other hand, relocation is seen as the way to go, economic, political and social conditions must be created so as to attract the population to the new sites (GFDRR, 2011). The on-site reconstruction strategy utilized in Chile was very successful in rural areas and small towns, with the construction of thousands of prefabricated houses that contributed to regularizing land tenure rights across the affected area. Despite this fact, the complexity of implementing this strategy was evidenced by the slower pace of reconstruction of city cores, such as in Talca, and the need for defining criteria to inhabit tsunami risk coastal areas, as seen in Dichato. The coastal land-use policy, defined by MINVU, allowed most land owners to rebuild on their original sites using government subsidies in order to protect their attachment to the land and preserve their social networks, highlighting the challenges and tradeoffs that policymakers face in the aftermath of disasters.

5 *Integrate risk assessments with urban planning to improve urban resilience.* Disaster related UN publications underline the increment in the frequency and severity of natural disasters around the world, urging governments to invest in risk reduction, focusing on risk mitigation and emphasizing the cost-effectiveness of such measures. The effects of climate change, such as extreme weather and sea level rise, have raised global awareness about how cities should be better prepared to confront disaster challenges and achieve successful recovery. The growth in popularity of the concept of urban resilience on the planning agenda of many cities and worldwide campaigns led by international organizations show the importance of addressing this matter. The recognition that large-scale disasters cause increasing amounts of property damage and extensive disruption to economies, but that they also present opportunities for greater improvements has underpinned the use of the motto 'build back better' as a common driver of recovery plans. This goal involves some cross-cutting dilemmas that need to be carefully balanced, such as planned redevelopment and mitigation which require displacements of communities or changes in lifestyles, or improvements in construction codes that affect housing affordability.

6 *Determine deadlines and benchmarks to achieve completion, considering that quality is as important as quantity.* While reconstruction is generally measured by the amount and

speed of construction, a successful reconstruction unquestionably requires building safe, culturally appropriate dwellings. Such dwellings have or will acquire social meaning in terms of both the materials of which they are built and their location. Consequently, successful reconstruction also involves the long-term viability of a settlement and its potential to sustain further social development, a condition that is as dependent on arrangements in social space as on the cultural appropriateness of each individual dwelling or the safety of the terrain (Oliver-Smith, 1990). Therefore, the criteria upon which the success or failure of a reconstruction project is assessed must include impacts on the social fabric of the community. Different models of reconstruction strategies after earthquakes have been implemented around the world. Hayles (2010) suggests that strategies must find a balance between affordability, technical feasibility and quality of life, and that they must also recognize the end-users as active stakeholders, aware and conscious of their own needs and wants, rather than as passive recipients. The Chilean experience reinforces these points.

7 *Recognize and address the limitations of physical reconstruction and complement any approach with initiatives that promote social and economic recovery.* Physical reconstruction cannot solve all of the needs that arise after a disaster. The complexity of disaster recovery requires multiple approaches to rebuild the lives of the ones affected. The Chilean governmental response demonstrated that the government was very effective in the immediate aftermath of the disaster, providing leadership and rebuilding critical infrastructure and housing (Useem et al., 2015). Helping families and communities stitch their social and economic fabrics back together takes much more, however (Ahlers, 2013). Consequently, reconstruction should be accompanied with other programs and strategies to fulfill those needs. Moreover, the fulfillment of these needs should allow extending the recovery period beyond the limits of the construction phase. Reconstruction strategies and livelihoods should not be separated.

Conclusions

Despite the devastation and loss of life, the experience of the February 2010 Chilean earthquake and tsunami showed that Chile could recover from extreme natural events relatively well, thanks to strong institutions and financial resources, as well as to the integration of lessons learned from previous disasters. In the short term, the recovery plan emphasized the quick reconstruction of physical losses, and in the long term the plan included goals for improved design and construction of buildings, updated zoning plans, road and infrastructure improvements, heritage recovery and new master plans for impacted cities which would seek sustainable development.

Two aspects of the recovery were particularly important. First, almost all housing reconstruction was completed within the four-year timeframe established by the government. The government set very ambitious housing benchmarks to measure the progress of the plan, and this sense of momentum was fundamental to achieve high rates of completion of housing delivery. The leadership of the government in designing the reconstruction and acting as intermediary between different stakeholders strengthened the ongoing decentralization process and consolidated the role of local authorities, a crucial piece for successful implementation with a fast pace of construction.

Second, the development of sustainable strategic urban planning in the frame of the reconstruction process contributed to ensuring a long-term perspective for recovery, which also laid the foundation for the progressive integration of tsunami risk conditions into planning instruments. The experience indicated the need of more advanced planning tools in order to confront future urban challenges beyond the frame of recovery. Moreover, the 27F reconstruction experience promoted community participation, following the government's agenda of shifting from a top-down to bottom-up approach. This remains an ongoing challenge for Chilean policymakers, where the poorest populations are highly vulnerable and often excluded from the decision-making processes.

In terms of reconstruction strategies, the three cases analyzed highlight the importance of avoiding displacement and prioritizing on-site reconstruction for better post-disaster recovery. The analysis highlights the need to consider context-specific challenges and difficulties. In the case of Talca the complexities of urban recovery and the need of integrating contemporary urban planning instruments to ensure neighborhood recovery are revealed. Dichato shows that the disaster could be a transformative event for a city with high levels of destruction. In this case the coastal land-use policy was key to foster timely reconstruction instead of hindering development. Vichuquén indicates the importance of heritage reconstruction to preserve a coherent urban image and tourism-based economies. These different strategies and challenges share the common denominator of the key role of partnerships among different stakeholders and the flexibility provided by the reconstruction plan to innovate and respond to specific contexts.

Finally, while these lessons extracted from the recent Chilean experience are intended to guide others confronting similar challenges, they are also considerations that must be made for future reconstruction processes in Chile itself. The 27F disaster may have a legacy far beyond a successful recovery story in Chile, by contributing to improved learning for better future reconstruction programs and disaster response in Chile more generally and in the world at large.

Notes

1 Munich Re – Weather Resilience and Protection (WRAP) – 2015 Natural Catastrophe Statistics: http://www.munichre.com/us/weather-resilience-and-protection/media-relations/news/160104-natcatstats2015/index.html
2 The *Global Assessment Report on Disaster Risk Reduction* was published by the United Nations in May 2009.
3 100 Resilient Cities initiative sponsored by the Rockefeller Foundation: www.100resilientcities.org.
4 Sustainable Development Goals by the United Nations: https://sustainabledevelopment.un.org/topics.
5 Pablo Ivelic, Chilean Housing National Reconstruction Coordinator. Opinion published in La Tercera newspaper. February, 2013.
6 The Chilean Ministry of Interior reports the data on earthquake losses.
7 The law is still pending for approval in the Chilean congress.
8 Structural and non-structural measures definition by the United Nations Office for Disaster Risk Reduction (UNISDR), January 15, 2009.
9 60 percent of the houses damaged corresponded to adobe constructions.
10 According to the 2002 census.
11 Reconstruction Plan of 18 coastal settlements/Plan de Reconstrucción de Borde Costero de 18 localidades.

References

Ahlers, D. (2013). *Genesis of Recupera Chile.* Cambridge, MA: Belfer Center for Science and International Affairs, Harvard Kennedy School.

Arrasate, M.I., Ivelic, P. and Allard, P. (2012). Innovations of the reconstruction. Constructing Chile: public policies in social housing *Libertad y Desarrollo*: 235–292.

Barakat, S. (2003). Housing reconstruction after conflict and disaster. *Humanitarian Policy Group, Network Papers* 43: 1–40.

Boano, C. (2011). Lost in translation? The challenges of an equitable post-disaster reconstruction process: lessons from Chile. *Environmental Hazards* 3: 293–309.

Bresciani, L.E. (2012). De la emergencia a la política de gestión de desastres: la urgencia de institucionalidad pública para la reconstrucción. *Emergencia y Reconstrucción: el antes y el después del terremoto y tsunami del 27F en Chile.*

Cartes, I. (2010). Plan Maestro de Reconstrucción de Dichato: del sitio cero a las plataformas de futuro. *Arquitecturas Del Sur* (38).

Comerio, M. (2013). *Housing Recovery in Chile: A Qualitative Mid-Program Review.* Pacific Earthquake Engineering Research Center Headquarters at the University of California.

Da Silva, J., Lubkowski, Z., Batchelor, V. and Disasters Emergency Committee (2010). *Lessons from Aceh: Key Considerations in Post-Disaster Reconstruction.* Rugby, UK: Practical Action Publishing Limited.

Fothergill, A. and Peek, L. (2004). Poverty and disasters in the United States: a review of recent sociological findings. *Natural Hazards* 32(1): 89–110.

Franco, G. and Siembieda W. (2010). Chile's 2010 M8.8 earthquake and tsunami: initial observations on resilience. *Journal of Disaster Research* 5(5): 577–590.

Global Facility for Disaster Reduction and Recovery (GFDRR) (2011). *Earthquake Reconstruction.* Washington, DC: The World Bank.

Hayles, C.S. (2010). An examination of decision making in post disaster housing reconstruction. *International Journal of Disaster Resilience in the Built Environment* 1(1): 103–122.

Hong, H.Y. and Brain, I. (2012). Land readjustment for urban development and post-disaster reconstruction. *Land Lines, Lincoln Institute of Land Policy* 24(1): 2–9.

Jha, A.K. with Barenstein, J.D., Phelps, P.M., Pittet, D. and Sena, S. (2010). *Safer Homes, Stronger Communities: A Handbook for Reconstructing After Natural Disasters.* Washington, DC: World Bank.

Loustalot, B.D. (2013). Beyond the appearance of heritage: reconstruction of historic areas affected by earthquakes in Chile. *Archnet-Ijar* 7(3).

Ministerio del Interior y Seguridad Publica (2014). *Diagnostico estado de la reconstrucción terremoto y tsunami, 27 de Febrero de 2010.* Santiago, Chile: Government of Chile.

Ministry of Housing and Urban Planning (MINVU) (2010). *Reconstruction Plan: Chile United for Better Reconstruction*, 1st edn. Santiago, Chile: Government of Chile.

Ministry of Housing and Urban Planning (MINVU) (2013a). *Reconstrucción Urbana Post 27F.* Santiago, Chile: Government of Chile.

Ministry of Housing and Urban Planning (MINVU) (2013b). *Reconstruyendo el patrimonio de Chile.* Santiago, Chile: Government of Chile.

Nigg, J.M. (1995). *Disaster Recovery as a Social Process.* University of Delaware Disaster Research Center, Preliminary Paper 219.

Oliver-Smith, A. (1990). Post-disaster housing reconstruction and social inequality: a challenge to policy and practice. *Disasters* 14(1): 7–19.

Rahman, Md.S. and Kausel, T. (2012). Disaster as an opportunity to enhance community resilience: lesson learnt from Chilean coast. *Journal of Bangladesh Institute of Planners* (5): 1–11.

Siembieda, W. (2012). Multi location disaster in three countries: comparing the recovery process in Japan, Chile and New Zealand. *Focus: Journal of the City and Regional Planning Department* 9(1): 15.

Siembieda, W., Johnson, L. and Franco, G. (2012). Rebuild fast but rebuild better: Chile's initial recovery following the 27 February 2010 earthquake and tsunami. *Earthquake Spectra* 28(S1): S621–41.

United Nations Office for Disaster Risk Reduction (UNISDR) (2009). *Global Assessment Report on Disaster Risk Reduction (GAR): Risk and Poverty in a Changing Climate, Invest Today for a Safer Tomorrow*. Geneva: United Nations.

Useem, Michael with Kunreuther, H. and Michel-Kerjan, E. (2015). *Leadership Dispatches: Chile's Extraordinary Comeback from Disaster*. California: Stanford University Press.

Chapter 4

Risk, resilience and the fragile city

John de Boer

Fragile cities: the epicenter of extreme vulnerability

> The challenge of knowing how to engage most effectively in concentrated urban areas characterized by violent criminal gangs, lawlessness, and extreme poverty cannot be overestimated.
>
> Peter Maurer, ICRC (2013)

Over the past 40 years the urban population in lower-income and fragile countries has increased by 326 percent (IDMC, 2014). Continuing population growth and urbanization are projected to add another 2.5 billion people to the world's urban population by 2050 and nearly 90 percent of that increase will be concentrated in Asia and Africa. Some of the world's most fragile and conflict-affected countries – Angola, Cote d'Ivoire, Iraq, Mali, Sudan and Uganda – are projected to add more than 20 million people each to their urban populations. Conflict- and disaster-prone countries such as Afghanistan, Burundi, Rwanda and Somalia will see their urban populations multiply fourfold over the next 30 years, possibly pushing cities in these countries to the brink of collapse (see Figure 4.1). Other already overburdened countries such as Bangladesh, the Democratic Republic of Congo, Pakistan and Ethiopia will each see more than 50 million people flood into their cities.

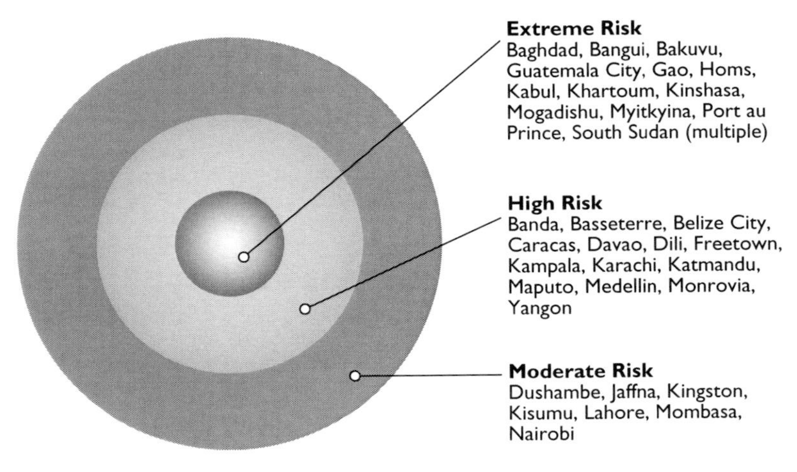

Figure 4.1 Indicative list of fragile cities[1]
Source: based on figures from UN DESA (2014)

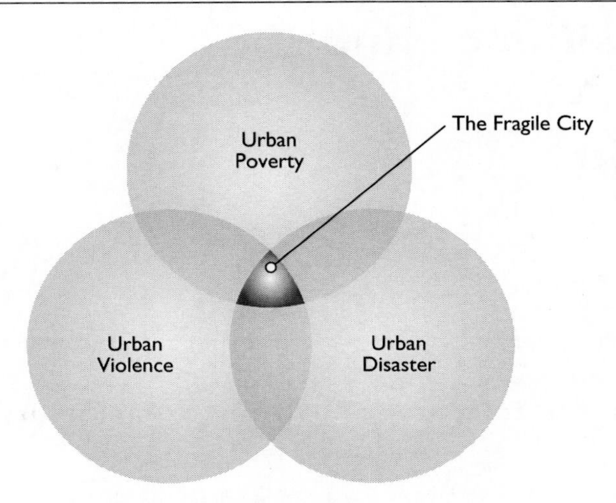

Figure 4.2 The fragile city – an analytical framework

How will these countries cope with such rapid urbanization? According to the World Bank's list of fragile situations,[2] these are some of the poorest, most violent and most disaster-prone countries in the world. As their populations aggregate in cities at a breakneck pace, it is plausible that the capacity of their governments at all levels to deliver services, respond to disasters, provide security and govern effectively will be pushed to the brink. What is certain is that the humanitarian crises of tomorrow will be more urban than rural and that the urban centers of fragile and conflict-affected countries are some of the world's most vulnerable zones (see Figure 4.2).

Yet notwithstanding the growing risks facing urban populations living in fragile and conflict-affected states, international organizations, governments and non-governmental organizations are ill-prepared to deal with this impending reality. Existing mechanisms for aid, disaster relief and security have traditionally been concentrated at the national level and have been limited to formal armed conflict. Today's risks, however, more often revolve around smaller, irregular armed groups and disaster-prone areas that are usually beyond the purview of international aid packages or peacebuilding activities and demand a more flexible and targeted response. Determining how to respond effectively in densely populated environments where violence intersects with disaster and extreme poverty is no simple task. To be effective, humanitarian and peacebuilding actors, along with development actors, need to develop and implement strategies to reduce the vulnerability and enhance the resilience of urban populations in fragile cities most at risk to multiple and interlocking crises.

What makes cities in fragile and conflict-affected countries so vulnerable?

Humanitarian and development communities are beginning to recognize that the causes and nature of vulnerability are multiple and interlocking. Emerging studies tell us that it is the aggregation of risk, i.e. the cumulative effects of multiple risks, that results in the greater likelihood and intensity of urban vulnerability to disaster, extreme poverty and violence (Muggah, 2012). The rapid accumulation of risks, which happens in contexts of violent conflict and humanitarian crises, often overwhelms local coping systems. A major factor shaping violence and vulnerability to disaster in these contexts is the inability of government institutions to respond appropriately. In some cities systems of law and order, ranging from the police, judiciary, penal systems and other forms of legal enforcement are dysfunctional and considered illegitimate by the citizens they are intended to serve. There is also often a serious capacity gap in providing basic and accountable security and other services that would otherwise reduce the city's vulnerability to extreme poverty, violence and disaster.

Increased recognition of the multiple and interlocking dimensions of risk is promoting a new understanding of fragility, one that goes beyond a single categorization of fragile states, toward measures that capture how diverse aspects of risk make a variety of populations more vulnerable to natural and man-made disasters. The Organisation for Economic Co-operation and Development's (OECD's) 2015 report, *States of Fragility*, reflects this new approach by proposing a working model that assesses fragility across five clusters of indicators. This goes beyond traditional notions that largely limited the understanding of fragility to political and security risks all the while neglecting the impact of social, economic and environmental shocks and disasters on the ability of the state to meet and protect the basic needs of its citizens. Despite progress, however, notions and measures of fragility remain limited to a state level analysis, failing to acknowledge that fragility is an issue of universal character that can challenge countries on multiple fronts and at multiple levels.

The 2010 *World Disasters Report*, for instance, warned that the world's 2.6 billion urban dwellers living in low- and middle-income countries were particularly exposed to disaster risk (IFRC, 2010). It went on to note that those worst affected by disasters triggered by natural events are vulnerable city dwellers living in slums and unplanned settlements. The report asserted that the world should expect three to five large-scale urban disasters in the next ten years and urged the international humanitarian community to work to reduce the vulnerability of the 1 billion or more people who live in urban slums worldwide. Since then, the world has witnessed a number of significant interlocking urban crises that have cost hundreds of thousands of lives and forced millions to flee their homes in Haiti, Indonesia, Myanmar, Nepal, Pakistan, the Philippines, Somalia and Syria.

As stated above, the number of people affected by disasters in fragile and conflict-affected states is disproportionately high. Somalia tops the list of conflict-affected countries with the highest level of disaster risks (see Figure 4.3). When one considers that 80 percent of the countries on this list will have the majority of their populations living in urban centers by 2050, the need to find feasible approaches that reduce vulnerability and promote resilience in fragile urban contexts becomes even more obvious and pressing.

One outcome of this heightened vulnerability to disaster and violence among fragile countries has been a record number of refugees and internally displaced persons (IDPs) (see Figure 4.4). According to the Office of the United Nations High Commissioner for Refugees (UNHCR) the world in 2013 had an estimated 51 million refugees and IDPs.[3] The Internal Displacement Monitoring Centre (IDMC) notes that approximately half of them are in urban areas. In countries such as Iraq, Jordan, Lebanon, Pakistan, Somalia, Sudan and Syria, the vast majority of IDPs (between 60 and 95 percent) reside in urban settings. This influx of refugees not only places an added burden on already overwhelmed cities but puts vulnerable IDPs in situations where they are unable to access social support or afford the cost of adequate housing, forcing many to occupy private and public property without permission. This makes people already vulnerable even more vulnerable, especially prone to deprivation, disease and violence and often exposes them to forced evictions and repeated displacement (IDMC, 2014).

#	*Country*	*% of urban pop'n by 2050*
1	Somalia	58%
2	Afghanistan	45%
3	Niger	35%
4	Guinea-Bissau	65%
5	Burundi	26%
6	Chad	37%
7	Sudan	50%
8	Democratic Republic of Congo	60%
9	Guinea	56%
10	Haiti	76%
11	Zimbabwe	44%
12	Ethiopia	38%
13	Central African Republic	57%
14	Bangladesh	56%
15	Liberia	65%
16	Sierra Leone	57%
17	Timor-Leste	48%
18	Burkina Faso	52%
19	Burma/Myanmar	55%
20	Rwanda	53%

Figure 4.3 Ranking of fragile countries with high disaster risk
Source: adapted from Harris et al. (2013: 9). See also OCHA (2012)

In the case of the 2011 East African humanitarian crisis,[4] a combination of natural hazards, violence and weak government responses led to catastrophes that spilled over to neighboring countries. In humanitarian circles it is widely acknowledged that more needs to be done to proactively tackle the risks posed by interlocking crises of disaster, violence and extreme poverty through preventive programming; however, in practice as little as 1 percent of official development assistance is invested in reducing risks associated with humanitarian crises and violence.

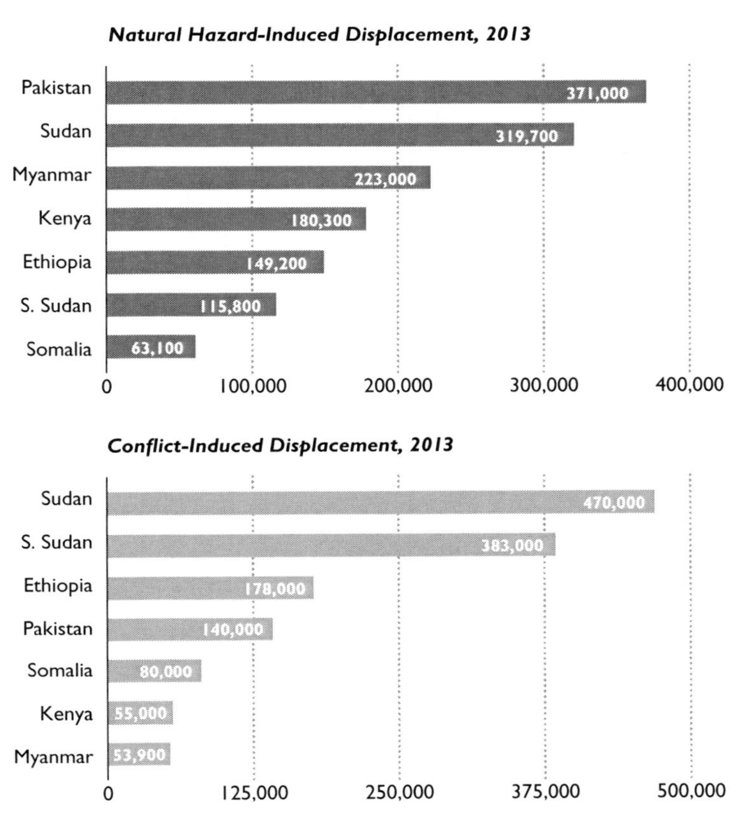

Figure 4.4 Confluence of natural and conflict-induced displacement
Source: IDMC (2014)

Can cities promote resilience and drive development in fragile and conflict-affected countries?

Not everything is doom and gloom. National governments and international organizations, such as the United Nations, are increasingly coming to recognize that cities possess the potential to play a transformative role in promoting resilience and development. The agreement within the UN Open Working Group on Sustainable Development Goals to establish a stand-alone goal on cities (Goal 11)[5] reflects this greater interest in cities as fonts of solutions. Part of this realization builds on the fact that cities are central to future global development. According to the McKinsey Global Institute (2011), cities generate more than 80 percent of global GDP today. While this wealth has been disproportionately concentrated in the developed world's largest cities this reality is about to shift radically with nearly 40 percent of global growth expected to come from cities in emerging markets by 2025.[6]

While this trend bodes well for cities such as Bursa, Delhi, Hangzhou, Istanbul, Izmir, Kuala Lumpur and Kunming, which are all in the top 20 fastest growing metropolitan economies in the world, the key question is what this means for fragile cities.[7] In other words, what are the implications for cities mired by unanticipated disasters and violent conflict? Can we expect to see fragile cities perform the same role driving national and regional development across conflict- and disaster-prone countries in Sub-Saharan Africa, Southeast Asia, the Middle East and North Africa?[8]

The answer according to well-respected observers is yes. By their account cities will drive development even in fragile contexts. A variety of international consulting firms unanimously support the idea that cities in these regions will dominate economic growth. According to the McKinsey Global Institute (2011) 70 percent of total GDP growth in Sub-Saharan Africa between 2010 and 2025 will be generated by cities in the region. In the Middle East and North Africa this figure will rise to 80 percent and in Southeast Asia, cities will constitute 66 percent of regional economic growth. One of the fastest growing cities in Sub-Saharan Africa is Khartoum (Sudan), which is expected to more than double its GDP within the next 10 years. In Southeast Asia, Yangon (Myanmar) is projected to grow even more dramatically from its current GDP of US$8 billion to $24 billion by 2025. According to A.T. Kearney's *Global Cities Index* (2014), Kinshasa and Karachi, both of which are located in fragile and conflict-affected countries, are ranked within the top 80 global cities worldwide (see Figure 4.5).

These projections of robust urban growth and economic activity highlight urbanization itself as a potential pathway out of poverty and extreme vulnerability for some of the most fragile and conflict-affected countries. Evidence shows that no country has ever achieved sustainable economic growth without urbanizing (Kacyira, 2012). Cities have historically been where most employment opportunities are located. They are often the engines of creativity and wealth generation and have served as important hubs for technology and transportation. Cities are where government and commerce are centered and have been associated with higher levels of literacy, better health, enhanced political participation and greater access to social services.

While economic and social upsides to urbanization undoubtedly exist, real-life downsides must be recognized as well. Many urban dwellers living in fragile and conflict-affected countries may actually be experiencing an urban disadvantage. Population growth in many of these fragile cities has been unplanned and as a result the majority of urban residents live

City	*Total GDP*	*Population*
Baghdad (Iraq)	2010: US $17 billion	2010: 5,000,000
	2025: US $46 billion	2025: 9,000,000
Khartoum (Sudan)	2010: US $43 billion	2010: 9,000,000
	2025: US $93 billion	2025: 14,000,000
Karachi (Pakistan)	2010: US $28 billion	2010: 13,500,000
	2025: US $67 billion	2025: 20,200,000
Kinshasa (DRC)	2010: US $17 billion	2010: 8,000,000
	2025: US $48 billion	2025: 15,000,000
Yangon (Myanmar)	2010: US $8 billion	2010: 4,300,000
	2025: US $24 billion	2025: 6,300,000

Figure 4.5 Projected growth in GDPs of select cities in fragile states
Source: based on data from McKinsey Global Institute (2011)

in precarious informal settlements characterized by poor housing, a lack of access to adequate sanitation and public services, rampant crime and violence and significant pollution. According to UN-Habitat (2014), over 75 percent of urban populations in countries emerging from conflict live in slums. This amounts to approximately 1 billion people who are not benefiting from the projected economic growth of these cities.

Furthermore, as noted in the 2014 report of the Intergovernmental Panel on Climate Change (IPCC), risks related to climate change are concentrated in urban areas.[9] Such risks are amplified for those lacking essential infrastructure and services or living in poor-quality housing and exposed areas (IPCC, 2014). Homicide also appears to be largely an urban phenomenon. According to the United Nations Office on Drugs and Crime's (UNODC) Global Homicide Report (2014), homicides in the national capital regions of countries such as Haiti, Liberia and Sierra Leone significantly outstrip national averages. In 2012 the Haitian capital of Port-au-Prince accounted for some 75 percent of national homicides. Additionally, extreme inequality is a reality in many of these cities. The African Development Bank (ADB, 2012) notes that inequality in African cities is the second highest in the world after Latin American cities. Given these realities the optimistic prospects for growth in fragile contexts put forward by the aforementioned reports must be tempered.

Investing in urban resilience: existing challenges and some ideas to build on

The extent to which cities in fragile and conflict-affected contexts can be resilient and catalysts for sustainable development will depend on two key factors: first the degree of exposure and susceptibility to risks that can derail growth (major disasters, extreme violence, disease epidemics, political instability and extreme poverty); and second the degree to which their governments, institutions and residents develop coping and adaptive capacities to mitigate these risks.

The question of whether individual countries and cities are able to harness urban opportunities largely depends on the development and implementation of effective risk governance strategies and capacities.[10] As the IPCC 2014 report puts it, a real paradigm shift is needed to address the growing accumulation of disaster risks now and in the future in urban centers (IPCC, 2014). For this, political, social, ecological and economic innovation is required.

As described above, urban disasters and violence are increasingly on the agendas of humanitarian and development agencies (Muggah and Savage, 2012). Yet, many questions remain as to how best to situate agencies within these new urban spaces and adapt methods for providing assistance that have traditionally been modeled around rural contexts. In cities, development and humanitarian agencies need to account for a number of factors, such as highly diverse populations (including those belonging to both displaced and host communities), the presence of a wide variety of existing state and non-state actors (armed and not-armed, licit and illicit) and formal and informal institutions that all play roles (whether positive or negative) in disaster response.

To be effective, a practical and context-driven understanding of the range of actions available in this new setting is required. Some of the recently issued recommendations are simply not useful in these contexts. For example, the United Nations Office for Disaster Risk Reduction's ten point essential checklist to make cities resilient calls for cities to create and budget for an entity responsible for disaster risk reduction (DRR). It also encourages cities to provide incentives for homeowners and businesses to upgrade their facilities.

Furthermore, it asks cities to assess the safety of all schools and health facilities, to apply and enforce realistic risk-compliant building codes and land-use regulations, to implement education programs on DRR, to protect ecosystems and emergency management capacities, to install early warning systems and to invest in and maintain critical infrastructure.[11] While these may indeed be the first-best measures, they are simply not feasible for most fragile cities, many of which have slum populations that exceed 50 percent of their total populations and, at the best of times, have difficulty delivering even the most basic services.[12]

Public authorities and residents of fragile cities will need to develop ways to better absorb disruption and to operate under a wide variety of conditions that may arise as a result of exposure to disaster and violence. Fragile cities need to anticipate risks with the resources they have. They need to foster and harness protective factors, i.e. characteristics that strengthen the ability of individuals, communities and states to confront stresses, without resorting to violence, that already exist within their societies. These factors include reducing the exposure of children to violence and promoting their interaction with positive family role models, supporting proactive community associations and engaged schools, promoting links between neighboring communities and increasing productive employment opportunities, among others.

While still a comparatively nascent area of study, there is a growing body of evidence documenting the role that protective factors can play to enhance the resilience of vulnerable urban populations in contexts of violence, disaster or extreme poverty. For instance urban pacification and policing interventions that combine the re-assertion of state authority with efforts to reinstall social services in neglected areas have produced some promising results in places such as Rio de Janeiro and Medellin (Muggah, 2015). Youth risk reduction programs that aim to stimulate income opportunities for youths through job training, cash transfer schemes, micro-enterprise development and the provision of childcare have also produced positive results.

Urban humanitarian interventions that have reinforced existing public services in cities rather than supplanting them have proven especially effective in strengthening healthcare and key services such as water and sanitation. Cities such as Nairobi and Johannesburg have experimented with market-based approaches to enhance the value of slum land by providing low-interest loans, tax rebates and grants to rehabilitate houses and attract businesses to revive decaying urban areas. Finally, programs that support the devolution and decentralization of certain core governance functions from national and regional governments to municipalities are also being experimented with in cities in Asia and Africa.[13]

In an ideal world these investments should be coupled with multi-level urban risk governance mechanisms and policies that provide incentives for risk reduction, strengthen local government and help communities develop adaptation capacity in collaboration with the private sector. However, these options may not be realistic for cities in fragile contexts. They need plans that are feasible, incremental and strategic. To get there, learning from research on counterfactuals (i.e. cities that have resisted or exited from fragility in the face of multiple crises) will be essential. Cities such as Amman, Beirut, Kinshasa and Yangon currently serve as sanctuaries for millions of refugees that have fled conflict and disaster. Despite the massive influx of refugees that has placed added stress on aging and inadequate infrastructure and limited government capacity, these cities are islands of relative political stability and sources of economic growth for their residents. These cities have demonstrated significant adaptive capacity to respond to crises without provoking political upheaval or social conflict. Kigali is another interesting example. Despite its many challenges, this once war-torn city may be emerging as a hub for development and security. There is an increasing push away from the ethnic politics that once led to genocide toward a more inclusive social and political environment in the city. Whether this trend will continue is unknown; however, it is essential to monitor and assess the extent to which what is being experimented with in Kigali is working and whether principles and lessons can be adapted to other fragile city contexts.

In conjunction, researchers and practitioners have to be better at identifying proven interventions that can be brought to scale. Doing so is challenging yet necessary. The reality is that very little is known about what interventions are most effective in reducing vulnerability, saving lives and rebuilding livelihoods in urban contexts during and after crises. The evidence on the required quality and nature of institutional and governance frameworks in relation to a country/city's capacity to reduce risk is extremely thin. Similarly very little is known about the role that resilient and adaptive infrastructure can play in preventing disasters in one part of the city system from cascading through the larger whole.

In support of such adaptive capacity, new technologies and solutions are emerging that may prove useful in fragile cities. These include open data initiatives that can help cities monitor and evaluate interventions, the development of critical infrastructure (electrical grids, water, telecommunication, banking and finance systems) with an embedded capacity to adapt and reconfigure in times of disaster, and predictive modeling as a result of scalable 'smart' innovations such as the US Geological Survey's Twitter Earthquake Detector[14] or Oracle's socially enabled policing.[15] The role that cloud computing can play[16] in supporting a dynamic Common Crisis Information Management System (CCIMS) for decision-makers and communities in times of crisis should also not be underestimated. Established approaches such as land-use planning, insurance schemes, education and community mobilization must also be part of the mix.

To be sure, the answers are not all technical or top-down. Resilience in fragile cities cannot be imposed from above. Instead it needs to be, and often is, found already in the relationships that mediate people's everyday lives. In many cases fragile cities have already developed some of these capacities through informal networks. Research has shown that some of the most resilient people and communities are those in places that have experienced deep challenges (i.e. fragile cities and countries).[17] These capacities have developed as a result of having overcome repeated disruptions and challenges to the point where a culture of resilience has emerged through informal networks rooted in trust. While one does not wish for multiple disasters as training grounds for future resilience, resilience in fragile cities needs to build on whatever intrinsic qualities and assets they have developed within their unique environments over time.

Moving forward

The resilience of cities is a crucial feature from which important lessons can be drawn. The concept of resilience has increasingly appeared in humanitarian, development and climate change circles as an organizing principle in relation to preventing, preparing for and responding to disasters. This concept's use in relation to disasters and violence is relatively recent and how best it can help to catalyze more effective responses remains an open question. The value of the concept, however, is that it offers an avenue to promote better linkages between humanitarian and development actors in their efforts to help affected communities and individuals reduce their vulnerability to multiple and interlocking disasters.

If managed well, cities can be engines of growth and provide workers and residents with quality job opportunities, better healthcare, improved housing, safety and social development. Cities can help contribute to national growth through increased revenue generation, political stability and post-conflict reconciliation. Opportunities do exist to harness the transformative potential of cities to promote development, implement effective disaster response systems and reduce violence.

An increasing number of initiatives are investing in and testing smart and scalable solutions that promote resilience at the city level, including the joint United Nations University and World Bank initiative on 'Resilience and the Fragile City,' the Rockefeller Foundation's 100 Resilient Cities Initiative, the DFID and IDRC-funded Safe and Inclusive Cities initiative, the C40 Cities Climate Leadership Group, the Ford Foundation's Just Cities Initiative, the Siemens SENSable City Lab and IBM's Smarter Cities program. Together, these initiatives are promoting a new approach to assess vulnerability and promote resilience at the city level. This includes helping to identify and assess the effectiveness of Big Data analytics, technology, innovative land-use policy and planning, infrastructure design, new financing and insurance products and common crises information management platforms as well as smart and predictive policing. Through these initiatives, researchers are teaming up with policymakers and private sector actors in a multi-disciplinary way to explore solutions that will make cities more resilient to disaster and violence.[18]

While this represents a good start, more work is especially needed to determine what works best to reverse fragility in cities already pushed to the brink. Cities that are on the front lines of the struggle against disaster, violence and extreme poverty may require specially conceived solutions that, while drawing on the increased knowledge about urban resilience, account for heightened burdens that vulnerability places on strategy, implementation and scalability.

Notes

1 The figures used in this chapter were originally published in an article by the author in *Stability: International Journal of Security & Development*, http://doi.org/10.5334/sta.fk.

2 See the World Bank's Harmonized List of Fragile Situations available at: http://siteresources.worldbank.org/EXTLICUS/Resources/511777-1269623894864/HarmonizedlistoffragilestatesFY14.pdf.

3 See www.unhcr.org/pages/49c3646cbc.html.

4 The 2011 East African humanitarian crisis was provoked by the worst drought experienced in the region in 60 years. The crisis began in July 2011 and threatened the livelihoods of some 13 million people. The crisis was unique in that, for the first time, a significant number of people in crisis were the urban poor, who struggled to cope with sustained hyperinflation in food prices. The urban food crisis was widespread, affecting 25 percent of the total urban population, or 705,000 people, of which 565,000 were identified as in acute food and livelihood crisis and 140,000 in humanitarian emergency. In addition, according to UNHCR, over 1 million people were internally displaced and concentrated in cities such as Afgoye and the Somali capital of Mogadishu.

5 See the final draft of the United Nations 2030 Action Agenda for Sustainable Development called 'Transforming our world: the 2030 Agenda for Sustainable Development,' available at: www.un.org/pga/wp-content/uploads/sites/3/2015/08/120815_outcome-document-of-Summit-for-adoption-of-the-post-2015-development-agenda.pdf.

6 See the Brookings Institution's 2014 *Global Metro Monitor: Uncertain Recovery* available at: www.brookings.edu/~/media/Research/Files/Reports/2015/01/22-global-metro-monitor/bmpp_GMM_final.pdf?la=en.

7 Ibid.
8 For more on fragile cities see de Boer (2014).
9 Cities are also responsible for some 70 percent of global greenhouse gas emissions. See data from C40, available at: www.c40.org/.
10 See UNU-EHS, *2014 World Risk Report*, Bonn, October 16, 2014 available at: http://ehs.unu.edu/news/news/world-risk-report-2014.html#info.
11 See UNISDR, 'Toolkit for Local Governments,' available at: www.unisdr.org/campaign/resilientcities/toolkit/essentials.
12 In some cities, those living in slums form the majority: 70.1 percent of Port-au-Prince's population lives in slums, 66 percent of Calcutta and 60 percent of Bogotá (see UN DESA, 2014).
13 For projected urban populations see UN DESA (2014). For more detail on the examples see Muggah (2012). Also see: IDRC and DFID's Safe and Inclusive Cities Initiative; the Harvard Humanitarian Initiative's Urbanization and Emergencies work; the Humanitarian Action in Situations other than War project led by the Igarape Institute; Robert Muggah's TED Talk on 'How to Protect Fast-Growing Cities From Failing' (October 2014).
14 For the US Geological Survey's Twitter Earthquake Detector visit: https://twitter.com/usgsted.
15 For more on socially enabled policing see: www.linkedin.com/pulse/20140928004129-185500037-what-is-social-enabled-policing.
16 On this see the World Disaster Report available at: http://worlddisastersreport.org/en/chapter-4/index.html.
17 See Zolli and Healy (2012).
18 See for instance the knowledge-sharing partnership between Swiss Re and the International Committee of the Red Cross. Another example is the Global Assessment Report on Disaster Risk Reduction, which brings together numerous UN agencies with the private sector and other multilateral organizations to assess risk and build a data base on vulnerability.

References

African Development Bank (ADB) (2012). *Urbanization in Africa*. December 13. Available at: www.afdb.org/en/blogs/afdb-championing-inclusive-growth-across-africa/post/urbanization-in-africa-10143/.

A.T. Kearney (2014). *Global Cities, Present and Future: 2014 Global Cities Index and Emerging Cities Outlook*. Available at: www.atkearney.com/research-studies/global-cities-index/2014.

de Boer, J. (2014). *The Fragile City: The Epicentre of Extreme Vulnerability*. UNU-CPR, March 9. Available at: http://cpr.unu.edu/the-fragile-city-the-epicentre-of-extreme-vulnerability-2.html.

Harris, K., Keen, D. and Mitchell, T. (2013). *When Disasters and Conflicts Collide: Improving the Links Between Disaster Resilience and Conflict Prevention*. London: Overseas Development Institute. Available at: www.odi.org.uk/sites/odi.org.uk/files/odi-assets/publications-opinion-files/8228.pdf.

IFRC (International Federation of Red Cross and Red Crescent Societies) (2010). *World Disasters Report 2010 Focus on Urban Risk*. Geneva: IFRC. Available at: www.ifrc.org/Global/Publications/disasters/WDR/WDR2010-full.pdf.

Internal Displacement Monitoring Centre (IDMC) (2014). *Global Estimates 2014: People Displaced by Disasters*. Available at: www.internal-displacement.org/publications/2014/global-estimates-2014-people-displaced-by-disasters.

IPCC (2014). *Climate Change 2014: Impacts, Adaptation, and Vulnerability*. Available at: https://ipcc-wg2.gov/AR5/images/uploads/IPCC_WG2AR5_SPM_Approved.pdf.

Kacyira, A.K. (2012). Addressing the sustainable urbanization challenge. *UN Chronicle* XLIX(1 & 2). Available at: http://unchronicle.un.org/article/addressing-sustainable-urbanization-challenge/.

Maurer, P. (2013). *The Challenges of the Evolving Battlefield*. NYU School of Law, March 20. Available at: http://intercrossblog.icrc.org/blog/icrc-president-on-the-challenges-of-the-evolving-battlefield#sthash.4B3IFfac.dpbs=.

McKinsey Global Institute (2011). *Urban World: Mapping the Economic Power of Cities*. Available at: www.mckinsey.com/insights/urbanization/urban_world.

Muggah, R. (2012). *Researching the Urban Dilemma: Urbanization, Poverty and Violence*. Ottawa, Canada: IDRC. Available at: www.idrc.ca/EN/PublishingImages/Researching-the-Urban-Dilemma-Baseline-study.pdf.

Muggah, R. (2015). Fixing fragile cities: solutions for urban violence and poverty. *Foreign Affairs*, January 15. Available at: www.foreignaffairs.com/articles/142760/robert-muggah/fixing-fragile-cities.

Muggah, R. and Savage, K. (2012). Urban violence and humanitarian action: engaging the fragile city. *Journal of Humanitarian Action*, January. Available at: http://sites.tufts.edu/jha/archives/1524.

OECD (2015). *States of Fragility 2015: Meeting Post-2015 Ambitions*, rev. edn. Paris: OECD Publishing.

UN-Habitat (2014). Number of slum dwellers grows to 863 million. *Urban Matters*, February 10. Available at: www.cordaid.org/en/news/un-habitat-number-slum-dwellers-grows-863-million/.

United Nations Department of Economic and Social Affairs (UN DESA) (2014). *World Urbanization Prospects 2014*. Available at: http://esa.un.org/unpd/wup/.

United Nations Office for the Coordination of Humanitarian Affairs (OCHA) (2012). *World Humanitarian Data and Trends*. Available at: https://docs.unocha.org/sites/dms/Documents/World%20Humanitarian%20Data%20and%20Trends%202012%20Web.pdf.

United Nations Office of Drugs and Crime (UNODC) (2014). *Global Study on Homicide*. Available at: www.unodc.org/gsh/.

Zolli, A. and Healy, A.H. (2012). *Why Things Bounce Back*, New York: Simon & Schuster Paperbacks.

Part II

People, places, complex systems and regulation

Chapter 5

Urban disaster resilience

Learning from the 2011 Bangkok, Thailand, flood using morphology and complex adaptive systems

Pamela Sitko

Introduction

This chapter describes research undertaken by the author that explores the resilience of low-income neighborhoods after a large-scale flood. The neighborhoods also have a history of eviction threats. Complex adaptive systems (interdependent systems that adapt and co-evolve with their changing environment) and urban morphology (the study of changes in urban form) are combined to interrogate humanitarian and built environment drivers of urban disaster resilience within three cases, demonstrating that these two urban approaches can be employed to reveal patterns of urban resilience, vulnerability, capacity, risk and opportunity.

Morphology and complex adaptive systems (CAS) are combined as an investigative approach for three reasons. First, analysis of the morphological layers and their relationships with complex adaptive systems generates an understanding about the interactions that shape risk, opportunity and vulnerability in the built environment and the degrees of influence each system has at different physical scales. Second, the approaches analyze both disaster and chronic risks, striving to overcome the traditional silos of 'disaster' and 'development' approaches. Third, the combined approach helps identify issues about which urban actors can collaborate across vertical and horizontal scales that include policy and practice. While neighborhoods and urban professionals recognize the importance of working together, they face challenges in doing so. Leeson (2014) notes that while 'planners and the humanitarians were not speaking the same language, both groups recognized the incredible wealth of expertise that the other could bring to their work.'

Due to its broad range of applicability, it is imperative to define resilience *for whom,* and *to what,* in order to speak about the concept with clarity. The research undertaken as the basis for this chapter is focused on learning about the flood and eviction challenges faced by three low-income neighborhoods in Bangkok, Thailand.

An urban morphological and CAS approach to resilience

Urban disaster resilience can be more accurately analyzed when based within a framework that acknowledges and accommodates overlap, complexity and adaptive behavior (Anderies et al., 2006; Da Silva, 2014). Hence, the approach used in this research is based on two approaches. The framework uses morphological layers on one axis, reflecting a built environment language and way of thinking (Butina Watson and Bentley, 2007; Moudon, 1997; Whitehand, 2012), and a CAS approach on the other, which reflects the humanitarian and development language of assets (Moser, 1998) and livelihoods (Carney, 1998; Chambers and Conway, 1991; Sanderson, 2009; Scoones, 1998) (see Figure 5.1).

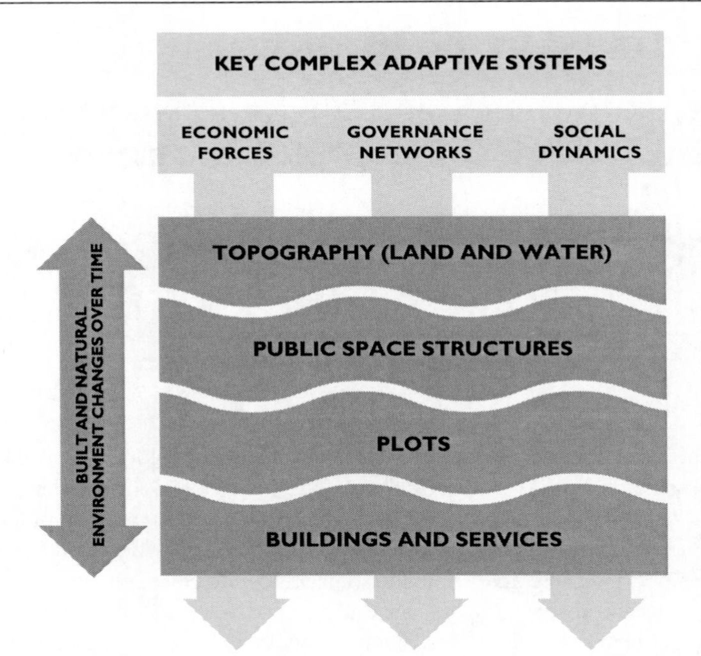

Figure 5.1 A framework for urban disaster resilience that blends urban morphology and complex adaptive systems. The horizontal axis represents non-physical complex adaptive systems. The vertical axis represents built and natural environment changes

Urban morphology is the study of how urban form is shaped by social, political and economic factors (Whitehand, 2012). Urban morphology engages with history, seeking to draw connections between historical and modern day transformations at different layers (scales) and resolutions in order to identify underlying factors that shape physical infrastructure and natural ecosystems (Warner and Whittemore, 2012). The historical dimension of morphology is powerful when seen through a resilience lens because, as Levine et al. (2012) argue, resilience alone lacks a historical dimension resulting in the repetition of mistakes. Understanding the creation of urban form is essential to the success of future molding and reshaping of cities and their component parts, making morphology essential to urbanism and urban design (Kropf, 2005). To this end, the vertical axis of the framework traces changes in the spatial relationships between the physical and natural form of a city over time. For example, the buildings and services layer changes more quickly over time than rivers in the topography layer. Four morphological layers are used: a topographical layer that explores land and water (Bolio Arcaeo, 2012); a public space layer that investigates the impact of streets and spaces under public ownership (Truong, 2013); a plots layer that analyzes the way in which small or large parcels of land change over time (Kropf, 2009); and a buildings and services layer that explores the ways in which buildings and access to utilities such as water and electricity impacts upon disaster safety and security. While each of these layers has been presented and defined as distinct, individual layers, it must be emphasized that all of the layers integrate across space and time, creating dynamic intersections (Gauthiez, 2004).

The second approach recognizes cities and neighborhoods as complex adaptive systems. This means that they exemplify a high degree of order while appearing chaotic (Bar-Yam,

1997), non-linear in their operation (Folke, 2006) and complex and interdependent (Wallace and Wallace, 2008). Such systems also possess fuzzy boundaries about where they stop and are influenced by a plethora of factors that create feedback loops, which cause a system to adapt and change (Da Silva et al., 2012; Holling, 2001).

The horizontal axis is host to three key interdependent complex adaptive systems, which are economic forces, governance networks and social dynamics. Economic forces are defined as economic benefits such as money, markets, businesses, rent, jobs, savings, loans, credit, ownership and skills. Governance networks involve the organization of power and decision-making such as government, institutions, leaders, networks, planning policies and legal frameworks (Resilience Alliance, 2007). Social dynamics are defined by social interaction such as networks, social capital, discrimination, culture and values. Social dynamics also include social services such as education, welfare and healthcare (Resilience Alliance, 2007).

Bringing together concepts of morphology and complex systems aims to provide a more powerful context analysis and a more accurate identification of the interaction of the built environment and the systems that influence it.

Bangkok's 2011 flood and the Bang Bua Canal

Bangkok's 2011 flood began when flooding started in northern Thailand in early July due to five consecutive rainstorms. By the end of the year more than 600 people had died (Associated Press, 2011). The flooding affected 13 million people in 66 out of 77 provinces, causing an estimated US$46.5 billion in damage (World Bank, 2012).

Many people interviewed by the author[1] believed the root cause of the flood was political, as a change in government had occurred around the time the floods began. Boonyabancha and Archer (2011) describe water management in Thailand as a 'sensitive political matter.' The coordination of the flood involved 16 organizations from four ministries (Boonyabancha and Archer, 2011). Effective disaster response collaboration in Bangkok was hindered due to the tenuous relationship between the governing Democratic opposition party and the Pheu Thai central government (Barber, 2012; Pongsudhirak, 2011), giving rise to what Boonyabancha and Archer (2011) describe as 'political games'. The 'games' involved politicians and other influential actors allegedly exerting their power to protect wealthier areas from flooding, at times resulting in community protests that led to the dismantling of flood protection barriers (Kwankijswet and Janssen, 2011).

The densely populated Bang Bua Canal in north-western Bangkok is home to more than 17,000 people (Wungpatcharapon and Tovivich, 2012). A narrow three-kilometer strip of land lining the canal is host to 12 low-income neighborhoods, described by one resident as 'ghetto-like' before a national slum and squatter upgrading program dramatically changed the physical, social and economic conditions of some of the neighborhoods. The incremental upgrading program, which began in 2004, is still taking place in some neighborhoods today. Three of the neighborhoods that the author undertook research in are as follows.

Bang Bua neighborhood is well known for its upgrading success (see Plate 11) and is often visited by others as a study of good practice. There are 229 households, all of which have been reconstructed within three years of the start of the upgrading based on a collaborative neighborhood vision and a series of land sharing negotiations amongst residents (Wungpatcharapon, 2012). Residents from the neighborhood formed a cooperative and have a 90-year lease agreement on all the land in the neighborhood.

Saphan Mai neighborhood started upgrading in 2007 but parts of the neighborhood did not trust the process. When the 2011 flood occurred many of the homes that had not previously been upgraded were severely damaged or destroyed due to their low quality. The flood created an opportunity for people to unite and begin to trust one another through collective actions to meet individual needs (see Plate 12). Since then, the final 45 homeowners have been granted access to loans to reconstruct their homes, resulting in an upgrading rate of 100 percent. Saphan Mai is also a neighborhood cooperative and has a 90-year lease agreement on the land.

Roi Krong neighborhood (see Figure 5.2) is divided between those who participate in upgrading (approximately 40 percent) and those who oppose it (approximately 60 percent). The neighborhood has 135 houses and is a mix of affluent and low-income people living together. Land tenure has not been secured in this neighborhood. Informality seems to best suit the affluent people in the neighborhood who earn income from renting rooms in dormitories that have been abandoned by a nearby university. It also suits poorer people who do not want to go into debt or believe they cannot afford to. Many of the upgrading opponents say they are prepared to be evicted rather than voluntarily give up income and land. Roi Krong has created a cooperative but it is currently too small and too undersubscribed to be able to afford to rent the land. Only 25 houses have been upgraded out of a total of 135 homes; 12 have been repaired.

Figure 5.2 Roi Krong neighborhood (to the left)
Source: the author

Exploring resilience using morphology and CAS

While each of the three neighborhoods has its own unique history, the three together reveal a broader story, one of the Bang Bua Canal as a whole and its struggle to exist in the face of eviction in the early 2000s and the 2011 Bangkok flood. Exploring chronic stresses and disaster risks from a macro to micro scale provides valuable insights into root causes of more systemic vulnerabilities that exacerbated the impact of the flood. This section analyzes the four morphological layers, namely topography, public space structures, plots, and buildings and services, and the ways in which they intersect with systems of economic flows, governance networks and social dynamics to create a picture of the Bang Bua Canal (see Plate 13).

Topography (land and water)

The topographical layer, meaning land and water, is investigated first because it is the largest, most permanent morphological layer where changes manifest across centuries (Bolio Arcaeo, 2012). Analysis of the topographical layer adds value by investigating the terrain and soil of pre-urban structures (Koster, 1998). Historical analysis of how people affect change at a topographical level can shed light on modern day challenges and opportunities related to quality of place (Bolio Arcaeo, 2012; Choi, 2011) and the subsequent need to investigate other morphological elements (Butina Watson and Bentley, 2007). The topographical layer is important in this framework because it accounts for changes in political, economic and social CAS that take place at a macro scale across centuries through such elements as weather patterns, sea level change and land subsidence. While analysis of the topography layer reveals patterns of vulnerability and a predisposition to flooding, it also identifies the formation of the Bang Bua Canal upgrading network as a key driver of resilience.

Bangkok, including the Bang Bua Canal, is rooted in an agricultural past of rice farming and political power battles (Raochanakanan, 1999). Much of the city is below sea level (World Bank, 2010), with some parts as low as 1.5 meters below (Philip, 2011). In 1953 Bangkok covered 67 square kilometers; rice paddies surrounded the Bang Bua Canal and flooding was on a seasonal basis, creating an ideal environment for rice farming (Raochanakanan, 1999). Historically canals in Bangkok were used for transportation, irrigation and as a flood prevention mechanism.

In the 1950s, people from provinces outside of Bangkok began to migrate to the Bang Bua Canal in search of jobs, many of which were related to what was then Bangkok's only airport, which had been expanded and declared an international travel hub (Raochanakanan, 1999). Plate 14 is a historical land-use map that depicts the Bang Bua canal in 1968, reflecting a primarily rural landscape with few houses next to the canal (Royal Thai Survey Department, 1968).

Decades of weak urban planning and lack of enforcement of land-use regulations in Bangkok led to the uncontrolled growth of under-serviced neighborhoods and settlements (UNESCAP, 2014), including the Bang Bua Canal. Modernization and rapid economic growth accompanied by unenforced environmental regulations left the Bang Bua Canal heavily polluted.

Eviction threat

Residents in the canal have often faced eviction threats, and in 2004 the National Government's Treasury Department, the land owner, communicated plans to replace the homes around the canal with a new highway to alleviate the traffic congestion. Moreover, flooding downstream was being blamed on river bank houses for stifling the flow of water. Increasing levels of water pollution due to the practice of dumping untreated sewage and wastewater directly into the canal also were blamed on canal dwellers.

Ultimately, the neighborhoods in the Bang Bua Canal avoided eviction by joining the national government's slum and squatter upgrading program, *Baan Mankong*, which translates as 'secure housing' (Wungpatcharapon and Tovivich, 2012). The Baan Mankong program successfully advocated to the Bangkok Metropolitan Authority (BMA) that slum upgrading instead of eviction was in the best interest of canal residents and the city as long as the following three conditions were agreed to: land rental was paid; houses were moved off the river bank and onto proper land; and environmental pollution was reduced.

Upgrading and the formation of the Bang Bua Canal Network

During the upgrading the neighborhoods in the canal formed 'the Bang Bua Canal Network' and partnered with architects, planners, district authorities, the municipality, aid agencies and universities to meet the upgrading criterion listed above. For a period of 10 years relationships grew.

When the 2011 flood occurred, the network and its partners adapted the ways they worked together. For example, medical students from universities provided healthcare advice and engineering students taught people how to prevent electrocution. In fact, during the flood the Bang Bua Canal Network rivaled local district governments in terms of having the ability to quickly procure aid and effectively distribute it. The effectiveness of the Bang Bua Canal Network was recognized with an increase in membership from 18 to 38 neighborhoods by the end of the flood.

Therefore, through analysis of the topography layer it can be observed that Bangkok has a predisposition to flooding. Years of unenforced urban planning regulations have resulted in the growth of informal settlements addressed by eviction. However, upgrading and the development of the Bang Bua Canal Network gave people a sense of agency, i.e. the ability to collectively organize and self-represent.

Public space structures

The second morphological layer investigates movement networks and public open spaces as part of public space structures. Economic and social use of movement networks and public open spaces offers insights into power dynamics. Who is included in the social and economic interactions that take place on roads and in public open spaces demonstrates that power is a relational effect, an outcome of social interaction. The ways in which spaces are constructed, their layout and their uses serve not only as a resource of power, but also as a means through which power is exercised (Allen, 2003).

Movement networks are defined as mobility infrastructure such as streets, large highways and small pedestrian lanes (Kropf, 2009) as well as water channels used for transportation, commercial activities or socializing (Truong, 2013). The design of movement networks impacts safety and permeability of an area and increases legibility of an area (Carmona et al., 2003). Public open spaces are open to the air spaces that are accessible to the general public and often host social and economic activities (Carmona et al., 2003). Examples of public open spaces are informal marketplaces, playgrounds, parks and squares. Public spaces 'mirror the complexities of urban societies'; they can be impersonal, fragmented, contested or exclusive

(Madanipour, 2010). Alternatively, when public spaces are accessible and inclusive (Madanipour, 2010) they can create a safe environment for strangers to connect and for friendships, cultural attitudes and identities to be strengthened. The movement networks and public open spaces layer reveals three drivers of resilience: safety, inclusivity and income generation.

Since 2004, the incremental upgrading in the canal prioritized the creation and improvement of roads and public open spaces which contributed to a greater sense of safety and security. For example, major pedestrian lanes were expanded and lights were installed creating better visibility and more permeability. Smaller alleys were designed with a high degree of connectedness to the major pedestrian lane in each neighborhood, arguably contributing to safety by increasing footfall in previously isolated areas. The increased width of the road also increased the capacity for socializing. The roads were enablers for people to generate income; therefore income generation is included as the third driver of resilience at the movement networks and public open spaces layer. In Bang Bua neighborhood the creation of a canal-based pedestrian lane resulted in an increase of vendors accessing the area with goods to sell. Small portions of the road in Bang Bua and Saphan Mai neighborhoods are used for storing goods related to income generation such as vending carts or goods for recycling. In Roi Krong the main road remains narrow and accommodates few vendors.

When the 2011 flood struck, roads were completely submerged. Neighborhood leaders participating in Baan Mankong prioritized mobility in their preparedness efforts through the decision to pre-position one boat per neighborhood in order to assist with the management of distributions. Free public transportation was offered at a city level by the military, which enabled some of the urban poor to continue working at their regular jobs or to innovate ways to earn money by traveling great distances to markets and reselling goods on boats. Overall, mobility was underscored as extremely important to residents because they needed to access different parts of the city to support every aspect of their lives, including access to food, education, healthcare, jobs and other such daily routines that support survival and well-being. After the flood waters receded, Bang Bua neighborhood resumed patterns of economic and social activities that took place before the flood. The robust roads sustained little to no damage, aiding in a quicker recovery. Meanwhile, Saphan Mai placed great emphasis on rebuilding roads after the flood, having the opportunity to widen parts of the primary pedestrian lane and create smaller alleys due to an increase in participation in upgrading.

Examination of public open spaces also reveals findings about the experience of inclusion in the Bang Bua Canal. As discussed above, children are included through the intentional creation of open space. Children's right to play in safe, child-friendly spaces was prioritized through the design of public open spaces at the center of all three neighborhoods. Prior to the upgrading children used to play in parking lots, at risk of vehicular-related accidents and within reach of strangers, if the playtime was unsupervised by adults. Assimilating children through safe places to play in their neighborhood creates spatial autonomy for social interaction, and turns public open spaces into grounds where children can develop and test their identity in relation to their peers (Travlou, 2007). Their caregivers, usually elderly relatives, are also included because the space is within a short walking distance of all neighborhood homes and is a pleasant area for elderly people to gather, socialize and supervise younger children. In Saphan Mai neighborhood adults use the open space for formal neighborhood meetings. During the 2011 flood, water submerged the public open spaces. However, had there been a different kind of crisis, an earthquake, for example, public open spaces may have been used for shelter, distributions and activities.

In summary, thoughtfully designed and well-maintained roads and public open spaces accommodated a panoply of social and economic activities that promoted safety, inclusivity and income generation for the users. Analysis of the interconnected economic, governance and social CAS and the ways in which they shape movement networks and public open spaces in crisis and non-crisis periods therefore offers a way in which key drivers of disaster resilience can be identified.

Plots

The third morphological layer focuses on analysis of plots in order to identify changes in access to and quality of a piece of land, its use and ownership. Once street patterns are established, plots begin to appear (Koster, 1998), hosting people settling or working on parcels of land (Whitehand, 2001). Plots are defined by land use and their physical form (Kropf, 2009). This approach includes plots as a separate layer of analysis because it allows investigation of ownership and control, providing an essential insight into socially defined relationships between the controller and the user (Kropf, 2009). It is widely recognized that many towns and cities lack regulated plot dimensions (Whitehand, 2001), and thus they vary in shape and size. In urban areas where land is a scarce resource and land rights in informal settlements are frequently contested, it is important to analyze the use and access to specific plots of land at a neighborhood and household scale in order to identify how CAS shape specific aspects of plots over time. In Bang Bua Canal four key drivers of resilience were found to be essential to the transformation of the plots, namely land tenure, access to loans, governance mechanisms and social capital.

The transformation of individual and neighborhood plots within Bang Bua Canal through settlement upgrading is an example of using development mechanisms to reduce disaster risk and manage crises. The first driver is land tenure and the ways in which chronic stresses and disaster shocks prompted the need for canal residents to rethink tenure security. In the early 2000s the looming threat of eviction instigated a multi-sectoral upgrading approach between 12 neighborhoods. Without tenure security, investments in buildings, roads and public spaces are risky.

In Bang Bua neighborhood secure land tenure resulted in the reconstruction of all of its 229 houses within two years, after a year of planning had taken place. In Saphan Mai neighborhood, tenure security was an important driver for investment in buildings and common infrastructure. Other drivers, however, impeded progress such as trust in financial and governance mechanisms related to the upgrading program, which prevented the neighborhood from collectively renting the land for almost nine years. In Saphan Mai the 2011 flood became an opportunity to work together collectively and build trust. After the flood 45 houses that had not undergone reconstruction before the flood joined the upgrading program, some because they saw the long-term investment reduced disaster risk and others because the Saphan Mai cooperative threatened to sue the remaining 17 houses that were living on cooperative land without paying rent. Meanwhile, in Roi Krong neighborhood tenure security was important but formalization was resisted partly because of fragmented social capital but primarily because a minority group of people controlling plots in the area risked losing significant financial income generated through rent.

The second driver of resilience is access to loans. For the urban poor individual financial access is often dependent upon collective activity and social capital at the neighborhood level. At the neighborhood plot level, savings groups set up and run by the cooperative enabled people to collectively pool their resources to access loans with low interest rates. The loans were provided by Community Organizations Development Institute (CODI),[2] the national government's implementing partner responsible for facilitating the upgrading process, and afforded canal residents the opportunity to re-parcel their individual plots, reconstruct their homes, invest in common urban infrastructure such as public spaces, and initiate a social welfare fund. During the 2011 flood the savings groups in Bang Bua and Saphan Mai neighborhood set up food kitchens. The savings group in Roi Krong was unable to afford a food kitchen due to low membership numbers. After the flood the savings groups provided small loans with a low interest rate to members who needed money to invest in activities valued by the neighborhood such as restarting livelihoods or paying school fees. The savings group worked as a mechanism for building social capital because of the collective way in which people worked together to manage their money. Transparent and accountable processes and management committees earned trust amongst members and formed relationships and bonds. Those who did not participate in savings groups either had alternative means of accessing finances (through loans or family members, for example) or felt they could not afford to participate because the investment cost was too high.

The third driver is that of governance mechanisms. Cross-case study analysis found that democratic formal and informal governance mechanisms are amenable to power sharing and adaptable to crisis and non-crisis situations. Each neighborhood had a formally elected leader recognized by the local district government. The neighborhoods also had an informal leader elected to run the upgrading process. Both types of governance mechanisms were successful if they were transparent, accountable and equitable. For example, in Bang Bua neighborhood there appeared to be a large level of satisfaction with the governance structure, which was decentralized and therefore enjoyed high levels of participation in activities such as census data collection. When the 2011 flood occurred, the method for collecting census data was adapted for assessing needs and monitoring distributions. To this end, the leader in Bang Bua was able to seek appropriate donations from partners and networks. This type of adaptive governance arguably builds resilience by strengthening local capabilities beyond 'managing' informal settlements to positively integrating into the wider city (Seeliger and Turok, 2014).

The fourth driver of resilience identified at the plots layer is social capital. A pattern of three types of social capital can be witnessed: bonding through intra-communal relations within a neighborhood; bridging through inter-communal relations between neighborhoods; and linking, a function of neighborhood relations with the state (Archer, 2009). The first level of social capital, bonding, was evidenced most when neighborhoods took action to address social and financial inequities between individuals and improve the overall livability of the area. For example, through the savings group, each neighborhood has its own social welfare system to assist unstable or depleted individual financial assets. Furthermore, neighborhoods worked together to plan new roads, re-parcel plots of land and design public open spaces as discussed above.

The bridging form of social capital builds horizontal linkages between neighborhoods within the canal and is demonstrated through the Bang Bua Canal Network of 12 neighborhoods that have worked together since the early 2000s to address drug-trafficking, pollution and land tenure security. Mere weeks before the flood struck Bangkok, the Bang Bua Canal Network sent its leaders to assist other neighborhoods participating in the upgrading in flood-affected cities in northern Thailand in order to learn how to implement key preparedness and response activities. When the flood reached Bangkok the network of neighborhoods collaborated to procure donations from a range of partners and personal friends.

Evidence of the linking form of social capital can be observed during the upgrading when neighborhood leaders worked with government district authorities to arrange regular garbage collection. During the flood, the Bang Bua Canal Network liaised with district authorities, at times rivaling the government in regards to efficiency and effectiveness, according to interviews with key government informants and Bang Bua Canal Network leaders.

Analysis at the plots layer therefore demonstrates that land tenure, access to loans, governance mechanisms and social capital are key drivers of urban disaster resilience. Furthermore, development approaches were successfully adapted to the flood context, improving the way people survived the flood.

Buildings and services

The final layer is buildings and services, and is used to identify opportunities for improving quality in order to improve overall human well-being. The buildings and services layer is the most rapidly changing of the physical layers, and arguably one of the most fundamental layers in morphological analysis for understanding the social, political and economic factors that influence a neighborhood (Bolio Arcaeo, 2012; Whitehand, 1987). So important are buildings and services such as water and electricity, that UN-Habitat describes them as the 'bedrock of prosperity' (UN-Habitat, 2013), arguing that 'inadequate infrastructure is a major impediment to the prosperity of cities' (UN-Habitat, 2013, xvii). Access to adequate housing and utilities promotes competitiveness and economic growth, improves urban connectedness, reduces poverty and contributes to safer, more sustainable cities. Investing in and maintaining critical infrastructure and utilities are listed by the United Nations Office for Disaster Risk Reduction (UNISDR, 2015) as one of ten essentials in its Making Cities Resilient campaign. Linking this particular layer with all of the other layers in the framework recognizes that in a crisis, people who live in neighborhoods rely on the city to maintain a low-level functionality of basic utilities such as power and water in order to survive. In non-crisis periods, people not only require access to utilities, but also to quality houses that are affordable (Lucci, 2014).

Cross-case analysis of the buildings and utilities layer reveals three key drivers of resilience that are essential to transformation of inadequate buildings and utilities, namely access to loans, inclusive planning and community centers.

Quality of houses

Poorer urban dwellers were disproportionately affected by the floods due to the low quality of the buildings they lived in. Quality is assessed through characteristics such as durability, affordability, layout, structure and materials used to construct the buildings. The poor quality of building construction can be traced back to financial vulnerability; inexpensive building materials such as bamboo, corrugated iron and timber were deliberately used to best cope with the weather, offer privacy and accommodate construction on marginalized, risky land. Some neighborhoods, such as Saphan Mai, have had electricity since 1974, despite their informal status. According to one leader in the area, politicians traded the offer of access to utilities in return for votes. Most of the houses had access to water and electricity before the upgrading. However, each house that participated in the upgrading has its own meter and is responsible for paying bills. The district government in all three case studies collects rubbish once a week. Sewage treatment tanks are installed in the reconstructed homes.

Thailand's National Housing Authority estimates that approximately 73 percent of Bangkok's low-income population were affected by the flood (UNESCAP, 2014). In the

Bang Bua Canal, the most vulnerable people were those who lived in one-story homes, people who were unemployed, illegal migrant workers and/or people who generally required more protection such as children, the elderly or those with mobility challenges. One-story homes were particularly vulnerable because they were often made of wooden flooring and walls, which often rotted during the three months of flooding. Stilt houses built over the canal experienced subsidence. Moreover there were limited places to store valuables such as beds, TVs and motorcycles out of the reach of the flood water due to the lack of a second story. Figure 5.3 depicts flooded single-story homes. Many of the houses with corrugated iron quickly rusted when the flood water receded. Figure 5.4 shows the inside of one woman's single-story home. The walls are rusted corrugated iron. The home

Figure 5.3

Figures 5.3 and 5.4 Bang Bua Canal during the 2011–2012 floods
Source: Pattawan Lamjiek

has limited space to store valuables. There are a few elevated planks of wood (to the right) to store things. The flood water remained at waist height for over a month. People living in low quality housing sought shelter and assistance from evacuation centers if they could not stay with family or friends. Meanwhile, well-constructed two-story homes that met planning regulations and risk reduction measures were instrumental in enabling some flood survivors to remain at home, very often with access to running water and electricity.

Inclusive planning and reconstruction processes

Planning policies at a city scale and the upgrading activities that have taken place at a neighborhood scale greatly influenced buildings and access to utilities. A historic lack of enforcing planning regulations at a city level has resulted in the construction of vulnerable buildings in the Bang Bua Canal. Flexible planning policies were applied to houses in the canal in order to enable people to legitimately build their homes closer together, waiving on-site sanitation regulations and making an exception to Bangkok's Comprehensive Plan's land-use controls (Usavagovitwong et al., 2013). Flexibility in the planning process was important at the policy level as well as in the participatory neighborhood level activities.

Community centers

Other high quality buildings included community and health centers in all three neighborhoods. Before the floods occurred, the centers were used to host meetings, manage savings groups and, in some cases, conduct livelihood activities. When the flood struck, the location of the community centers played a factor in their usefulness. Centers that were located next to major roads were used as a donation drop-off point for vehicles. Moreover, centers with two stories were used to store and distribute goods. A public loud-speaker was set up and managed at the community centers reverting to traditional ways of sharing information.

In summary, analysis of the building layer demonstrates that access to quality homes and adequate services is an important driver of disaster resilience. Moreover, flexible planning policies contribute to the development of safer, well-planned neighborhoods. Lastly, community centers provide space for neighborhoods to engage on social and economic levels as well as offering a central meeting point for running collective activities in response to chronic stresses and disaster shocks.

Discussion

At its core, resilience is about more than merely surviving; it is about thriving. The opportunity to build resilience occurs at every stage of the disaster management cycle, from mitigation to preparedness to response and recovery (Bahadur et al., 2010). While disaster risk reduction is about removing or reducing risk, resilience frames problems in a positive light (Manyena, 2006).

A morphology and CAS approach puts people at the center of building urban disaster resilience. It prevents urban actors from making the assumption that intervention in the built or natural environment alone will improve urban disaster resilience. Instead, the approach highlights the ways in which the built form interacts with three complex adaptive systems, namely economic, governance and social.

Moreover, it analyzes disaster and development risk together, recognizing that the separation of types of risk, ranging from the chronic to the acute, is largely an academic exercise, and that in reality people from low-income neighborhoods do not separate the two (Bene, 2013). The approach demonstrates that in order to identify drivers of resilience it is crucial to analyze everyday and disaster risks together.

Using morphology to interpret the qualities of human interaction within a city's urban fabric allows a flexible approach for analyzing different scales of the built and natural environment (Moudon, 1997). Meanwhile, a systems approach that analyzes access to power and the distribution of resources at a range of scales can identify factors internal and external to the scale of analysis (Tyler and Moench, 2012).

The approach seeks to demonstrate that intersections between morphology and CAS identify drivers of risk, vulnerability, capacity and resilience at a range of scales across disaster and development contexts. The intersections between the built and natural environment and CAS are where drivers emerge. Drivers are identified through analyzing complex interactions between CAS and morphology, and deconstructing complicated feedback loops (Juarrero, 2000) with fuzzy boundaries affecting where interactions begin and end within seemingly chaotic and non-linear patterns of behavior (Bar-Yam, 1997) that have inter- and intra-dependent causal relationships (Wallace and Wallace, 2008).

Furthermore, the intersections in the theoretical framework assist to identify issues for intervention at different morphological layers from an economic, governance and social perspective. Identifying key issues within different morphological layers has the potential to assist with the identification of appropriate actors to collaborate on the issue, be it at a practical level or through policy-based work. Recognizing the rate of change of each morphological layer can also better inform disaster recovery planning by a range of diverse actors such as urban planners and designers, architects, politicians, governments (district, city and national levels), the private sector, universities, emergency personnel (police, fire and ambulance), the army and aid agencies, just to name a few. Ultimately, resilience becomes useful when users of the term are clear about its application by defining *resilience for whom* and *to what*. The urban morphology and CAS approach can assist with operationalizing resilience by identifying drivers and entry points for interventions that build stronger, safer neighborhoods and cities.

Notes

1 Ninety residents from three neighborhoods in Bangkok's Bang Bua Canal participated in interviews, focus group discussions and participatory techniques, such as household vulnerability assessments, ranking, brainstorming, timelines, transect walks and mapping over a two-month period in 2014. The data were analyzed and tested through further focus group discussions with representatives from each neighborhood. A further 50 interviews were conducted with key informants to seek an external perspective on the ongoing development and disaster management work in the area. The CAS and morphology approach was tested with 69 participants from 15 countries. The participants were from two universities and one aid agency.

2 CODI is a public organization under the Ministry of Social Development and Human Security.

References

Allen, J. (2003). Power as an immanent affair: Foucault and Deleuze's topological detail. *Lost Geographies of Power*. Oxford: Blackwell Publishing, pp. 65–92.

Anderies, M., Walker, B. and Kinzig, A. (2006). Fifteen weddings and a funeral: case studies and resilience based management. *Ecology and Society* 11(1): 21.

Archer, D. (2009). *Social Capital and Participatory Slum Upgrading in Bangkok, Thailand.* PhD Thesis. University of Cambridge.

Associated Press (2011). *Thailand Flooding 2011: Death Toll Above 600.* Bangkok: Huffington Post. Available at: www.huffingtonpost.com/2011/11/20/thailand-flooding-2011-death-toll_n_1103930.html (accessed January 8, 2015).

Bahadur, A., Ibrahim, M. and Tanner, T. (2010). *The Resilience Renaissance? Unpacking of Resilience for Tackling Climate Change and Disasters. Strengthening Climate Resilience Discussion Paper 1.* Brighton: Institute of Development Studies.

Bar-Yam, Y. (1997). *The Dynamics of Complex Systems.* Reading, MA: Addison-Wesley.

Barber, R. (2012). *Responding to Emergencies in Southeast Asia: Can We Do Better?* Melbourne: Save the Children Australia; Save the Children Asia Regional Office.

Bene, C. (2013). *Towards a Quantifiable Measure of Resilience.* London: Institute of Development Studies (IDS).

Bolio Arcaeo, E. (2012). *Urban Transformations and Place-Identity: The Case of Merida, Mexico.* PhD Thesis. Oxford Brookes University.

Boonyabancha, S. and Archer, D. (2011). *Thailand's Floods: Complex Political and Geographical Factors Behind the Crisis.* International Institute for Environmental Development. Available at: www.iied.org/thailands-floods-complex-political-geographical-factors-behind-crisis (accessed January 8, 2015).

Butina Watson, G. and Bentley, I. (2007). *Identity by Design.* Oxford: Elsevier.

Carmona, M., Heath, T. and Tiesdell, S. (2003). *Public Places Urban Spaces.* Oxford: Elsevier.

Carney, D. (1998). *Sustainable Rural Livelihoods. What Contributions Can We Make?* London: DFID.

Chambers, R. and Conway, G. (1991). *Sustainable Rural Livelihoods: Practical Concepts for the 21st Century.* University of Sussex: Institute of Development Studies.

Choi, H. (2011). *Place Identity in 21st Century Contemporary New Town Development in South Korea: Using the Case of the Proposed Multifunctional Administrative City in South Korea.* PhD Thesis. Oxford Brookes University.

Da Silva, J. (2014). *City Resilience Framework.* London: Arup and The Rockefeller Foundation.

Da Silva, J., Kernaghan, S. and Luque, A. (2012). A systems approach to meeting the challenges of urban climate change. *International Journal of Urban Sustainable Development* 4(2): 1–21.

Folke, C. (2006). Resilience: the emergence of a perspective for socio-ecological systems analysis. *Global Environmental Change* 16: 253–267.

Gauthiez, B. (2004). The history of urban morphology. *Urban Morphology* 8(2): 71–89. Available at: www.urbanform.org/online_public/2004_2.shtml (accessed January 23, 2013).

Holling, C.S. (2001). Understanding the complexity of economic, ecological, and social systems. *Ecosystems* 4: 390–405.

Juarrero, A. (2000). Dynamics in action: international behaviour as a complex system. *Emergence* 2(2): 24–57.

Koster, E. (1998). Urban morphology and computers. *Urban Morphology* 2(1): 3–7.

Kropf, K. (2005). The handling characteristics of urban form. *Urban Design*, Winter (93): 17–18.

Kropf, K. (2009). Aspects of urban form. *Urban Morphology* 13(2): 105–120.

Kwankijswet, S. and Janssen, P. (2011). Thai floods claim almost 500 lives. *Deutsche Presse Agentur*, November 6.

Leeson, K. (2014). *Fitting into the Cityscape: How Can We Improve Crisis Prevention and Response in Urban Settings?* International Rescue Committee. Available at: www.rescue.org/blog/fitting-cityscape-how-can-humanitarians-improve-prevention-preparedness-and-responses-urban-set (accessed April 24, 2015).

Levine, S., Pain, A., Bailey, S. and Fan, L. (2012). *The Relevance of 'Resilience'?* London: Humanitarian Policy Group.

Lucci, P. (2014). *An Urban Dimension in a New Set of Development Goals.* London: ODI

Madanipour, A. (2010). Public space and everyday life in urban neighborhoods. In Madanipour, A. (ed.) *Whose Public Space? International Case Studies in Urban Design and Development.* London: Routledge, pp. 107–110.

Manyena, S. (2006). The concept of resilience revisited. *Disasters* 30(4): 433–450.

Moser, C. (1998). Reassessing urban poverty reduction strategies: the asset vulnerability framework. *World Development* 26(1): 1–19.

Moudon, A. (1997). Urban morphology as an emerging interdisciplinary field. *Urban Morphology* 1: 3–10. Available at: www.urbanform.org/online_public/1997_1.shtml (accessed January 22, 2013).

Philip, B. (2011). Bangkok at risk of sinking into the sea. *The Guardian*, September 13.

Pongsudhirak, T. (2011). The politics behind Thailand's floods. *The Guardian*, October 21.

Raochanakanan, T. (1999). *Bangkok and the Second Bangkok International Airport: Politics of Planning and Development.* PhD Thesis. Australian National University.

Resilience Alliance (2007). *Research Prospectus: A Resilience Alliance Initiative for Transitioning Urban Systems towards Sustainable Futures.* Available at: http://www.citiesforpeople.ca/wp-content/uploads/2014/02/urbanresilienceresearchprospectusv7feb07.pdf.

Royal Thai Survey Department (1968). *Historical Map of Bangkok: L7017.* Bangkok: Bangkok Metropolitan Administration.

Sanderson, D. (2009). *Integrating Development and Disaster Management Concepts to Reduce Vulnerability in Low Income Urban Settlements.* PhD Thesis. Oxford Brookes University.

Scoones, I. (1998). *Sustainable Rural Livelihoods: A Framework for Analysis. Working Paper 72.* Brighton: Institute for Development Studies.

Seeliger, L. and Turok, I. (2014). Averting a downward spiral: building resilience in informal urban settlements through adaptive governance. *Environment and Urbanization* 26(1): 184–199.

Travlou, P. (2007). Mapping youth spaces in the public realm: identity, space and social exclusion. In Thompson, C. and Travlou, P. (eds) *Open Space People Space.* Abingdon: Taylor and Francis, pp. 71–81.

Truong, H. (2013). *The Quality of Public Open Spaces in Hochiminh City, Vietnam.* PhD Thesis. Oxford Brookes University.

Tyler, S. and Moench, M. (2012). A framework for urban climate resilience. *Climate and Development* 4(4): 311–326.

UN-Habitat (2013). *State of the World's Cities 2012/2013.* New York: UN-Habitat.

UNESCAP (2014). *Bangkok 2011 Flood Case Study.* Bangkok: UNESCAP.

UNISDR (2015). *The 10 Essentials for Making Cities Resilient.* Available at: www.unisdr.org/campaign/resilientcities/toolkit/essentials (accessed April 30, 2015).

Usavagovitwong, N., Pruksuriya, A., Supaporn, W., Rak-U, C., Archer, D. and McGranahan, G. (2013). *Housing Density and Housing Preference in Bangkok's Low-Income Settlements. Urbanization and Emerging Population Issues Working Paper 12.* London: International Institute for Environment and Development (IIED).

Wallace, D. and Wallace, R. (2008). Urban systems during disasters: factors for resilience. *Ecology and Society* 13(1).

Warner, S. and Whittemore, A. (2012). *American Urban Form: A Representative History.* Cambridge: MIT Press.

Whitehand, J. (1987). *The Changing Face of Cities: A Study of Development Cycles and Urban Form.* Oxford: Basil Blackwell.

Whitehand, J. (2001). British urban morphology: the Conzenian tradition. *Urban Morphology* 5(2): 103–109.

Whitehand, J. (2012). Issues in urban morphology. *Urban Morphology* (16): 55–65. Available at: www.urbanform.org/online_public/2012_1.shtml (accessed January 24, 2013).

World Bank (2010). *Climate Risks and Adaptation in Asian Coastal Megacities.* Washington, DC: World Bank.

World Bank (2012). *Thai Flood 2011: Rapid Assessment for Resilient Recovery and Reconstruction Planning*. Bangkok: World Bank.

Wungpatcharapon, S. (2012). *Participation and Place-Making in Thailand*. PhD Thesis. University of Sheffield.

Wungpatcharapon, S. and Tovivich, S. (2012). *Baan Monkong at Klong Bang Bua Community Guidebook*. Bangkok: Community Organizations Development Institute, Community Act Network, Asian Coalition for Housing Rights.

Chapter 6

Regulatory barriers and the provision of shelter in post-disaster situations

Housing, land and property (HLP) issues in the recovery of Tacloban, the Philippines, after 2013 Typhoon Haiyan

Victoria Stodart

Introduction

Following many naturally induced disasters, legal and regulatory frameworks have constituted substantial obstacles to the rapid and equitable provision of shelter solutions to persons whose homes have been damaged or destroyed. In particular there is often a dilemma about how and where to house people who lack documented legal title to the homes in which they lived prior to a disaster. Renters sometimes receive lesser and slower assistance than property owners. Informal settlers (the most vulnerable) often struggle to receive anything more than emergency humanitarian assistance. Property owners are often hesitant to allow even temporary use of their land for settlement when this might interfere with more profitable uses. States sometimes lack clear procedures or are reluctant to invoke their powers of eminent domain[1] to make appropriate land available for settlement. Dispute resolution procedures related to land ownership or control are often not well suited to a crisis setting (IFRC, 2011a).

In both the conflict and developmental contexts, HLP issues are now an established focus of activity for a number of leading agencies, and many initiatives have been launched in recent years. However, specific attention still needs to be given to the post-disaster context, where although the vast majority of those affected may only be displaced for a short amount of time (if at all) their HLP status and whereabouts are likely to cause an increase in their vulnerability, particularly when faced with a lack of assistance or threat of relocation. The immediacy of response means that the existing developmental and/or conflict guidance around HLP may not be appropriate. Moreover, with little operational guidance offering practical means of addressing such issues, shelter practitioners are left to deal with, at times, a very complex issue with little means of support or technical knowledge. Experience shows that HLP issues can become one of the major barriers to a post-disaster response and yet with a lack of appropriate capacity, understanding or guidance in the shelter sector to address these barriers there is also an increased chance of further vulnerabilities being created once programs have finished.

What is HLP?

Disasters affect a broad array of human rights, including rights to adequate housing, an adequate standard of living, freedom of movement and non-discrimination, among others. The constellation of these (sometimes disparate) rights most relevant to shelter is often referred to by professionals as HLP rights – housing, land and property rights.

HLP rights are the collective bundle of human rights laws, standards and principles that have a direct bearing upon the residential conditions in which people live and the rights they possess as dwellers. HLP rights are applicable at all times, whether in peace, conflict or disaster. Organizations providing assistance to people affected by naturally induced disasters should respect the human rights of those affected and advocate for their promotion and protection to the fullest extent (IASC, 2006: 13). More particularly, the following are key HLP principles that are applicable in post-disaster shelter responses and to which shelter providers should be mindful and supportive of:

- Everyone has the right to adequate housing.
- The shelter response should be free from HLP discrimination and should ensure the rights of the most vulnerable – this is especially relevant when considering beneficiary selection criteria.
- All affected people should have access to information and the right to participate.
- Affected people should have the right to choose between return, local integration and relocation.

The right to adequate housing is much more than a shelter commodity; it is the right to live somewhere with security, peace and dignity (CESCR, 1991). The criteria for an adequate standard of housing includes security of tenure, cultural adequacy, affordability, availability of services, materials, facilities and infrastructure, habitability, accessibility and location (CESCR, 1991). Of the seven criteria that lead to 'adequate housing', security of tenure is arguably the most complex as a concept. There are a multiplicity of legitimate tenure arrangements besides private ownership, such as public or private rental accommodation, cooperative housing, leasehold, emergency housing, occupation/rent of land or property in informal settlements, and other user or occupancy rights through statutory, customary, religious or hybrid arrangements all with varying degrees of formality or informality (Shelter Cluster Philippines, 2014).

Notwithstanding the type of tenure, all persons should possess a degree of security in their tenure which guarantees legal protection against forced eviction, harassment and other threats. The complexity of security of tenure as a concept and the vast diversity of tenure forms within, as well as among, countries may be contributing to the emergence of registered title as the de facto preferred tenure form in humanitarian settings, (IFRC and NRC, 2014) which is at odds with the need to provide assistance without discrimination and, indeed, with the very conditions of fluidity that arise in many humanitarian settings. At base, this tenure preference raises the questions whether the most vulnerable and marginalized groups are being adequately targeted and assisted.

In accordance with the Inter-Agency Standing Committee (IASC) Operational Guidelines, all affected groups and persons should have access to information and be able to participate meaningfully in the planning and implementation of the shelter response (IASC, 2011: 41). In particular, all affected persons should have the opportunity to participate in the identification and determination of tenure rights, in the planning and implementation of temporary shelter and permanent housing programs, in the choice of durable solutions (return, local integration, relocation) and in decisions over land-use planning and restrictions (IASC, 2006: 28).

Urban HLP complexities

Urban areas are frequently characterized by a relatively high percentage of renters, some of whom may have formal agreements while others may occupy through more unofficial means such as verbal agreements in multiple occupancy buildings or in informal settlements. In some areas informal settlements outnumber legally planned developments and are increasing more rapidly (USAID, 2005: 12). Not only does the overwhelming number of undocumented dwellers in urban areas present challenges for the humanitarian community, so too does the physical lack of space. Space is at a premium in any urban area, leading to an increasing need for multiple-occupancy and multi-story dwellings, house/flat shares and the sharing of single bedrooms. This results in several forms of tenure co-existing on the same plot. For instance, in India's Kolkata, 'thika' tenants rent plots and then sublet rooms to others who sublet beds on a shift system, with each party entitled to certain rights (Payne, 2000: 3). With such complicated, overlapping arrangements existing before a disaster, it is hardly surprising that the issue of land tenure in an urban context presents substantial challenges to the humanitarian community. In urban areas it is not just tenure complexities that cause challenges for agencies responding but also the nature of informal settlements, including the lack of planning, poor infrastructure and construction methods and lack of critical services which again are all exacerbated in times of disaster. This is exemplified by the response to the 2010 earthquake in Haiti[2] (IFRC, 2011b) and more recently in 2013/2014 with Typhoon Haiyan in the Philippines.

Given the co-existence of different tenure arrangements, the informalities of housing markets and the constantly changing environment of urban areas there is a distinct need to understand the 'de jure' and 'de facto'[3] tenure systems which exist (including individual or collective security of tenure arrangements), along with the political systems that accompany them. In addition to this are the challenges that local governments face, where power may have been devolved from national governments but often resources, knowledge and capacity have not followed, especially in urban areas where legal and regulatory complexities are magnified and frameworks are more numerous than in rural areas. The UN Special Rapporteur for Adequate Housing in her 2014 report to the Human Rights Council identified the challenges of local government as one of the key barriers to the implementation of the right to adequate housing (OHCHR, 2014). Such challenges are increased in times of disaster response and even more so when new settlements are considered.

Implications of 'no build zones'

One of the lengthiest barriers to the provision of shelter post-disaster can often be seen in the imposition, post-disaster, by a host government of a 'no build' or 'buffer' zone (a designated area where the construction of some dwellings or all buildings is prohibited), justified as a means of reducing future disaster risk and the consequential need to relocate those who originally inhabited such areas. However, such decisions should only be enforced in limited circumstances and only where international and national (if provided) standards are met. In particular, the restriction must be: provided for by law; necessary and solely implemented to protect the lives and health of the affected population; and only imposed where the risks to lives and health could not be mitigated by other adaptation or less intrusive protective measures (IASC, 2011: 48). Where this restriction results in either the voluntary or forced relocation of populations, specific international and national standards must be met, including:

- Forced evictions and relocations should be a measure of last resort and should not render persons homeless or vulnerable to the violation of other rights (IASC, 2011: 42).
- Affected populations must be provided with adequate information on the eviction/relocation process, the reasons for the decision and the future use of the land (IASC, 2011: 47).
- Affected persons must be genuinely consulted during all phases of the relocation, including the choice of site and the construction of housing, services and livelihoods; this consultation should include vulnerable and marginalized groups (IASC, 2011: 48).
- Adequate and reasonable notice must be given prior to the date of eviction/relocation.
- Legal remedies that respect due process guarantees should be provided, including the right to be heard and the right of access to an independent court or tribunal, as well as to appropriate compensation (IASC, 2011: 49).

These protections apply to all affected persons, irrespective of their tenure status. It must also be guaranteed that conditions at the site of relocation are adequate under national and international standards, including that proposed relocation sites are not exposed to secondary impacts of the disaster and are safe from recurrent disasters, and affected persons have access to adequate housing, water, sanitation and hygiene (WASH), health services and education and livelihoods without discrimination.

Experience shows that relocating people involves large costs in terms of infrastructure and services and can also severely disrupt people's livelihoods and community lives (World Bank, 2006: 46; ALNAP, 2008: 21). Settlement and housing patterns are not random but reflect a specific economic and social fabric that may be difficult to replicate elsewhere, (OHCHR, 2011: 48) and if relocation plans are not appropriate then there is a high risk that those who are due to be relocated will abandon the sites and return to areas where there may be inadequate provisions for them or ongoing unsafe conditions. Responsible settlements are about more than the construction of shelter: they are about creating a safe environment for the entire community where everyone not only has access to an adequate standard of housing but also to utilities, critical infrastructure and livelihood opportunities. Adopting a settlements perspective therefore involves the consideration of other aspects of community life beyond shelter and how these aspects all fit together physically and functionally (IFRC, 2012: 7). Furthermore, sustainable settlements must include the meaningful involvement of affected communities at all stages including site selection, identification of basic needs, settlement planning and housing designs.

The Philippines and Typhoon Haiyan

In the Philippines, unregulated urban growth and acute poverty have resulted in severe housing problems. Of the 10 million Philipino families (approximately 50 million people) living in cities today, an estimated 3.1 million families (around 15 million people) lack formal security of tenure (UN-Habitat, 2012). As a result of the complicated, expensive and lengthy legal processes involved in formalizing tenure, a dynamic informal land market thrives. This informal system operates by exchanging 'land rights' or the right to use land without the benefit of a formal document or process (UN-Habitat, 2012), a recognized informal system until such times as it is called into question for ulterior gain. Moreover, the geographic nature of the country (7,107 islands) combined with its topography (not only are the islands volcanic in origin but numerous active volcanoes remain) and its geophysical location (exposed regularly to over 20 typhoons a year along with the consequences of being located on the Ring of Fire) means that HLP issues are always going to be one of the biggest challenges to any form of response in the Philippines.

Typhoon Haiyan (locally known as Yolanda and a Category Five typhoon) hit central Philippines on 8 November 2013. As one of the largest typhoons ever to make landfall it brought unprecedented levels of damage across a vast area of the country. With sustained wind speeds of over 235 kilometers per hour, gusts over 300 kilometers per hour and a tidal surge of up to 5 meters in some areas, over 6,000 people lost their lives with over 25,000 injured. The government identified a priority corridor covering 171 municipalities in 14 provinces and 4 regions, with estimates that over 14 million people were affected.

Over 1.1 million houses were damaged in the priority corridor with more than 50 percent of these totally destroyed.[4] Damage levels and typology varied greatly across the affected areas, which included highly impacted dense urban and peri-urban areas such as Tacloban, Guiuan and Ormoc through to remote isolated island and mountain communities. Informal settler communities by waterways were some of the most heavily affected due to storm surges.

Over 4 million people were displaced by the typhoon with many taking initial refuge in emergency evacuation centers and larger public facilities, or, where possible, evacuating to safe areas including Manila and Cebu. Over the coming months many found themselves living in small tent cities, government-managed bunkhouses (emergency collective centers) or with host families, though the majority returned to live and build self-made makeshift shelters (IFRC et al., 2014) (see Plate 15).

Within a couple of weeks of Haiyan the president of the Philippines recommended that a 40-meter no build zone[5] (NBZ) in all Haiyan-affected coastal areas be enforced by local government units as a means of protecting citizens from future storm surges. The government subsequently identified 205,000 families to be permanently relocated.[6] The government's intention to protect its population from further disasters was well respected; however, it was the pace at which the announcement came with seemingly little consideration for what the impact of this actually meant at ground level that caused concern, along with a lack of credible evidence on which to base such a decision.

The proposed NBZ has been one of the biggest challenges not only for the humanitarian community but also for local government, none more so than in Tacloban. Tacloban was one of the hardest-hit cities by the typhoon (see Plate 16). Tacloban is the capital of the Eastern Visayas, designated as Region VIII within the country. It has a population of approximately 220,000 people and around 45,000 homes (PSA, 2010) rising to a purported 1.2 million people during the day. Of the 45,000 homes, approximately 21,000 were totally destroyed by the typhoon, with 10,000 of those belonging to the urban poor, the overwhelming majority of which were along the coast and consequently in the proposed NBZ. It was estimated by the Tacloban City Government that if the recommendation of the national government were enacted at least 14,000 families would need to be relocated. Such numbers caused substantial problems for all organizations and authorities involved in trying to encourage durable shelter solutions for those affected, not least because of a lack of available, appropriate and affordable land.

Advocacy as a means of overcoming HLP challenges

With so many houses completely destroyed and the uncertainty generated by the NBZ announcement, many people had nowhere to return to and initially remained in evacuation centers. One of the strategies of the government was to provide temporary shelter for affected people known as bunkhouses, multi-family units with a proposed timeframe of six months to provide a temporary shelter solution for internally displaced persons (IDPs) and for those in proposed NBZs, until durable solutions could be attained. There was a rapid construction of 222 bunkhouses across Region VIII (see Figure 6.1 and Plate 17). These were initially designed to house 24 families each. In December 2013 it became apparent that in some instances structures were being built without any knowledge of international minimum standards (units were $8.4m^2$ per family, as opposed to the recommended $3.5m^2$ per person (The Sphere Project, 2011: 258)). Many bunkhouses were built in concentrated sites due to limited amounts of identified available land, large caseloads and a pressing timeframe owing to the ongoing rains.

As the construction progressed, issues arose particularly with regards to site preparation and design and common facility provision. Humanitarian partners from across sectors and clusters consequently engaged with national and local authorities on necessary modifications to improve site conditions so as to reach Sphere standards and recommendations that units be modified to provide two units per large family (Shelter Cluster Philippines et al., 2013). In addition to improvements and modifications there were concerns around the lack of consultation with communities, lack of suitable alternatives being sought and consequently questions being raised around the voluntary nature of the relocation. In response, humanitarian agencies worked with the City Government to ensure that movement of people was carried out in the proper manner (Shelter Cluster Philippines et al., 2014a).

In addition to the construction of bunkhouses came plans for the development of transitional sites as an option for those residing in evacuation centers or in proposed NBZs in order to relocate people away from perceived danger and offer livelihood opportunities

Figure 6.1 Construction of bunkhouses, Tacloban, December 2013
Photo: Victoria Stodart/IFRC

through the building of permanent houses (see Plate 18). At the request of the City Government guidance was put together jointly by five IASC clusters,[7] namely Camp Coordination and Camp Management (CCCM), Shelter, Protection, WASH and Early Recovery (Shelter Cluster Philippines et al., 2014a). This included guidance on voluntary and informed decision-making for relocation, beneficiary selection, participatory and community-based approach for planning and management and how to achieve a sustainable settlement. Additional guidance was provided on site selection, site planning and shelter design.

Figure 6.2

Figures 6.2 and 6.3 The way in which people were informed as to whether they were living in a NBZ
Photo: Victoria Stodart/IFRC

Regardless of the numbers identified as potentially being in an NBZ and the temporary solutions available, the vast majority of people wanted to return or remain in their original home or site. However, not only did the government state that no shelter assistance would be provided in such areas[8] but there was also reluctance by some local government units to allow the provision of assistance (of any sort) by humanitarian agencies owing to fears that this would encourage people to remain and not move voluntarily (Figure 6.4). With a considerable lack of available and appropriate land and also the length of time any relocation would take, humanitarian agencies felt trapped between wanting to respect and support local governments but recognizing the substantial humanitarian need that existed with those remaining in the proposed NBZs having to fend for themselves. An inter-cluster advisory to the Humanitarian Country Team (Shelter Cluster Philippines et al., 2014b) questioned not only the arbitrary use of a law designed to protect water sources from people as a means of installing an NBZ, but also recommended that any relocation should be voluntary, unless it was justifiable on the grounds of public safety evidenced by geo-hazard mapping. Moreover the importance of risk reduction measures was highlighted, including early warning systems, robust evacuation centers, raised housing and mangrove planting.

This advocacy did have some positive results with the government declaring in March 2014 that NBZs, then known as no dwelling zones, would have to be evidenced by hazard mapping. By August it was agreed that hazard mapping would establish safe, unsafe and controlled zones with residential property being allowed on the first floor or above in controlled zones with appropriate evacuation routes, centers and early warning systems in place. Finally November 2014 saw a joint government department circular *Adoption of Hazard Zone Classification in Areas Affected by Typhoon Yolanda* [the local name for Typhoon Haiyan] *and Providing the Guidelines for Activities therein* (Government of the Philippines, 2014).

Even though national policy may have been altered slightly to ensure equitability, this does not mean that the challenges have been removed at the local level. The ability of local governments to enact such an NBZ policy, especially when combined with the challenges of appropriate land availability and the cost of developing that land, still remains questionable for reasons previously stated as well as the time it will take and the continued exposure people have to the elements when they are still living in temporary self-built shelters facing the continual weather cycles (see Figure 6.5).

The NBZ is not something new to the Philippines and the Water Code of 1976 has been used many times before. In Typhoon Sendong (2011) a 20-meter no build zone/ danger zone was attempted to be imposed, and in Typhoon Pablo (2012) a 40-meter no build zone was considered in some places along riverways. Neither was properly imposed nor enforced, primarily due to political reasons and so questions remain as to how the Haiyan no build zone chapter will end. This is one of the main difficulties, not just in the Philippines but in any country in the world: land is political and valuable. Governments are stuck between a rock and a hard place, knowing that, especially in the Philippines, climate change is inducing more disasters and therefore there should be a moral responsibility upon governments to protect their people against consequential harm. The question is, however, how to go about this when land is a finite resource.

For the Philippines, the international community is supportive of the government in its attempts to carry out its duty to protect civilians, while remaining mindful of the need to ensure that this is done in a fair and equitable way and, moreover, in compliance with the Philippines' own comprehensive laws. For instance the Urban Development Housing Act 1992

Figure 6.4 A community in the NBZ in Anibong, Tacloban, where no assistance was allowed to be provided
Photo: Victoria Stodart/IFRC

outlines the procedures that must be followed as and when an eviction for public safety must be undertaken and such mention is even included in the Philippine Constitution, Section 10 of Article XIII:

> Urban or rural poor dwellers shall not be evicted nor their dwelling demolished, except in accordance with law and in a just and humane manner. No resettlement of urban or rural dwellers shall be undertaken without adequate consultation with them and the communities where they are to be relocated.
>
> (Government of Philippines, 1987)

However, only time will tell whether good governance will prevail and peoples' rights will be respected.

Raising awareness and supporting local governments

Tacloban was not the only urban center to be damaged: many other urban and peri-urban areas across the regions were affected, all facing similar challenges especially regarding the question of relocation. The Philippine Commission on Human Rights, supported by the Protection and Shelter Clusters, held a number of roundtables with local mayors and local NGOs to discuss the impact of the proposed NBZ and consequential relocation requirements. At these roundtables national laws, regulations and international standards were presented and discussed, with the primary focus being upon the respect for the right to adequate housing. Additionally it provided a forum for mayors to discuss the challenges that they foresaw in implementing the national government's recommendation, while sharing strategies and best practices aimed at finding durable solutions. Critical points of action to ensure a comprehensive relocation strategy that would guarantee safe and secure access to basic living standards for those relocated were considered as well as the challenges to the creation of livelihoods for predominantly coastal communities who were to be moved inland and thus away from more traditional livelihoods such as fishing.

These roundtables culminated in the attending mayors adopting a common declaration of principles so as to inform national authorities on gaps in or problems with the implementation of such a NBZ policy and expressing additional concerns around good governance (The Inquirer, 2014). Relevant provisions of the Declaration included the need to safeguard the right to adequate housing, it acknowledged that the NBZ policy did not meet the Philippines' constitutional provisions for protecting such a right and stated that the impact of any such relocation could potentially increase poverty and reduce developmental gains. The mayors' collective urged the national government to identify best practices to achieve comprehensive hazard and vulnerability, as well as economic and livelihood sources, mapping so as to justify the need to relocate people and to ensure the legality of the process; to respect the need to maximize livelihood opportunities; and to ensure adequate community services in the new sites. Finally, they expressed a need for genuine consultation and participation by and with local government units and the affected population, including information sharing with the affected population and that adequate compensation was provided where appropriate.

This combined with advocacy at the national level resulted in the national government agreeing that any proposed NBZs should be decreed by hazard mapping and any movement of people should be done in accordance with national and international standards. At the time of writing, the impact of the newly termed 'safe/unsafe' policy is still emerging; however, it is hoped that through the extensive work done with local actors that people's rights are more fully understood and these will be respected in the process going forward.

Practical support for operational agencies

In November 2011, the 31st International Conference of the Red Cross and Red Crescent including all state parties to the Geneva Conventions adopted Resolution 7 by which the States with support from their National Societies, the IFRC and partner agencies, were encouraged to review and address the regulatory barriers identified above. Additionally the Resolution (paragraphs 11 and 12)

> affirmed the importance of finding practical solutions (both formal and informal) for quickly addressing regulatory barriers related to the provision of emergency and transitional shelter after disasters, and called on states, the components of the International Red Cross and Red Crescent Movement and relevant humanitarian organizations to make every effort to assure equitable shelter assistance as between all persons in need, including as between those who possess formal legal title to land or real property and those who do not, as well as between women and men.
>
> (IFRC, 2011c)

Through its work in this area, it has become clear that the means of practically addressing HLP in a post-disaster situation is threefold; first understanding the HLP legal and regulatory context (both formal and informal); second how this contextual information is translated into operations; and finally practical guidance on how to respect and improve a person's HLP rights in an operation. An example of this can be seen in methods of beneficiary selection. In the humanitarian sector there is often a leaning towards the requirement for legal proof of ownership (registered title) so as to provide assurances around beneficiary selection (IFRC and NRC, 2014). However, with only approximately 30 percent of land, in the developing world, registered (UN-Habitat, 2013) this very often means that the most vulnerable are overlooked. IFRC and the NGO Norwegian Refugee Council (NRC) are working together to develop a 'secure enough' approach whereby alternative means of verification can be carried out and thus the most vulnerable more readily supported with shelter (IFRC and NRC, 2014).

One aspect that is considered a key indicator in determining the 'secure enough' approach is an understanding of the community norms on forms of ownership and occupancy rights. In response to this the Global Shelter Cluster developed a 'Due Diligence Checklist for Land and Shelter' (Global Shelter Cluster, 2013) which provides the questions that should be asked in the various phases of a shelter program. This area needs to be developed further with considerations around how an assessment could be done as a preparedness measure with local professionals. In doing this it would mean that the shelter sector would be much better equipped and knowledgeable about the legal and regulatory frameworks in which they are responding. Consequently such knowledge would ensure that as and when the shelter is handed over it is done with the appropriate documentation in place, thus upholding and respecting the rights of the beneficiary.

Reflections

As can be seen from this chapter, HLP rights are complex and made even more so in an urban environment. With the immediacy of a post-disaster response, HLP considerations often get pushed back to the six-month marker and seen as more of a recovery activity. However, as has been seen with responses in Haiti to the 2010 earthquake, and more recently in the Philippines, there is a need to engage with HLP from the outset. HLP is not just about restitution of property or protracted legal claims over land; if it is not considered properly it can truly hamper the whole response.

Why then have things taken time to move in the Philippines? Since February 2014 when it was announced that the originally announced, less than systematically determined 40-meter NBZ would be superseded by classifications of unsafe and safe zones established by comprehensive hazard mapping, until the end of November 2014 not much had happened and frustration and confusion ruled at the municipality level. However, mapping at this scale takes time and the presentation of the findings at times takes longer. The information found must be understood and then presented in a way in which people, other than geographic information system (GIS) specialists, can understand, along with financial ramifications. With the decentralized nature of the Philippines it is the local government unit that needs to understand the process and the results so as to be able to amend its Comprehensive Land Use Plan – the official documentation that gives credence to a genuine no build zone – and only they have the power to impose and enforce it. But such delays do not bring relief to those who remain in makeshift shelters.

One hindrance in this whole process has been a lack of communication between the national and local level. This has not just been reserved for decisions and ramifications around the post-disaster NBZ but also in the delivery of government programs. Even if

Figure 6.5 An example of self-built shelters in the NBZ in Tacloban
Photo: Victoria Stodart/IFRC

there are not comprehensive answers, communication is still reassuring to those who are in the front line (Regional and Local Officers) and more importantly those who are due or likely to be impacted by any government decision. Without knowledge, however vague that it may be, rumour pervades and consequently uncertainty and upset are caused – this becomes a difficult situation to manage with often the ill-informed leading the ill-informed and the real key decision-makers not ensuring consistent messaging.

In the Philippines, it is up to the local government unit to enact national government recommendations and yet there was a lack of consultation at that level when the policy was announced. Consequently availability of appropriate land was given little consideration before such edicts were given and more importantly, the question of who is financially responsible for such relocation processes – for instance who bears the responsibility of skills retraining for fisherfolk who will invariably be removed from their coastal access, habitation and livelihood? Another difficulty concerns managing expectations: the international humanitarian community is driven by a desire to assist and to do so as quickly as possible. Yet when land issues are put in the mix, speed and consideration are two very different aspects. For a government (of whatever nationality) to move on issues such as land takes time. Finance and politics need to be considered and such deliberations will never match the hunger of the humanitarians whose primary objective is driven by the humanitarian imperative to provide assistance wherever it is needed (ICRC and IFRC, 1994).

Furthermore, in the Philippines, there is a perception issue. The Philippine Government is constantly applauded for its disaster risk reduction (DRR) and disaster response mechanisms and yet what is often overlooked is the disparity of those who have and those who have not. This becomes ever more apparent after a disaster; a year after Typhoon

Haiyan struck, shelter agencies were finding it hard to distinguish between those who were in genuine need of humanitarian assistance, i.e. still living in an emergency or makeshift shelter as a result of Haiyan as opposed to the more fundamental problem of people living continuously in a makeshift or what could be considered 'emergency' shelter regardless of the impact of a disaster. Where is the line drawn between emergency response and development?

Perhaps one consideration that should be highlighted is that while a lack of clarity continues around the NBZ there is a need for evacuation routes and centers to be repaired and improved irrespective of locality. Regardless of relocation unless rigorous enforcement measures are imposed, land that is emptied will always be filled, especially in urban and peri-urban areas that offer more of a chance vis-à-vis livelihoods. What happens then when an area is deemed a danger area to begin with and yet nothing happens, i.e. there is no assistance, no risk reduction, no preparedness measures, essentially no hope given to those living in informal settlements who will continue to inhabit the space and continue to remain the most vulnerable in the next storm, let alone typhoon? Governments need to accept that without powers of enforcement at the local level this issue will remain for many years to come. Consideration needs to be given to alternatives to relocation and, for national government and other actors, to support local governments in the provision of robust early warning systems, evacuation routes and centers, while in the meantime allowing assistance to be provided throughout the affected area, regardless of location.

Conclusion

In summary therefore, four key points stand out. The first is that regulatory and HLP barriers are common in post-disaster responses, especially in urban environments which require an increased engagement with a complex governance structure and an understanding of the legal and regulatory frameworks. Second, understanding context is imperative. In addition to more responsible programming, this can result in much more effective advocacy and relationship building. Understanding the context of the Philippine Constitution and legal frameworks for example, is important (it is there if you look). Third, a joint humanitarian position leads to a much more impactful message, whereby all responding agencies come together with the same voice. Finally, HLP challenges in urban response are threefold, and include: how to support a challenged local government; advocacy to support HLP rights in cases of resettlement; and practical responses to improving HLP rights of those that are able to remain, i.e. securing tenure.

Notes

1 'Eminent Domain' or 'Compulsory Purchase' is the power to take private property for public use by the state, while respecting due process and ensuring the payment of just compensation to the owner of the property.
2 The 2010 earthquake displaced over 1.2 million people. In Port-au-Prince, the capital, an estimated 70 percent of the population lived in slums. Many were undocumented tenants with an average living space of less than $2m^2$.
3 In this instance, de jure, means the law of the state and, de facto, is the reality on the ground.
4 Taken from the Philippine Government's Department for Social Welfare and Development's DROMIC data on December 9, 2013.
5 The recommendation was based upon Article 51 of the Presidential Decree No. 1067 or the Water Code of the Philippines (1976). The purpose of the Water Code is to protect and conserve

water sources from human impact (Article 2) not to ensure public safety. Article 51 of the Water Code mandates the creation of public easements next to water sources, specifically 3m in urban areas, 20m in rural areas and 40m in forest areas.

6 The Office of Civil Defense estimates there to be 205,128 families living in 'unsafe zones' in Region IV-B (8,760), V (102), VI (117,203), VII (22,423) and VIII (56,140); see the 2014 Resettlement Cluster Recovery and Rehabilitation Action Plan (http://president.gov.ph/wp-content/uploads/2014/08/Revised-DraftYolanda-Rehab-Briefer-as-of-1-Aug-2014-w-status-report.pdf). This includes both Haiyan-affected and non-affected households.

7 For the Haiyan Response, specific government departments led relevant clusters supported by: the International Organization for Migration (IOM) for CCCM, IFRC for Shelter, UNHCR for Protection, UNICEF for WASH and UNDP for Early Recovery.

8 DSWD's Emergency Shelter Assistance Guidelines (Memorandum Circular 24, 2014) expressly stated that ESA was not allowed to be provided to anyone in an 'unsafe' area.

References

ALNAP (2008). *Responding to Earthquakes: Learning from Earthquake Relief and Recovery.* Available at: www.alnap.org/resource/5239.aspx (accessed July 21, 2015).

Global Shelter Cluster (2013). *Due Diligence Checklist for Land and Shelter.* Available at: www.sheltercluster.org/sites/default/files/docs/Due%20diligence%20in%20shelter-A5.pdf (accessed July 22, 2015).

Government of the Philippines (1987). The 1987 *Constitution of the Republic of the Philippines – Article XIII.* Available at: www.gov.ph/constitutions/the-1987-constitution-of-the-republic-of-the-philippines/the-1987-constitution-of-the-republic-of-the-philippines-article-xiii/ (accessed July 23, 2015).

Government of the Philippines (2014). *Adoption of Hazard Zone Classification in Areas Affected by Typhoon Yolanda and Providing the Guidelines for Activities Therein.* Available at: http://pcij.org/wp-content/uploads/2015/01/Joint-DENR-DILG-DND-DPWH-DOST-Adoption-of-Hazard-Zone-Classification.pdf (accessed July 22, 2015).

IASC (2006). *Operational Guidelines and Field Manual on Human Rights Protection in Situations of Natural Disasters.* Washington: Brookings.

IASC (2011). *Operational Guidelines on the Protection of Persons in Situations of Natural Disasters.* Washington: Brookings.

ICRC and IFRC (1994). *Code of Conduct for the International Red Cross and Red Crescent Movement and Non-Governmental Organizations (NGOs) in Disaster Relief.* Available at: www.icrc.org/eng/resources/documents/publication/p1067.htm (accessed July 21, 2015).

IFRC (2011a) *Addressing Regulatory Barriers to Providing Emergency and Transitional Shelter in a Rapid and Equitable Manner After Natural Disasters.* Available at: www.ifrc.org/PageFiles/86607/IC31_5_5_3_barriers_shelter_2Oct_EN.pdf (accessed July 21, 2015).

IFRC (2011b). *Evaluation of the Haiti Earthquake 2010: Meeting Shelter Needs, Issues, Achievements and Constraints.* Available at: www.ifrc.org/docs/Evaluations/Evaluations2011/Global/HTShelterClusterReview11.pdf (accessed July 21, 2015).

IFRC (2011c). *Resolution 7: Strengthening Normative Frameworks and Addressing Regulatory Barriers Concerning Disaster Mitigation, Response and Recovery.* Available at: https://fednet.ifrc.org/PageFiles/82294/31IC_R7_disaster%20laws_adopted_12Dec_clean_EN.pdf_(accessed July 21, 2015).

IFRC (2012). *Post-Disaster Settlement Planning and Guidelines.* Geneva: IFRC

IFRC and NRC (2014). *Security of Tenure in Humanitarian Shelter Operations.* Available at: www.ifrc.org/Global/Documents/Secretariat/201406/NRC%20IFRC%20Security%20of%20Tenure.pdf_(accessed July 21, 2015).

IFRC, UN-Habitat and UNHCR (2014). *Shelter Projects 2013–2014.* Geneva: IFRC.

OHCHR (2011). *Report of the Special Rapporteur on Adequate Housing as a Component of the Right to an Adequate Standard of Living*. Report to the General Assembly 66th Session, UN Doc. A/66/270.

OHCHR (2014). *Report of the Special Rapporteur on Adequate Housing as a Component of the Right to an Adequate Standard of Living*. A/HRC/28/62.

Payne, G. (2000). *Urban Land Tenure Policy Options*. Available at: http://citeseerx.ist.psu.edu/viewdoc/download?doi=10.1.1.202.6387&rep=rep1&type=pdf (accessed July 21, 2015).

Philippines Statistics Authority (PSA) (2010) *Population and Housing Census 2010*. Available at: http://web0.psa.gov.ph/sites/default/files/attachments/hsd/pressrelease/Eastern%20Visayas.pdf (accessed July 21, 2015).

Shelter Cluster Philippines (2014). *Key HLP Principles for Shelter Partners*. Available at: www.sheltercluster.org/sites/default/files/docs/Key%20HLP%20Principles%20for%20Shelter%20Cluster%20Partners.pdf (accessed July 21, 2015).

Shelter Cluster Philippines et al. (2013). *Recommended Minimum Standards for Bunkhouses*. Available at: www.sheltercluster.org/sites/default/files/docs/Bunkhouse%20standards%20FINAL.pdf (accessed July 21, 2015).

Shelter Cluster Philippines et al. (2014a). *Inter-cluster Advisory Note on Transitional Sites for Tacloban North Relocation*. Available at: www.sheltercluster.org/sites/default/files/docs/Final%20Technical%20guidance%20for%20the%20provision%20of%20temporary%20shelter%20solutions%20in%20relocation%20sites.pdf (accessed July 21, 2015).

Shelter Cluster Philippines et al. (2014b). *Inter-cluster Advisory on Provision of Assistance in No Build Zones*. Available at: www.sheltercluster.org/sites/default/files/docs/Advisory%20Note%20-%20No%20Dwelling%20Zones.pdf (accessed July 21, 2015).

The Inquirer (2014). *No Dwelling Zones Stump Mayors*. March 22. Available at: http://newsinfo.inquirer.net/587945/no-dwelling-zones-stump-mayors (accessed July 21, 2015).

The Sphere Project (2011). *Humanitarian Charter and Minimum Standards in Humanitarian Response*. Southampton: Practical Action Publishing.

UN Committee on Economic, Social and Cultural Rights (CESCR) (1991). *General Comment No. 4: The Right to Adequate Housing (Art. 11 (1) of the Covenant)*. December 13. E/1992/23.

UN-Habitat (2012). *Innovative Urban Tenure in the Philippines – Challenges, Approaches and Institutionalisation*. Available at: http://mirror.unhabitat.org/pmss/listItemDetails.aspx?publicationID=3144 (accessed July 21, 2015).

UN-Habitat (2013). *Global Report on Human Settlements 2013: Planning and Design for Sustainable Urban Mobility*. Available at: http://unhabitat.org/planning-and-design-for-sustainable-urban-mobility-global-report-on-human-settlements-2013/ (accessed July 21, 2015).

USAID (2005). *Land Tenure and Property Rights, Volume 1: Framework*. Available at: http://usaidlandtenure.net/sites/default/files/USAID_Land_Tenure_Framework_Tool_0.pdf (accessed July 21, 2015).

World Bank (2006). *Hazards of Nature, Risks to Development: An IEG Evaluation of World Bank Assistance for Natural Disasters*. Available at: http://documents.worldbank.org/curated/en/2006/06/6891782/hazards-nature-risks-development-ieg-evaluation-world-bank-assistance-natural-disasters (accessed July 21, 2015).

Chapter 7

How does reconstruction after disaster affect long-term resilience?

Theo Schilderman

What do we know about the impact of disasters?

On August 15, 2007, an 8.0 Magnitude earthquake struck the coastal area of Peru just south of Lima. Leticia Quispe lived with her family in El Carmen, an informal settlement just outside the town of Chincha, that was heavily affected by the earthquake. She and her husband had put all their savings into a house for which they were still paying off a mortgage loan. They saw it crumble before their eyes in just three minutes. While losing their dwelling was bad enough, it meant an even greater loss for Leticia. She had been running a nursery in her house, so she also lost her workplace and source of income (Schilderman and Watanabe, 2014).

Earthquakes and other naturally triggered disasters destroy not only houses, but also infrastructure, livelihoods and social assets. They kill and injure people, and if they strike heavily populated urban areas, this can affect large numbers, as in the case of the 2010 Haiti earthquake. Even under normal circumstances, the urban poor face many problems. Their poverty and vulnerability are multidimensional. Naturally induced disasters are just one of the many risks they face. For many, daily survival is a greater challenge than the distant threat of disaster. A wish to live close to employment locations, for instance, may encourage them to settle on dangerous sites, prone to flooding, landslides and earthquakes (see Plate 19). When disasters ultimately do arrive, they only make matters worse for them (Schilderman, 2010).

Reconstruction traditionally focuses on building back safer houses and sometimes infrastructure. It is usually far less concerned with the non-physical aspects of recovery, such as regenerating livelihoods or restoring social networks. This was recognized as a serious problem in a report to the United Nations by its special rapporteur on adequate housing in 2011 (UNGA, 2011). The emphasis of reconstruction has been overwhelmingly on making structures more resilient, where instead much more attention should go to making people and their communities more resilient.

What is more, our common knowledge of the impact of reconstruction stems largely from end-of-project reports and evaluations. As those involved in development know, the overall impact of projects only becomes evident at a later stage. The resilience of housing, for instance, only becomes apparent with time, when climate, insects and hazards have tested them. And whether the limited socio-economic support provided by some projects pays off in terms of more empowered communities able to undertake their own initiatives and households with a better standard of living will not immediately be evident.

As part of our research, we reviewed 99 documents describing the impact of reconstruction. Only 15 of those were produced more than five years after projects had ended. When reconstruction stops, the bulk of the agencies involved leave, and they rarely return to assess the long-term impact of their work. Researchers with an interest in this question generally find it hard to access funding for such research. The information we found in literature was therefore biased towards short-term impact. In terms of resilience, it recognized, for instance, the importance of participation to get projects right and generate ownership, but it also found that communities have rarely become truly empowered by a project only lasting a few years.

Beneficiaries also valued quality, for example how well houses were finished and looked, and disaster resistance, but not if they came at a cost too high for them to carry in the future. Often, it paid off to start with technologies known to residents and their builders, and improve those in terms of quality and resistance, as that tended to promote replication. There was evidence of reconstruction projects generating employment in construction, but this was not always sustained, while livelihood support in other sectors was rare and had mixed outcomes (Schilderman, 2014).

A longer-term look at the impact of reconstruction

If we want reconstruction to become more effective in generating resilience in the long term, we need to start with gaining a better understanding of the long-term impact of past projects. With this in mind, Building and Social Housing Foundation (BSHF) initiated a research program in 2013. BSHF is an independent UK-based NGO established to identify and transfer innovative housing solutions worldwide. It undertakes research and runs an annual World Habitat Awards competition to help it do so. Some of the good practices identified exist in reconstruction of and disaster mitigation in housing. BSHF approached organizations that had undertaken projects it had previously recognized as good practice, asking them to join in an effort to assess the long-term impact of those. Seven agreed to do so, and three of those offered to look at more than one project. This gave us case studies in ten countries: El Salvador, Guatemala, Honduras, Nicaragua, Peru, Pakistan, India, Sri Lanka, Vietnam and Indonesia, going back between 4 and 35 years.

With these cases we had sufficient end-of-project information to serve as a historical 'baseline' to compare with a status quo to be established through fieldwork. BSHF discussed a research methodology with those partners that became further refined with members of the broader reconstruction community in meetings of the UK Shelter Forum and the Shelter Centre in Geneva. We decided to focus on five broad thematic areas of research, under which there were a number of questions to explore: user satisfaction; beneficiary targeting; replication; technical performance (covering the resilience of structures); and livelihoods development (including people's resilience). The research used qualitative methods, interviewing limited numbers of beneficiaries, local builders and authorities, with at least two focus group discussions, as well as documenting change visually, all the while verifying information through triangulation.

The findings of this fieldwork were discussed among the research partners, compared with two similar initiatives and shared with others in an international conference in early 2014. They were subsequently published in a book that also provides further details on the methodology (Schilderman and Parker, 2014).

Our case studies covered reconstruction in both rural areas and the towns servicing those areas; the largest of these was Banda Aceh, Indonesia, with over 220,000 inhabitants when the 2004 Indian Ocean tsunami struck, but none were large cities. They looked back over widely varying periods, stretching as stated earlier from 4 to 35 years, which made comparison between them difficult, as we found that impact can change over time. And they took place in different contexts, and these kept changing too. For instance, where economies stagnated after the reconstruction boom, as in Sri Lanka and Nicaragua, we found that employment generated during reconstruction could not be sustained, but where economies continued to flourish, as in India, Peru and El Salvador, many of those trained by projects continued to be employed in construction. A flourishing economy can also encourage people to improve or change their housing.

Revisiting a reconstruction project of the early 1990s in the Alto Mayo of Peru, Guzmán Negrón (2010) reported that in the booming towns about a third of beneficiaries had replaced their post-disaster improved *quincha* (timber frame with soil infill) reconstructed houses with concrete and brick ones, while the improved *quincha* technology kept replicating in rural areas. Political changes could lead to oppression that squashes empowerment, as happened in Guatemala, or it could enable it. And a lot depended also on beneficiaries' own initiatives after reconstruction ended.

We noticed in urban Peru, where a project targeted only those heavily affected by an earthquake within a larger settlement where others suffered much less, that lethargy among that broader community and the authorities discouraged further initiatives. But Duyne Barenstein (2014) found in a relocated village in India, where beneficiaries had been very dissatisfied immediately after reconstruction, that they had managed to turn their housing into a flourishing settlement at their own initiative seven years after.

There are important lessons in all of this for urban reconstruction, but each context is different, and therefore lessons will have to be adapted to new contexts. What follows is a selection of findings from our research that may be of particular relevance in making urban communities and housing more resilient.

Making urban housing more resilient

The vast majority of the houses reconstructed in our case studies have proven to be very resilient; even the improved adobe houses in Guatemala have stood firm for 35 years (see Figure 7.1). They have withstood the weather and wear and tear, as well as similar hazards as those that caused the initial disaster.

However, in a few cases there have been problems with hazards of a different nature, for example flooding where houses had been rebuilt solely to withstand earthquakes, as in El Salvador where some houses were swept away from flooding during a hurricane. Following the Indian Ocean tsunami, in Aceh, da Silva (2010) found that several projects had designed housing to withstand tsunamis, but not the much more frequent earthquakes, as the codes did not require that for simple housing. In designing reconstruction projects, agencies therefore need to take all potential hazards in the project location into account, not just the most recent one.

Problems such as flooding that affect the resilience of housing also arise where projects have provided no or insufficient infrastructure. As Maynard et al. (2014) and several other authors found, this happened sometimes in post-tsunami reconstruction in Aceh (see Plate 20). Too often, agencies provide only housing, but not the infrastructure that settlements require too, perhaps expecting the authorities or utilities to install it, but the latter are often overwhelmed and under-resourced.

The traditional approach to achieve resilience, advocated since the first major international efforts at reconstruction in 1970, has been to impose higher standards of construction, to have houses designed by professional architects and engineers, and built by contractors. It has been a top-down approach that often produced houses ill-suited to local conditions. It was expensive too, and as a result did not reach sufficient numbers,

Figure 7.1 Domingo built his house 35 years ago; it needs a bit of maintenance, but is sound
Photo: Kurt Rhyner

while beneficiaries struggled to maintain and replicate this standard of construction. And it did not necessarily guarantee better quality and safety from disaster. Rapid urbanization leading to densification stimulates vertical development, mostly in reinforced concrete. There is increasing evidence of such buildings becoming death traps, when earthquakes strike, because they often have been poorly designed, constructed or inspected.

Our case study in Guatemala, described by Rhyner (2014), showed how it could be done differently, by supporting a bottom-up approach that gave disaster victims and their local builders the knowledge to improve their vernacular adobe construction. In Peru, traditional *quincha* walls have proven to be more earthquake-resistant than *tapial* (rammed earth) or poorly executed adobe. The Alto Mayo reconstruction project reviewed by Guzmán Negrón (2010) used that experience and improved on it. Further improvements to *quincha* were made by the same NGO when reconstructing in Chincha (Schilderman and Watanabe, 2014). A timber-and-infill walling technology very similar to this, *dhajji dewari,* found a wide uptake after the Kashmir earthquake of 2005 in Pakistan. Some of our case studies introduced more radical innovations in technology, with far less success, e.g. the rat-trap bond brick walls in a project in Sri Lanka found no replication at all (Parker et al., 2014; see Figure 7.2) and Duyne Barenstein (2014) noticed the same with some flat concrete roofs in India.

The introduction of improvements to vernacular technologies has many advantages over more modern ones: it requires far less training, is more culturally acceptable and is invariably much cheaper. But one drawback of the vernacular approach is that it is generally less suitable for vertical development of more than a few stories which cities increasingly require. Another problem is that there is often no place for the vernacular approach in

Figure 7.2 Rat-trap bond brick wall used in post-tsunami reconstruction, Sri Lanka
Photo: Practical Action South Asia

standards and regulations; this particularly affects urban reconstruction. In Pakistan, after a year of wavering, the authorities accommodated *dhajji dewari* in their reconstruction program. But in both Guatemala and Peru, the use of improved vernacular technologies with proven disaster-resistance was prohibited for the extension or replication of houses by housing finance programs. Beneficiaries in Peru, though, trust the improved *quincha* more than modern concrete and bricks. As one interviewee stated:

> If there is an earthquake, the *quincha* part is safest. I know nothing is going to fall down there, not even the plaster. If I am in the brick section, and a tremor starts, I move to the room built with *improved quincha*.
>
> (Schilderman and Watanabe, 2014)

If only the authorities could believe that too; but those in power generally have had an education that pays scant attention to vernacular construction, and therefore prefer more modern technologies such as reinforced concrete that they know and trust; often, they are also not really in touch with low-income communities, and therefore do not know that people there favour technologies such as *quincha* (see Figure 7.3).

Many beneficiaries we interviewed valued good quality and safety of their housing. Unfortunately, poverty limits the quality they can afford. In several case studies, extensions to good quality houses were found to be haphazard and unsafe, because residents did not have the resources or skills to continue building in the same way. Housing finance is rarely accessible by the urban poor, and where it is, it often comes with restrictive conditions, e.g.

Figure 7.3 Reinforced concrete and brick extension to an improved *quincha* house in Chincha, Peru
Photo: Practical Action Latin America

restricting vernacular construction, as in Guatemala and Peru. But it can be done, as in Vietnam, where the Bank for Social Policy is running a scheme that makes small loans available to improve the typhoon-resistance of housing (MacLellan et al., 2014).

Making the urban poor more resilient

Instead of having to help those affected reconstruct their houses each time a disaster occurs, a more effective long-term approach is to increase the resilience of the poor to withstand and recover from future shocks and changes. We have to achieve this in a context where the urban poor are vulnerable to several shocks and changes, not just natural hazards. In order for them to better cope with disasters, a more holistic approach is needed: it is for instance just as important to help them gain more secure and diversified livelihoods as it is to provide information and training on safer construction, or cash to achieve that. The literature mentions several examples where projects focused only on giving cash for shelter after disaster, where some of that cash was diverted into livelihood activities, or occasionally food. Our case study in Sri Lanka even found a few beneficiaries who went as far as selling their allocated houses and living for a while with family, in order to get the funds needed to get their businesses going again (Parker et al., 2014).

Resilience is increasingly being pursued by development agencies arising out of the growing threat of climate change. We still find it hard to agree on its definition. Resilience is most commonly seen as people's ability to resist, cope with and recover from the effects of hazards. But agencies turn this into their own speak and adjust it to their own objectives, thus varying and expanding the definition. Whether the urban poor have been asked for their view on it remains debatable. We did not try in our research, as there is often no clear term for it in local languages, but we did talk to them about their concerns, and the overwhelming impression emerging from that is one of being able to achieve security and safety. In Peru, that included a house one can sleep in safely; all ten case studies managed to achieve that. An underlying concern for people to realize better urban housing is that of securing tenure; without it, investments can go to waste and finance is hard to access. Some of the cases assessed made a big effort of achieving that too. Having a secure income is another major worry of beneficiaries; they may not survive without it, nor will they be able to afford safer housing. All projects provided training, of varying levels of intensity, to beneficiaries as well as local builders (see Figure 7.4); that often provided some form of income during reconstruction and, where economies continued to flourish, even a permanent source, but projects put far less effort and often struggled to diversify into other forms of income generation. And people value a living environment free from oppression and violence. In Guatemala, government oppressed the empowerment of communities achieved during reconstruction and forced some leaders to flee the area altogether (Rhyner, 2014). In El Salvador, the empowerment of community-based organizations was allowed to flourish into an umbrella movement now influencing national housing policy; but a few beneficiaries there left or sold their houses due to the insecurity caused by the infiltration of criminal gangs (Blanco et al., 2014).

The urban poor face many such insecurities and projects that tackle only one of them, such as unsafe housing, often provide only short-term and incomplete solutions. There is an overwhelming case to be made for reconstruction agencies to take a more holistic approach, based on a full understanding of all vulnerabilities, not just the risk of naturally triggered disasters. Depending on the local context, such a type of reconstruction may need to cover safe housing; infrastructure and facilities; information and training; livelihood support; and the strengthening of social capital. That may not be easy for many of the agencies traditionally involved in reconstruction, as their missions and mandates are often restricted. Thus, they will either have to change or seek to collaborate with other agencies that can complement them.

Figure 7.4 Dual education of local builders in Guatemala
Photo: Kurt Rhyner

A good, albeit rural, example of how an agency specialized in livelihood support can branch out into reconstruction when the need arises is that of the Coffee Growers Association in Colombia described by Lizarralde (2010). The Association hired professional engineers and architects who assisted the coffee growers in designing new structures, and developed training and information materials. It also provided financial assistance for both housing and coffee infrastructure in the form of grants and additional loans. The reverse is also possible, with agencies specialized in housing branching out into livelihoods support. Among our case studies, branching out from housing happened in Gujarat (India), Aceh and El Salvador. The holistic approach taken by the latter project was very successful. In terms of livelihood support, a small business fund was established which particularly targeted persons otherwise unable to access finance; the fund gave on average US$57 per borrower. Many of the latter have gone on to form solidarity groups that continue to provide loans to their members. Some have ventured into new types of enterprises (see Plate 21). So far, more than 1,000 small enterprises have been established, many of them by women (Blanco et al., 2014).

Our case studies confirmed the importance of beneficiary participation to make projects a success. It increased user satisfaction and replication and made projects address needs outside housing. As a result of participation, designs became more flexible, which allowed a better adaptation to beneficiary needs, both initially and during subsequent changes or extensions. The right type of participation also helped to empower beneficiaries and their communities to tackle other concerns such as access to a better supply of water in Guatemala and Honduras (see Figure 7.5), or changes in housing policies in El Salvador. An example of what successful participation can achieve is provided by the reconstruction of 23 settlements in Aceh with support by Uplink after the Indian Ocean tsunami. Those settlements lost nearly half their population; rebuilding social capital and helping survivors overcome trauma became therefore as important as building thousands of safer houses. The initial phase of transitional housing was used intensively with survivors to jointly develop appropriate future plans and build community. Government policy was to relocate settlements to higher ground inland, but communities did not like that, and Uplink supported a coalition of them to work with others and achieve reconstruction in situ.

Communal land mapping helped with re-establishing former plots, and people participated in the design of the new settlements, including forms of protection from the sea and houses raised on columns. The intense involvement in this process, with others in similar circumstances, helped many overcome their traumas (Meilani et al., 2014). In reconstruction, process is as important as its physical end products, because it is the process that can empower people. This is, of course, not a new thought: Turner (1976) concluded much the same when observing informal housing in Peru. It is taking the reconstruction sector time to be convinced of the same.

Strong participation also generates ownership. This is important, as what happens after reconstruction depends on the initiatives of owners and their communities. Projects should prepare for that. Our research found that beneficiaries greatly valued house designs that were adaptable; this allowed them effectively to participate: to make easy extensions, or turn rooms to different purposes, to make space for activities such as income generation (e.g. opening a small shop) or family growth. When projects serve hundreds or sometimes thousands of households, they often end up developing a number of type plans, as it would become too expensive and time consuming to attend to household needs individually. To reach more people with limited budgets, some projects also develop house types of a minimum size that are meant to be extended at some stage by the inhabitants. Making those plans adaptable, allowing beneficiary participation, can make all the difference to

Figure 7.5 A community in Salamá, Guatemala, installing its own water supply
Photo: Kurt Rhyner

beneficiaries. As a result, many beneficiaries have been able to subsequently improve houses over time that initially fell in some way short of their needs (see Plate 22).

Beneficiaries also need to have the knowledge and skills required to make those changes, or at least know where to acquire these. Many of the cases had thoroughly trained beneficiaries and local builders, often trained early to implement some or all of the reconstruction to keep the costs down. This has paid off also in enabling them to continue building safely, creating extensions and new houses in the same settlements and surrounding areas. In a few cases, though, we noticed available amounts of time being a constraint, particularly in urban areas where people often work very long days, which can go against technologies that are too labor-intensive.

Ultimately, the future initiatives project beneficiaries can undertake largely depends on having the financial resources to do so. Adaptable design and training can only achieve so much in sustaining resilient housing. In our case studies, we have seen examples of excellent extensions and replication, but probably as many extensions that were poorly executed, mostly because beneficiaries lacked the resources to do so. This is one of the key reasons for projects to adopt a more holistic approach that incorporates livelihoods improvements. Making finance accessible in relatively small amounts to improve housing or boost and diversify livelihoods should be an important component, as the above examples of Vietnam and El Salvador demonstrate.

In some cases, such as in Aceh and Sri Lanka, extensions were made with materials recycled from transitional housing. This did nothing to improve the extensions, as transitional and permanent housing were designed separately and undertaken by different agencies, which did not allow design for recycling. Our case study in Peru showed a more joined-up approach. It was undertaken by a development agency already active in the Ica region before the 2007 earthquake, which enabled it to quickly get into the design and construction of temporary shelters and classrooms, and use that phase to design permanent housing with future beneficiaries. The temporary and permanent housing used different forms of the same technology, *quincha*, which allowed a certain amount of recycling; and training given on temporary construction could be expanded upon during the permanent phase; this joined-up approach saved money (Schilderman and Watanabe, 2014).

Achieving resilience at scale requires time, and this is beyond most reconstruction projects that have a typical duration of two to four years. It requires not only wide-scale replication of good practice but also transformation of those rules and policies that stand in its way. A typical example of the latter is the imposition of modern technologies through the financing of reconstruction or housing, as we have seen in the cases of Guatemala and Peru. Only a few of the cases we studied managed to move towards transformation, but this did require a commitment of the agency to remain involved in the long term. That is beyond the remit of most humanitarian agencies, but development agencies with a base in the disaster-affected country could. Our case studies in Vietnam, El Salvador and Pakistan are good examples of that.

In Vietnam, Development Workshop France (DWF) has been working on mitigating typhoon and flood risk to housing for 25 years, occasionally turning to reconstruction too when the need arose. It has taken a long time for them to prove to the authorities, through evidence from practice, that their ten principles of safer construction actually worked. That helped to convince the Vietnam Bank of Social Policy to establish a fund for small housing improvement loans, initially boosted by some guarantee capital provided by DWF and the Ford Foundation. The government has now invited DWF to become part of a commission establishing standards for wind and flood resistance of housing. Thus, some important constraints to wide-scale replication are being removed.

In El Salvador, the NGO FUNDASAL maintained a presence in the disaster district of La Paz after its reconstruction project ended. This was partly to undertake some other development work, but also to continue to build capacity in reconstructed communities. The NGO maintained its building materials production center, which greatly boosted appropriate replication. And it continued to support the umbrella organization created by local communities (ASPODEPAZ) until it became a voice influencing national housing policy.

The Building and Construction Improvement Program (BACIP) in Northern Pakistan provides a large range of small and affordable options for improving mainly rural housing; some of those are to mitigate disasters, quite a few others are to boost energy efficiency in this very cold region that is short of fuel. BACIP realized wide-scale uptake could only happen if the private sector would be enabled to undertake that role. To these ends the program built the capacity of many small enterprises to diversify their product range, and occasionally provided credits to enable investment. This has so far led to the installation of 40,000 of such improvements in the 120,000 houses the region counts (Khan and Parrack, 2014).

What does resilience mean for urban reconstruction?

Generating resilience that means more than just a safer house takes time. Reconstruction projects generally are too short to achieve that, and most do not have the mandate to do so. The urban poor we interviewed perhaps think more in terms of security than of resilience: a house they can sleep in safely; tenure that enables investment; income that guarantees survival; and an environment free from violence and oppression. They almost always face several insecurities at the same time, and struggle to address those simultaneously.

Projects that include participatory processes that can empower beneficiaries and their communities tend to be better at achieving that. In the long term, much hinges on beneficiaries of reconstruction taking ownership, finding a voice and developing their own initiatives. In that context, poverty can be a constraint, but this can be tackled by offering microfinance under conditions that do not enforce expensive solutions for both housing and livelihood activities.

If reconstruction is to generate resilience, not just of physical structures, but also of the urban poor, there is an overwhelming need for agencies involved to adopt more holistic approaches to reconstruction that tackle a range of vulnerabilities of the poor. They will also need to get better at addressing the risks of all disasters (not just the most recent one) and taking account of climate change. To achieve this, they need to develop a longer-term view than that required for a conventional reconstruction project of a few years duration. They will have to broaden their skills base or seek to work with other agencies that can complement them. They will also have to commit to a longer-term presence, or have partners who can do so. Only a few of the ten cases we studied managed to move in that direction, but they had some noticeable success that can stand as a foundation for future improvements.

References

Blanco, C., Rivera, A., Martinez, I. and Moring, J. (2014). A roof for La Paz: reconstruction and development in El Salvador after the 2001 earthquake. In Schilderman, T. and Parker, E. *Still Standing? Looking Back at Reconstruction and Disaster Risk Reduction in Housing*. Rugby: Practical Action Publishing, pp. 201–216.

da Silva, J. (2010). *Lessons from Aceh – Key Considerations in Post-Disaster Reconstruction*. Rugby: Practical Action Publishing.

Duyne Barenstein, J. (2014). Looking back at agency-driven reconstruction in India: case studies from Maharashtra, Gujarat and Tamil Nadu. In Schilderman, T. and Parker, E. *Still Standing? Looking Back at Reconstruction and Disaster Risk Reduction in Housing*. Rugby: Practical Action Publishing, pp. 39–58.

Guzmán Negrón, E. (2010). Peru: the long-term impact of short-term reconstruction work. In Lyons, M. and Schilderman, T. *Building Back Better: Delivering People-Centred Reconstruction at Scale*. Rugby: Practical Action Publishing, pp. 307–343.

Khan, N. and Parrack, C. (2014). A market-based programme to improve housing in the mountains of northern Pakistan: addressing seismic vulnerability. In Schilderman, T. and Parker, E. *Still Standing? Looking Back at Reconstruction and Disaster Risk Reduction in Housing*. Rugby: Practical Action Publishing, pp. 59–76.

Lizarralde, G. (2010). Decentralizing (re)construction: agriculture cooperatives as a vehicle for reconstruction in Colombia. In Lyons, M. and Schilderman, T. *Building Back Better: Delivering People-Centred Reconstruction at Scale*. Rugby: Practical Action Publishing, pp. 191–213.

MacLellan, M., Blackett, M., Chantry, G. and Norton, J. (2014). Reconstruction in Vietnam: less to lose! Examples of the experience of Development Workshop France in Vietnam. In Schilderman, T. and Parker, E. *Still Standing? Looking Back at Reconstruction and Disaster Risk Reduction in Housing*. Rugby: Practical Action Publishing, pp. 115–136.

Maynard, V., Parikh, P., Simpson, D. and da Silva, J. (2014). Emerging stronger? Assessing the outcomes of Habitat for Humanity's reconstruction programme following the Indian Ocean Tsunami. In Schilderman, T. and Parker, E. *Still Standing? Looking Back at Reconstruction and Disaster Risk Reduction in Housing*. Rugby: Practical Action Publishing, pp. 21–38.

Meilani, A., Hafidz, W. and King, A. (2014). Integrated people-driven reconstruction in Indonesia. In Schilderman, T. and Parker, E. *Still Standing? Looking Back at Reconstruction and Disaster Risk Reduction in Housing*. Rugby: Practical Action Publishing, pp. 137–152.

Parker, E., Ajantha, A., Pullenayegem, V. and Kamalaraj, S. (2014). Challenges for sustainability: introducing new construction technologies in post-tsunami Sri Lanka. In Schilderman, T. and Parker, E. *Still Standing? Looking Back at Reconstruction and Disaster Risk Reduction in Housing*. Rugby: Practical Action Publishing, pp. 97–114.

Rhyner, K. (2014). Guatemala: knowledge in the hands of the people. In Schilderman, T. and Parker, E. *Still Standing? Looking Back at Reconstruction and Disaster Risk Reduction in Housing*. Rugby: Practical Action Publishing, pp. 153–170.

Schilderman, T. (2010). Putting people at the centre of reconstruction. In Lyons, M. and Schilderman, T. *Building Back Better: Delivering People-Centred Reconstruction at Scale*. Rugby: Practical Action Publishing, pp. 7–37.

Schilderman, T. (2014). Introduction: what do we really know about the impact of reconstruction? In Schilderman, T. and Parker, E. *Still Standing? Looking Back at Reconstruction and Disaster Risk Reduction in Housing*. Rugby: Practical Action Publishing, pp. 1–20.

Schilderman, T. and Parker, E. (eds) (2014). *Still Standing? Looking Back at Reconstruction and Disaster Risk Reduction in Housing*. Rugby: Practical Action Publishing, pp. 247–251.

Schilderman, T. and Watanabe, M. (2014). Peru, building on the vernacular. In Schilderman, T. and Parker, E. *Still Standing? Looking Back at Reconstruction and Disaster Risk Reduction in Housing*. Rugby: Practical Action Publishing, pp. 217–232.

Turner, J. (1976). *Housing by People*. London: Marion Boyars Publishers Ltd.

UNGA (United Nations General Assembly) (2011). *Report of the Special Rapporteur on Adequate Housing as a Component of the Right to an Adequate Standard of Living*. New York: United Nations.

Chapter 8

Conflict and urban displacement

The impact on Kurdish place-identity in Erbil, Iraq

Avar Almukhtar

Place-identity and conflict

Most towns and cities have their own distinctive character and identity which distinguish one place from another. Spatial qualities of natural features and the built environment are what give places their special identity. Both the functional and symbolic qualities of place are the result of socio-cultural, economic and political processes and are crucial for the evolution and fostering of 'place-identity' (Dobbins, 2009; Butina Watson and Bentley, 2007).

Place-identity to a substantial degree is the result of urban development strategies (Hague and Jenkins, 2005) and can be defined as a set of meanings and the sense of belonging associated with a particular place (Bolio Arcaeo, 2012; Butina Watson and Bentley, 2007). The concept of place-identity can be approached from many different disciplines including urban design, architecture and planning, or from various perspectives such as the study of urban form. It is reflected in the physical setting that creates continuity across time and is linked to heritage as well as historical events (Graham and Howard, 2008). Furthermore, it is the physical representation of place, 'a collection of images that can transmit, at a glance, a suggestive reminder of the historical urban forms the city has acquired all along its evolution' (Castello, 2006: 62).

Many nations are composed of multi-ethnic cultural groups that share the same geographic location. In many cases, these ethnic groups, be they the majority or the minority, have their distinctive culture, history and local identity (Oliver, 1997). Unfortunately, when different political ideological movements practiced by dominant ethnic groups repress a minority group, the minority culture and identity is often neglected, changed or destroyed. In an attempt to protect their culture, traditions and identity, such groups sometimes resort to military armed conflict, which threatens livelihoods and causes displacement as people flee their homes seeking safety, shelter and opportunities elsewhere.

However, this attack on identity is not only on the human level. It also includes an attack on both intangible and physical elements such as traditions and historical values, heritage sites and architecture, as well as basic social services and infrastructure (Piquard and Swenarton, 2011). As the situation stabilizes and political, economic and social changes emerge, reconstruction efforts begin as a part of the post-conflict recovery process (Minervini, 2002). These changes can result in transforming the character and identity of place. Often less resilient and responsive to the local context, this evolving place-identity may threaten the local urban fabric. Therefore, in a conflict zone context there is a pressing need to address the issue of place-identity within a planning and urban design framework.

Background to the Kurdish conflict

While a deep political understanding is important to explain the Kurdish conflict, this is not the focus of this chapter. However, various political facts will be used to discuss the Kurdish context as foreground for the spatial consequences of the conflict.

Kurds are the world's largest ethnic group without a state to share a common and distinct culture, traditions, language and identity (Gunter, 2008; Aziz, 2011). The British Broadcasting Corporation reports the total Kurdish population to be 25–35 million (BBC, 2014). The historic area of Kurdistan is not easy to define, as it does not have an official boundary and is not an internationally recognized state (Diener and Hagen, 2010; Stansfield, 2003). It lies in the heart of the Middle East with an area of approximately half a million square kilometers (Polk, 2006; Jwaideh, 2006), distributed over four countries. The international boundaries of countries drawn after World War One did not account for various minority identities including the Kurds. Kurdistan as an area would now encompass the east and south-east of Turkey, the west of Iran, the north-east of Syria and the north of Iraq, which is the main focus of this study (Sheyholislami, 2011; Jwaideh, 2006).

Iraq is a country of nearly 32 million inhabitants (United Nations Iraq, 2015) and is shared between Kurds, Arabs, Turkmens and other ethnic minority groups (Stansfield, 2003). The ethnic boundary between the two groups is relatively clear, with Kurdistan officially an autonomous region in Iraq (Aziz, 2011).

In the early twentieth century, Iraqi architecture and city planning was largely the product of international consultants and reflected typical patterns of modern British town planning principles. The central authorities adopted this international planning system for developing the urban fabric of the cities in Iraq as part of the country's modernization process (Nooraddin, 2004). These planning and urban design policies and regulations were first applied in Baghdad, then to other cities such as Mosul and Erbil. The built environment was transformed with new streets and infrastructure that cut through the existing urban fabric rather than expanding and adapting to the existing structures within the city. Clear examples of developing parallel urban design systems can be found in the comprehensive town plans for cities including Baghdad, Erbil, Kirkuk and Najaf introduced by the well-known Greek architect and planner Constantine Doxiadis in the 1950s (Nooraddin, 2012). For example, the new proposal for Erbil was a modular grid system that ignored the original circular growth pattern of the city.

Iraq became a republic in 1958 (Anderson and Stansfield, 2005). Prior to that Kurds were involved in a political and military conflict with the Iraqi central government to protect their right to practice their culture and maintain their identity in the face of policies that were thought to favour Arabs (Stansfield, 2003). The national government's provisional constitution in 1958 recognized for the first time that Arabs and Kurds enjoyed equal citizenship in the same nation (Chaliand, 1994). The new government allowed Kurdish cultural activities and legalized the Kurdistan Democratic Party (KDP) but rejected the demand for total political autonomy for Kurdistan (Hiro, 2001; Tucker and Roberts, 2010).

In 1963 a Baa'thist coup overthrew the national government (Tucker and Roberts, 2010; Stansfield, 2003). The ideology and influence of the Baa'th Party called for Pan-Arabism (Arnold, 2008), claiming that all other non-Arab ethnic minorities who live on Arab soil should comply with the Arab way of life and culture (Manafy, 2005; Stansfield, 2007). 'Arabist' was then deemed the national identity for Iraq as a country and was imposed on all ethnic minorities existing within, including the Kurds (Kymlicka and Pfostl,

2014). The Baa'th Party and its policies and ideology resulted in nearly five decades of armed conflict, genocide, mass executions and human rights violations towards the Kurds.

The political ideology and Pan-Arabism of the Baa'th Party influenced many aspects of the country, including planning and urban design policies and processes, and architecture (Nooraddin, 2012). The urban fabric of towns and cities in Iraq are the result of different layers of ethnic cultures and civilizations evolving through several centuries. Applying Arab national policies and development patterns in the region represented an attempt to manipulate and change the local place-identity of the area, following colonial visions imposed early in the twentieth century. The traditional urban fabric of old towns and cities was demolished or replaced in the Citadels in Kirkuk and Erbil and some Kurdish villages. The trend of Arabic national ideology was also applied to the higher education system in all local architectural schools in Iraq. Architectural heritage for Arabic and Islamic towns was considered the national architectural heritage of the country, ignoring that Iraqi architectural heritage is a reflection of a multi-ethnic reality. Consequently, the architectural heritage of Kurdistan was ignored in the work of Iraqi architects and researchers (Nooraddin, 2012). Moreover, no architecture schools existed in the Kurdish Region up until the mid-1990s.

After an uprising in 1991, the Kurdistan Regional Government (KRG) was established in 1992 by a multi-party election, and the Iraqi Kurdistan Region become an autonomous region (Ahmed, 2012; Tucker and Roberts, 2010). However, the newfound autonomy was accompanied by limited new urban development due to the severe economic downturn resulting from international sanctions imposed by the United Nations. However, socially, Kurdistan witnessed significant growth in Kurdish Regional identity as there was more freedom to practice Kurdish culture, which took substantive and symbolic forms. The Kurdish language began to be widely used in the public domain, including in schools and educational institutions, in government administration and in broadcasting and media. Additionally, national symbols such as Kurdish flags and the construction of statues and portraits of Kurdish heroes increased (O'Leary et al., 2005).

For the first time in Iraq's recent history, the president of the country, Jalal Talabani, was Kurdish. The country became bilingual with Kurdish and Arabic both official national languages (Galbraith, 2006). Furthermore, this period experienced more freedom in practicing cultural rights such as celebrating the Kurdish new year 'Newruz.' Today Kurdistan is experiencing rapid economic growth. The extraction of oil from Kurdish-dominated areas has improved the economy of the region. Political stabilization has resulted in strong growth in the private sector, with local and international investment opportunities. The Kurdish government's efforts to develop and upgrade the region's infrastructure have transformed the urban environment (Almukhtar, 2010).

The spatial consequences of conflict

Erbil gained political significance as the capital of Iraqi Kurdistan in 1991 when the region became autonomous. Economic growth from oil revenues and UN support for rebuilding the area led the city to become the hub for investment, trade, tourism and development in the region (Almukhtar, 2010).

Erbil is roughly 6,000 years old. It comprises a fortified Citadel that includes multiple layers of different civilizations and historical periods. It is thought to be the oldest continuously inhabited settlement in the world. The city grew around the Citadel, whose rich and varied history contributes to the formation of its distinctive identity. It now stands as a symbol of Kurdish history, identity and the Kurdish nation within civil society and the government (High Commission for Erbil Citadel Revitalization, 2015). The southern part of the lower town and the eastern part of the city indicate that Erbil's identity and sense of place was first and foremost based on the Citadel. In interviews undertaken with residents by the author, many indicated that the Citadel is a source of pride and sense of belonging, especially after becoming an international World Heritage site in 2014. As one elderly man said, 'I feel nostalgic about the Citadel because my parents and grandparents were born there. I feel my roots are from the Citadel and that I belong here. It makes me feel proud to live in Erbil and be Erbili.'

Cultural identity is reflected in the building typology of the Citadel and the surrounding old town which includes elements that reflect the culture and lifestyle of inhabitants and both distinctive buildings and open spaces (see Plate 23). The area around the Citadel represents a unique semi-organic urban fabric that grew radially from its center. However, building typologies started to change dramatically towards the end of the twentieth century because of the different political ideologies, design standards and planning policies that the region experienced and their impacts on the economy, culture and lifestyles of the people inhabiting the area.

Typologies of spatial changes as the consequences of conflict

As outlined above, decades of conflict and political instability since the beginning of the last century resulted in a high influx of people being displaced as well as damage and destruction to infrastructure, buildings and services. This was followed by a period of economic growth after 2003 that led to rapid post-conflict reconstruction as part of the recovery process. Hence, displacement and reconstruction have been identified as the two main typologies of spatial change post-conflict that can transform local place-identity in the area.

Displacement

The mass displacement process that affected the region has changed considerably over the last few decades. On top of already weakened infrastructure, housing and public services after many decades of war and sanctions, displacement has evolved and shaped the city and its place-identity manifesting in the city's urban environment. This changing place-identity is now demonstrating fewer characteristics that reflect the cultural and historical values of the region. The three main elements of displacement – forced migration and relocation, internally displaced persons (IDPs) and refugees – are described below.

Forced migration and relocation

The displacement of Iraqi Kurds from their villages during the period of Saddam Hussain's government in the 1970s was a direct result of political, policy and military pressure in which the Baa'th regime used the built environment as a tool for demographic change. By the end of the 1980s, 3,000 villages were razed by the Iraqi government (Stansfield, 2003; Gunter, 2011) and around 600,000 men, women and children were forcibly relocated from their villages into modular settlement patterns (McDowall, 1992). Displaced populations were deported into new collective towns attached to existing cities in the region. These towns were located at a distance from the city but were still linked through clear transport access. The government rationale was to build cost-effective housing but it resulted in little or no consideration to the culture and identity of rural families in the area (Francesca, 2012). The collective towns were designed with wide roads in a grid system easily accessed by military tanks when needed. Houses were built with concrete in patterns that closely mimicked neighborhood blocks from urban areas, different from traditional Kurdish villages where houses are made of mud and stone which organically sprung up and created narrow alleyways and spaces for animal husbandry. Later on, as the collective towns expanded and the city grew, some towns such as Kasnazan merged with Erbil spatially but struggled to merge with Erbil's local place-identity as they were not part of the evolving process of Erbil's urban fabric.

Internally displaced persons

The second wave of displacement was during the post-Baathist regime which started after the 2003 invasion of Iraq. During this period, ethnic conflict erupted between Sunnis and Shia Muslim sects in different areas of the middle and south of the country. Fighting also began between the Iraqi security forces, Kurdish Peshmerga and armed opposition groups, which included the Islamic State of Iraq and Levant (ISIL) (Internal Displacement Monitoring Centre, 2015). As a result of this sectarian violence, many areas became politically unstable and lacked security and safety. Hundreds of thousands of families from these areas fled their homes, some even to neighboring states. More than 3 million Iraqis were internally displaced and relocated to Kurdish cities. With the present fighting and lack of security in Iraq's landscape in the immediate future, it is expected that this displacement will rise. The majority of the IDPs are Arabs, with some of them being relocated into temporary camps around the city, while others are being relocated to live in mosques, churches and public spaces like neighborhood parks. Those with better financial means either bought small residential units or benefited from the affordable housing scheme which was introduced by the Kurdish government and settled into different neighborhoods of the city, which is reshaping such neighborhoods (Marfleet, 2011). With IDPs being located in different pockets in the city, combined with no existing government long-term strategy to accommodate them, it will be difficult for the micro identity of these pockets to fit with the city's local place-identity.

Refugees

This displacement was followed by a wave of mainly Kurdish Syrian refugees escaping the Syrian civil war that started in 2011. The Syrian conflict has forced well over 2 million Syrian citizens to take refuge in neighboring states including Iraq. The majority of Syrian refugees in Iraq reside in Kurdistan, accommodated in camps and host communities around the cities of Erbil and Dahuk (see Plate 24), as they share the same ethnicity, religion and linguistic affiliations (Internal Displacement Monitoring Centre, 2015). Refugees are attracted to Kurdistan because the KRG introduced a policy of open borders which allowed individuals to enter the Kurdistan region (Middle East Research Institute, 2015) and the region offers greater stability, safety and livelihood opportunities. It is hard to predict when the Syrian civil war is going to end and whether the refugees will return or settle in the area because of better employment opportunities. How the presence of the Syrian population will affect the way people perceive Erbil's sense of place remains to be seen. Syrian refugees presently compete with local residents for jobs because they are willing to work for less.

Hosting large numbers of people puts pressure on the public services provided by the government of the host country, for example schools are overwhelmed and infrastructure like electricity is not meeting the demand of the city (World Bank, 2015; Norwegian Refugee Council, 2015).

Moreover, with the absence of clear, long-term planning strategies and policies from the Kurdish government (Middle East Research Institute, 2015) and the NGOs working in the area, the camps might become part of the city, integrating into its physical urban fabric. Without a strategic plan the different micro identities of the camps may not successfully integrate into the city's evolving place-identity, thereby placing pressure on the city's urban fabric over time.

Accommodating hundreds of thousands of displaced people as well as the 2003 post-conflict rapid economic growth has led to a massive reconstruction process. This rapid urbanization introduced many urban developments at different scales, from low-cost housing to luxurious globally influenced architecture and urban patterns, again placing the city's urban identity and historical values under threat (this is discussed below).

Reconstruction

Reconstruction after conflict is a critical issue for place-identity. As Barakat has shown, the choices made shape urban fabric, buildings and spaces, as well as social relationships, collective identities and the sense of belonging (Piquard and Swenarton, 2011). The Kurdish Region has recently experienced a rapid expansion of the region's urban fabric and infrastructure in order to respond to the rapid urban growth and the expansion of the city. The KRG has placed much effort into the development of city infrastructure and has made major improvements in terms of roads, flyovers, parks, footpaths and so on (Almukhtar, 2010). The reconstruction process includes three main themes – political redesign, implementing affordable housing and globally influenced developments – which are discussed as follows.

Political redesign

During the Baa'th political period, the architectural heritage of minority ethnic groups suffered from neglect, demolition and replacement. The national government imposed the use of Arabic-Islamic architectural elements in some of the institutional and governmental buildings as part of the Pan-Arabism national ideology, ignoring the multi-ethnic reality of the country. As a consequence, architectural heritage and local place-identity of non-Arab areas were weakened, threatened or ignored. In many cases, old cities and the traditional urban fabric were systematically demolished to expressly change their identity. Examples include the demolition of the Citadel of Kirkuk, the relocation of Kurdish villagers and the replacement of Erbil Citadel's gate.

In the 1960s, the gate of Erbil's Citadel was considered for generations to be the gate for the ancient Kurdish settlement. In the 1970s it was demolished and replaced with a new gate with architectural patterns imported from Babylonian design (see Plate 25). The new gate was a copy from the ancient Ishtar Gate in the city of Babylon, located in the center of Iraq (Nooraddin, 2012). In 2013, a debate within the Kurdish government started claiming that the 1970s Babylonian gate to Erbil's Citadel represented the last political regime and was an attempt to 'Babylonize' the Citadel. The Kurdish government believed that the new gate represented Mesopotamian civilization rather than Kurdish ancient history. Consequently, the Kurdish government decided to demolish the Babylonian gate and replace it with one that followed the original design. Furthermore, they did not consider the 1970s Babylonian gate as part of the Citadel's evolution process nor did they view it as a legitimate part of the city's transformed identity. However, until recently, representations of the Citadel have included the Babylonian gate in all administrative paperwork within the government, in schools and university logos, as well as in media and broadcasting.

Over 50 interviews undertaken by the author with local people, professionals and government officials suggested that the historical value represented in the Citadel has an important impact on people's perception on the city's identity, although such values are not reflected in newly developed areas of the city. As one middle-age architect said,

> When people in Erbil celebrate different events they go to the Citadel to express happiness and share sadness. We feel we belong to the Citadel and that it represents us and our city. This is why our Kurdish New Year celebration starts at the Citadel and where we hold many other events.

Implementing affordable housing

The provision of housing was one of the first steps after a long period of conflict and one of the first steps of the economic recovery. Due to mass displacement, housing remains a critical issue in the Kurdish Region. The large influx of IDPs led to a shortage of housing across the city of Erbil and an escalation in rental prices. As a response, the government introduced affordable housing schemes that allowed new buyers to take out a mortgage loan and repay through a long-term payment plan. These housing schemes are modular types of housing and gated developments designed and built by investors in order to accommodate the large demands on housing in such cities as Aynda and Lawan. These new residential developments are located around the cities and were designed to be cost effective without consideration of culture, local identity and the surrounding built form. The developers did not seek skills and awareness leading to consideration of 'place-identity' in design and planning from architects and urban designers and planners. Additionally, research interviews with the urban planning department revealed that the issue of place-identity was not considered in the development process of the city or when the department designs, assesses, reviews and approves schemes and developments outside the lower town. Moreover, it is important to note that most of the planning and urban design processes are top down rather than participatory. Consequently, these developments lack character, distinctiveness and connectivity to the surrounding urban fabric within the city.

Globally influenced developments

The end of long-standing conflict led to the removal of economic sanctions and ushered in a new era of relative political stability and strong economic growth that has attracted many international investors and developers through new investment policies and incentives. Most of the key developments follow new design ideologies that reflect global culture and architectural elements that are not consistent with the culture, climate and the existing context of the region. Furthermore, imported building materials and techniques have replaced those that have been traditionally used in order to be more attractive and appealing rather than relevant to the distinctive local culture (see Plate 26). While modern forms reflect international architectural norms, there is sprinkled within new developments a pastiche of traditional local architectural elements used as references to the past.

These new developments speak an urban language that is in stark contrast with historical and traditional Kurdish models of inhabitation and social interaction, thus ignoring the local place-identity of the area. These developments could belong in any part of the world. In housing developments named the 'English Village' and the 'Italian Village,' globally designed linear patterns of homes in communities with such Western names are common (see Plate 27). These developments are located within approximately two kilometers of the Citadel and are built next to each other. Their urban fabric and design typologies are segregated from each other and the surrounding context. These developments have mostly failed to provide locals with their basic housing requirements and have led to their use by business firms and are now mostly occupied by international expatriates. Furthermore, they are competing with each other by trying to be dominant individually and to celebrate a global image, introducing identities, mainly Western, that are different from the surrounding built form of the area. This has resulted in areas with a collage of multiple identities failing to represent themselves collectively as part of the city's local place-identity as well as a lack of distinctive character and sense of belonging.

Conclusion

Erbil is now a city with multiple identities of a global nature. Areas of the city are losing links with their historical past and are embracing micro-identities, which are anonymous and can be found in numerous places around the world. While multiple identities at a district and neighborhood level demonstrate Erbil's ability to embrace diversity, an overall strategy for uniting different areas could be developed by urban designers and planners in order to reduce the potential for identity confusion or destruction. The strategy should place emphasis on developing a local place-identity that respects and reflects historical and traditional values while presenting opportunities to recognize that change in design and function is a natural process in a city that embraces modern values.

Without a targeted strategy, the micro-identities of the districts and neighborhoods are at risk of evolving in a way that threatens Kurdish historical and traditional values and fails to reflect thoughtful ideals of adaptability and resilience of the city as a whole as it responds to rapidly changing political and economic conditions. Today it can be argued that Erbil's sense of place is heavily based on the Citadel. While the Citadel creates opportunities for diverse groups of people to connect, Erbil's sense of place goes beyond just there. It is therefore important for future urban design strategies and frameworks to consider ways to build a sense of place throughout the entire city instead of myopically focusing on the historic core and failing to honour it in any event.

In post-conflict Erbil, it is – and will be – important to emphasize and develop a deeper understanding of cultural traditions and enhance cultural continuity. Urban planning and design strategies can be used to assess, design and nurture the evolving process of place identity at the micro and city levels. Such strategies must include minority groups in the decision-making process in order to generate a feeling of ownership, inclusion and legitimatization. Urban actors such as NGOs, government officials, urban designers, planners, architects, developers and investors who are rebuilding the city must be especially aware of the multiple identities that exist in order to avoid spatially redesigning out of existence identities at neighborhood, district, city and regional levels. The argument in this chapter is that place-identity is an important strategy for contributing to the overall identity of a city, and that historical links can be important connectors between districts, ethnicities, regions and even countries. It is important for such strategies to be rooted in traditional culture, while at the same time being a part of global modernization processes that introduce economic and political opportunities that will inevitably transform the sense of place. Planning and urban design strategies to guide future development that upgrade, revitalize and enhance a resilient place-identity of the nation, responsive to rapid political and economic changes, should be employed for post-conflict zones.

References

Ahmed, M.M.A. (2012). *Iraqi Kurds and Nation-Building*. New York; Basingstoke: Palgrave Macmillan.

Almukhtar, A. (2010). *Urban Design Guidelines for Residential Neighbourhoods in Erbil*. Unpublished Master Dissertation, Oxford Brookes University.

Anderson, L.D. and Stansfield, G.R.V. (2005). *The Future of Iraq: Dictatorship, Democracy, or Division?* New York; Basingstoke: Palgrave Macmillan.

Arnold, J.R. (2008). *Saddam Hussein's Iraq*. Minneapolis: Twenty-First Century Books.

Aziz, M.A. (2011). *The Kurds of Iraq: Ethnonationalism and National Identity in Iraqi Kurdistan*. London: I.B. Tauris.

Bolio Arcaeo, E.A. (2012). *Urban Transformations and Place-Identity: The Case of Merida, Mexico*. Thesis (PhD), Oxford Brookes University.

British Broadcasting Corporation (BBC) (2014). *Who are the Kurds?* Available at: www.bbc.co.uk/news/world-middle-east-29702440 (accessed April 2015).

Butina Watson, G.B. and Bentley, I. (2007). *Identity by Design*. Amsterdam; London: Butterworth-Heinemann.

Castello, L. (2006). City and time and places: bridging the concept of place to urban conservation planning. *City & Time* 2: 59–69.

Chaliand, G.R. (1994). *The Kurdish Tragedy*. London: Zed Books in association with UNRISD.

Diener, A.C. and Hagen, J. (2010). *Borderlines and Borderlands: Political Oddities at the Edge of the Nation-State*. Lanham, MD: Rowman & Littlefield Publishers.

Dobbins, M. (2009). *Urban Design and People*. Hoboken, NJ: Wiley.

Francesca, R. (2012). *From Forced Displacement to Urban Cores: The Case of Collective Towns in Iraqi Kurdistan*. Erbil, Iraq and London, UK. Available at: http://architexturez.net/doc/az-cf-123984 (accessed November 30, 2015).

Galbraith, P. (2006). *The End of Iraq: How American Incompetence Created a War Without End*. New York; London: Simon & Schuster.

Graham, B.J. and Howard, P. (2008). *The Ashgate Research Companion to Heritage and Identity*. Aldershot: Ashgate.

Gunter, M.M. (2008). *The Kurds Ascending: The Evolving Solution to the Kurdish Problem in Iraq and Turkey*. Basingstoke: Palgrave Macmillan.

Gunter, M.M. (2011). *Historical Dictionary of the Kurds*. Lanham, MD: Scarecrow Press.

Hague, C. and Jenkins, P. (2005). *Place Identity, Participation and Planning*. London: Routledge.

High Commission for Erbil Citadel Revitalization (2015). *Erbil Citadel*. Available at: www.erbilCitadel.org/ (accessed April 24, 2015).

Hiro, D. (2001). *Neighbors, not Friends: Iraq and Iran after the Gulf Wars*. London: Routledge.

Internal Displacement Monitoring Centre (2015). *Iraq IDP Figures Analysis*. Available at: www.internal-displacement.org/middle-east-and-north-africa/iraq/figures-analysis (accessed April 2015).

Jwaideh, W. (2006). *The Kurdish National Movement: Its Origins and Development*. Syracuse, NY: Syracuse University Press (London: Eurospan distributor).

Kymlicka, W.and Pfostl, E. (2014). *Multiculturalism and Minority Rights in the Arab World*. Oxford: Oxford University Press.

Manafy, A. (2005). *The Kurdish Political Struggles in Iran, Iraq, and Turkey: A Critical Analysis*. Lanham, MD: University Press of America.

Marfleet, P. (2011). Displacement and denial: IDPs in today's Iraq. *International Journal of Contemporary Iraqi Studies* 5: 277–292.

McDowall, D. (1992). *The Kurds: A Nation Denied*. London: Minority Rights Group.

Middle East Research Institute (2015). *Impact of Displaced People on Kurdistan Region*. Available at: www.meri-k.org/?page_id=857 (accessed April 2015).

Minervini, C. (2002). Housing reconstruction in Kosovo. *Habitat International* 26: 571–590.

Nooraddin, H. (2004). Globalization and the search for modern local architecture: learning from Baghdad. In Elshishatawi, Y. (ed.) *Planning Middle Eastern Cities: An Urban Kaleidoscope in a Globalizing World*. London: Routledge, pp. 59–84.

Nooraddin, H. (2012). Architectural identity in an era of change. *Developing Country Studies* 2: 81–96.

Norwegian Refugee Council (2015). *No Escape: Civilians in Syria Struggle to Find Safety Across Borders*. Available at: www.nrc.no/arch/img.aspx?file_id=9187536 (accessed March 2015).

O'Leary, B., Mcgarry, J. and Salih, K.L. (2005). *The Future of Kurdistan in Iraq*. Philadelphia, PA: University of Pennsylvania Press; Bristol: University Presses Marketing.

Oliver, P. (1997). *Encyclopedia of the Vernacular Architecture of the World*. Cambridge: Cambridge University Press.

Piquard, B. and Swenarton, M. (2011). Learning from architecture and conflict. *The Journal of Architecture* 16: 1–13.

Polk, W.R. (2006). *Understanding Iraq: A Whistlestop Tour from Ancient Babylon to Occupied Baghdad*. London: I.B. Tauris.

Sheyholislami, J. (2011). *Kurdish Identity, Discourse, and New Media*. New York; Basingstoke: Palgrave Macmillan.

Stansfield, G.R.V. (2003). *Iraqi Kurdistan: Political Development and Emergent Democracy*, London: RoutledgeCurzon.

Stansfield, G.R.V. (2007). *Iraq: People, History, Politics*. Cambridge: Polity.

Tucker, S. and Roberts, P.M. (2010). *The Encyclopedia of Middle East Wars: The United States in the Persian Gulf, Afghanistan, and Iraq Conflicts*. Santa Barbara, CA: ABC-CLIO.

United Nations Iraq (2015). *Brief on Iraq*. Available at: www.uniraq.org/index.php?option=com_k2&view=item&layout=item&id=1078&Itemid=573&lang=ar (accessed April 26, 2015).

World Bank (2015). *The Kurdistan Region of Iraq Needs an Estimated US$1.4 Billion this Year to Stabilize the Economy*. Available at: www.worldbank.org/en/news/press-release/2015/02/12/kurdistan-region-iraq-stabilize-economy (accessed April 2015).

Plate 1 London today

Plate 2 Seoul's Cheonggyecheon, a new linear park

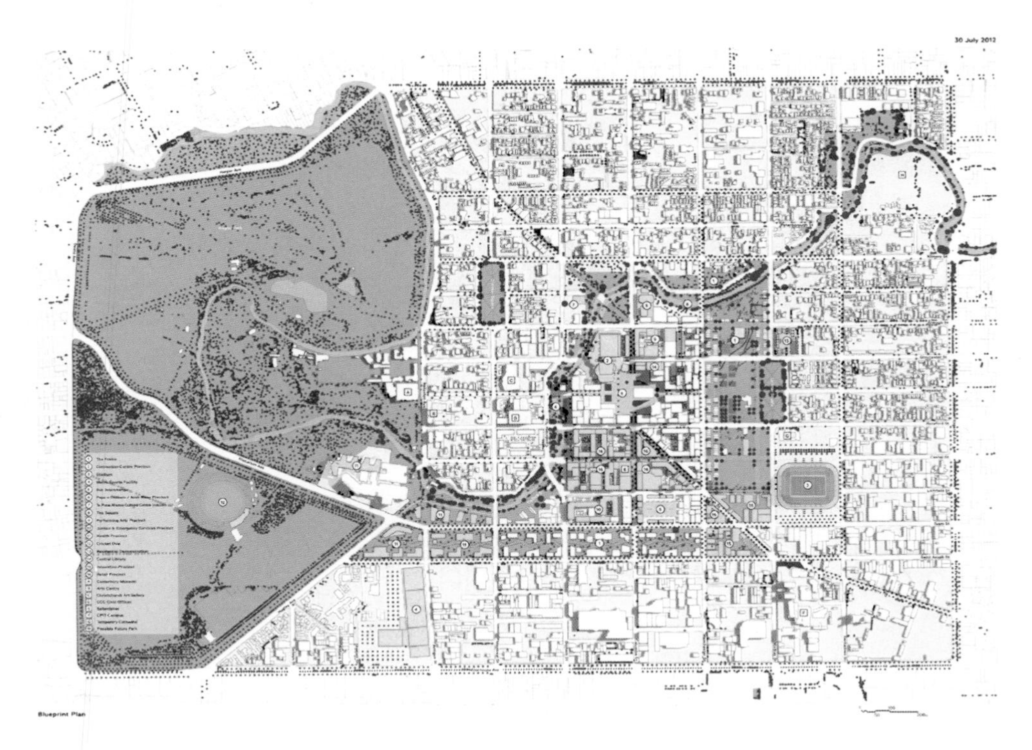

Plate 3 Blueprint for Christchurch Central Recovery Plan

Plate 4 Cardiff's visions

Plate 5 Houses on hillside, Port-au-Prince

Plate 6 Sewer construction in Delmas 19, Port-au-Prince

Plate 7 Housing damaged in the center of Talca and urban densification program polygon

Plate 8 Housing damaged in the center of Talca and urban densification program polygon

Plate 9 Tsunami-resilient housing designs in Dichato

Plate 10 Traditional corridors in Vichuquén town

Plate 11 Bang Bua neighborhood with all of its homes reconstructed and upgraded

Plate 12 Saphan Mai neighborhood carrying out upgrading and reconstruction activities

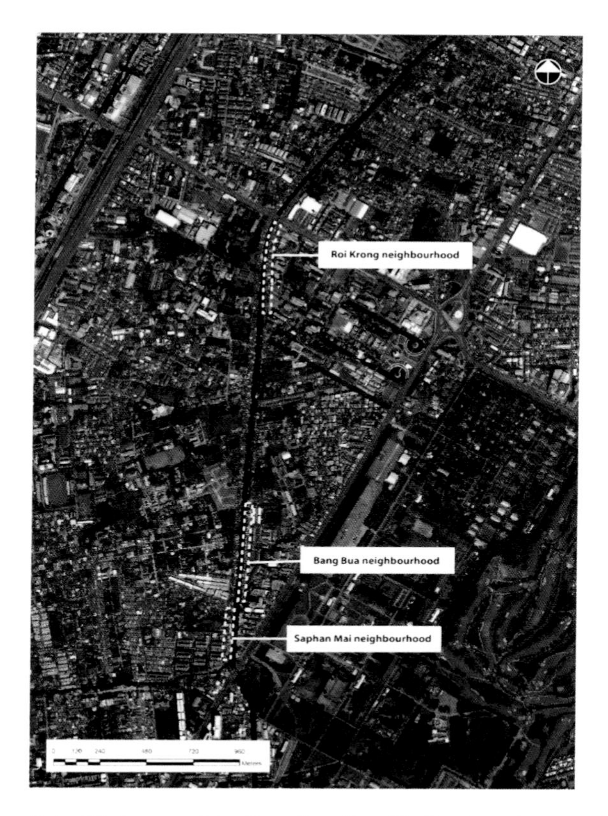

Plate 13 A map of the Bang Bua Canal indicating where each of the neighborhoods are located along the three-kilometer stretch of canal in northern Bangkok

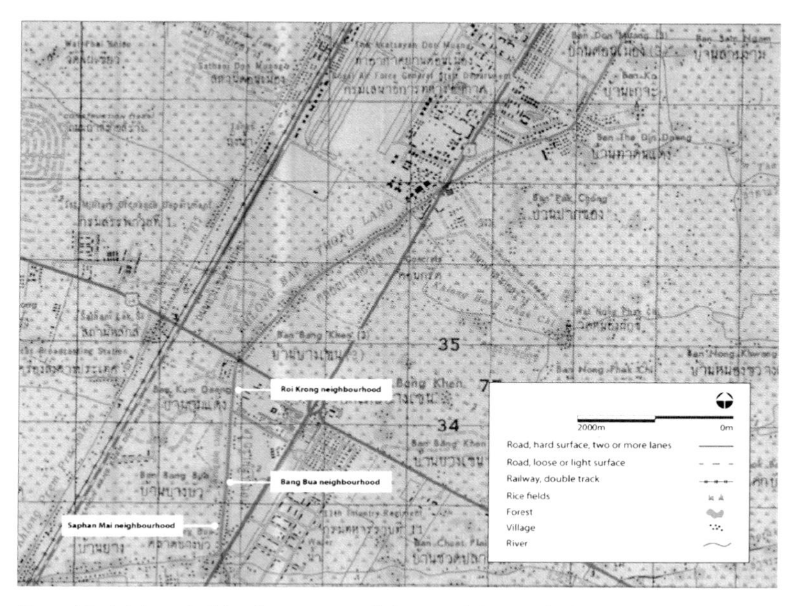

Plate 14 A historical land-use map of the canal from 1968 reflects a primarily rural landscape

Plate 15 Tacloban – Thousands of families made their own makeshift shelters

Plate 16 The destruction of Tacloban

Plate 17 Bunkhouses near completion in Ormoc, April 2014

Plate 18 Construction of transitional relocation sites outside Tacloban

Plate 19 Informal housing on a dangerously unstable slope in Lima, Peru, where the urban poor cannot afford better situated, less risky sites

Plate 20 Reconstructed houses in Aceh, flooded in 2013

Plate 21 House extended with a small shop, El Salvador

Plate 22 Stilt house with a ground floor modified into a restaurant in Aceh

Plate 23 Building typology in the Citadel

Plate 24 Refugee camp in North of Iraq, Erbil

Plate 25 New gate by the Kurdish government

Plate 26 Kurdistan International Bank

Plate 27 Italian Village, English Village and high-rise developments

Plate 28 Formalized stands typical of the four main sectors: food, hair and cosmetics, botanica and arts & crafts

Plate 29 Street market next to the Iron Market

Plate 30 A clearer division of the physical space raises vendors' social assets

Plate 31 Colorful informal markets occupying the streets surrounding the Iron Market

Plate 32 One of the two Digicel stands inside the Market

Part III

Urban markets, micro-enterprise, insurance and technology

Chapter 9

Linking response, recovery and resilience to markets in humanitarian action

Joanna Friedman

Urban markets: entry points for response and recovery

When it comes to disaster and conflict, affected populations and humanitarian agencies must navigate new and growing urban environments. From the Haiti earthquake, which devastated the capital of Port-au-Prince, to the Zaatari camp for Syrian refugees in Jordan[1] (Ledwith, 2014), crises since 2010 have affected, expanded and created dense populations centers. One of the major characteristics of these increasingly urban crises is the presence and diversity of markets, both old and new. A market is any formal or informal framework in which buyers and sellers exchange goods, labor or services for cash or other goods, and includes the institutions, infrastructure and rules that govern or enable these interactions.

The humanitarian think-tank Active Learning Network for Accountability and Performance (ALNAP) has highlighted the need for humanitarian agencies to work with markets as one of nine key lessons for urban disasters (Sanderson and Knox-Clarke, 2012). Working with markets during emergency preparedness, response and recovery actions in both urban and rural environments can contribute to humanitarian objectives of survival, recovery and the restoration of dignity (Sphere, 2011), in part through boosting the local economy on which communities, households and individuals rely. Sensitivity to markets and market strengthening can lay the groundwork for household recovery and resilience, local ownership and even longer-term development goals. Humanitarian agencies have developed market analysis tools and guidance and conducted numerous inter-agency and individual market assessments in emergencies, largely since 2010.[2] The translation of these studies into recommendations that may inform market-based programming in urban crises, however, remains inconsistent. The relative strength of markets in urban areas should encourage implementation and shared learning from market-based programs to make improvements in linking response, recovery and resilience.

While urban and rural areas are increasingly connected by markets and migration (Action Against Hunger, 2012), key differences remain between urban and rural markets. The cash-focused initiative, the Cash Learning Partnership (CaLP), has highlighted some distinct differences between urban and rural markets and economies, namely that there is a plethora of markets and actors in urban areas leading to more competition, and the capacity for resumption of trade is higher in urban areas due to this array of markets and actors and typically better infrastructure than in rural areas (Cross and Johnston, 2011). Most importantly, urban people and households, including those affected by disaster or crisis, the poor and those most vulnerable to shocks and stresses, have strong linkages to markets. Urban households depend on markets for survival through the purchase of basic goods and services as well as for their income or trade to maintain their livelihoods in the long term.

Urban households are often entirely dependent on procuring food from local markets. In 2013, Save the Children analyzed urban Household Economic Analysis (HEA) studies from 12 countries in Africa, Asia and the Caribbean. They found that urban households 'rely almost exclusively on purchasing their food from the market' and that the majority of very poor households in both urban and rural areas obtain food and cash income from 'sources other than their own crop production'[3] (Boudreau, 2013), meaning their incomes depend on markets. In a more recent example, Syrian refugees in urban areas of Jordan purchase water, electricity and shelter and access public services through markets, and competition has driven staple prices up and wages down. The refugee influx is straining the Jordanian labor market and public service delivery (UNHCR, 2014). Market-based solutions are imperative given the centrality of markets to the survival and livelihoods of crisis-affected urban populations. This also implies that government and international agencies need to closely examine urban market fluctuations in prices, actors and dynamics to understand the impact on livelihoods.

Dependency on markets can be a double-edged sword for urban households: they are vulnerable to crisis-related price shocks, but they can also benefit from the competitiveness of urban markets, numerous supply chains, and formal and informal financial services for livelihoods recovery. Affected populations and humanitarian actors can rely usually on decent network infrastructure for mobile phones and data connections to ensure a faster, wider-scale response, such as using mobile technology for family tracing and information updates, real-time mapping to assess physical damage and electronic transfers for delivery of assistance. In Port-au-Prince following the 2010 earthquake, humanitarian NGOs capitalized upon existing mobile networks to create economies of scale for one-time cash transfers to a large number of earthquake-affected households (CaLP, 2011). Development actors in urban areas typically aim to increase access for the poorest and most vulnerable populations to markets and public and private services. This can be a key entry point for humanitarian actors, who can capitalize on existing development programs to inform emergency preparedness as well as response and recovery.

Urban areas are also typically home to centers of various levels of government. Proximity to different government levels contributes to an increased information flow between affected populations and the government, but not necessarily to better access or opportunity for vulnerable urban households (Cross and Johnston, 2011). The poor and vulnerable segments of urban populations are almost always those with the least political capital and access to public services in 'normal' times (Pantuliano et al., 2012) and crisis does not automatically engender a stronger voice for marginalized people. Emergency response can and should feed into initiatives to reduce the marginalization of poor and vulnerable people, and should encourage government investment in public services and an enabling environment for enterprise development and employment creation. Market-based programming provides a natural link to recovery and development by supporting local economies so that they can return to functionality and by helping to rebuild the economic capacity of people affected by crisis. As market analysis requires going beyond a needs assessment to examine the pre-existing and current market systems, including relationships between market actors, regulators and consumers, market-based programming also encourages coordination and connection between short- and long-term actors, plans and activities (Pantuliano et al., 2012).

Temporary emergency cash transfer programs can lead to long-term cash transfer initiatives that support local government initiatives, technical expertise and financial services. Humanitarian agencies should consult national development plans to consider how they may help align response and recovery with development goals. Recent political and food security crises in Kenya have led to humanitarian-led cash-based safety net programs for poor and vulnerable households, and this is one type of market-based intervention that can serve as a pilot and lead into longer-term social protection initiatives to contribute to poverty reduction. Humanitarian agencies carried out cash-based safety net programs in response to the food price crisis in Kenya between 2008 and 2011, and in 2010 the government asked international humanitarian NGOs Concern Worldwide and Oxfam to carry out a pilot urban cash transfer safety net program in Nairobi slums (Concern, nd). The government then launched its own urban food subsidy cash transfer program and a National Social Protection Policy in 2011, in line with the government's poverty reduction and economic growth plan, Vision 2030 (World Bank, 2013). The National Social Protection Policy recognized the need to increase the scale of social assistance and the government of Kenya established a framework National Safety Net Programme in 2013 that encompassed multiple cash-based safety nets for different vulnerable groups. Cash-based safety nets are well suited to urban areas, and the Kenya case shows that humanitarian agency-led safety nets in urban crisis response can inform longer-term government social protection programs. Ideally, these programs would then be in place to contribute to preparedness for the next crisis, to mitigate future shocks to household economies.

Market analysis and market-based programming

Sudden-onset disasters such as the 2004 Indian Ocean tsunami, the 2010 Haiti earthquake, the 2011 Philippines typhoon and floods, and protracted conflicts in South Sudan and Afghanistan, with their devastating impacts on both urban and rural populations within affected countries, led to initiatives for better humanitarian coordination and response quality, including strengthening the linkages between basic needs, livelihoods and local markets in urban and rural areas. In these instances humanitarian agencies began to use cash-based interventions on a large scale in emergency response. Humanitarian actors acknowledged that economies continue to function during emergencies, that humanitarian action could profoundly impact local markets, and that market awareness was needed to improve lives and avoid harm to existing economic systems (SEEP Network, 2010).

Lessons learned from recent crises helped drive home the need to engage in economic recovery simultaneously with emergency response, and ideally specify economic recovery mechanisms and structures during the emergency preparedness phase, that is, before major crises happen, or, as is more often the case in reality, in contexts where climate-related disasters will continue to occur regularly, for example the floods in Pakistan and the Philippines, or in zones of protracted conflict such as Afghanistan and the eastern Democratic Republic of Congo. Market-based interventions fit into the early recovery approach championed by the United Nations Development Programme (UNDP) whereby development approaches are used within a crisis context to encourage a transition to economic recovery, participation by local authorities and communities, and a longer-term effect of post-crisis interventions (UNDP, 2008).

Minimum Economic Recovery Standards (MERS) have been developed by the SEEP Network, which brought together practitioners from 30 international humanitarian agencies in 2007 to define the technical scope of the standards for economic recovery in crises, with further consultation and iteration through 2010 (SEEP Network, 2010).[4] The

MERS guidance and the Emergency Market Mapping and Analysis (EMMA) toolkit are perhaps the best known and understood materials for humanitarian market analysis and programming to date, and the MERS materials are a companion to the Sphere standards for humanitarian action (Sphere, 2011).

How then do humanitarian actors understand markets and use market-based approaches in response and recovery programming? There are different levels of awareness and understanding and varying degrees of humanitarian engagement with markets.

Market awareness and market analysis[5]

Market awareness is a minimum standard for all humanitarian programming to consider markets throughout the project cycle and the potential impact of interventions on markets. Market analysis is the process of assessing and understanding the key features and characteristics of a market system so that predictions can be made about how prices, availability and access will develop in the future. From this information, decisions can be made about whether or how to intervene to improve humanitarian outcomes.

Over the past few years the inclusion of market analysis has become essential for humanitarian responders and their institutional donors (IRC et al., 2013). The question of market functionality may be seen as part of contextual or feasibility analyses, while damage to livelihoods should fall under needs assessment (have affected households, who may be traders or service providers, lost assets or clients critical to their income, or have they lost employment opportunities?).

Market analysis in protracted emergencies has begun to move beyond basic goods and services to include labor, credit and other critical markets that affect livelihoods and touch upon systemic issues, particularly in urban areas. An EMMA conducted in Lebanon in 2013 focused on critical markets, namely construction, agricultural labor and the service sector, for the livelihoods of Syrian refugees and host communities. The EMMA recommended 'market-smart humanitarian programs' to support local commodity and labor markets, and better informing refugees of employment opportunities and necessary skills, to improve labor market efficiency (Oxfam GB, 2013; Oxfam GB and WFP, 2013).

Market-based programming

Market-based programming is commonly understood in the humanitarian community as 'the practice of working through and supporting local markets in humanitarian response and recovery.' Market-based programming can be broken down into different levels of intervention in markets. In all cases the overarching goal is to rebuild and ultimately improve the lives and livelihoods of those people most affected by or most vulnerable to a crisis, although other segments of the population are likely to benefit as well.

There are three major areas within market-based programming:

- Market-integrated relief/market-sensitive interventions – humanitarian response activities that work through markets to provide basic goods and services to crisis-affected and vulnerable populations. An example is rental vouchers for disaster-affected urban households to access local shelter.
- Market support/indirect support through markets – humanitarian response activities that provide short-term support to market actors to restore market functionality after

a crisis and promote recovery, for example support to suppliers of key goods and services and grants to local grocery store owners to restock their supplies.

- Market strengthening and development – a long-term approach and related activities that aim for economic recovery, including the ability of markets to support livelihoods and contribute to resilience from future and recurrent shocks. An example is working with local microfinance institutions to expand their range of products and services for poor and middle-income groups, such as savings and loans for community-based savings and credit groups.

Using market-based approaches in response and recovery programming

Market-sensitive and market-supportive interventions can add value beyond an initial emergency response. Direct and indirect cash-based interventions in particular can help meet relief and recovery needs, maintain dignity and flexibility for aid recipients, and result in positive multiplier effects on the local economy (Cross and Johnston, 2011). A 2014 study by the NGO the International Rescue Committee (IRC) on cash-based assistance to Syrian refugees in Lebanon found that each dollar of cash assistance spent by a beneficiary household generated over US$2 of GDP for the Lebanese economy (Lehmann and Masterson, 2014).

Market strengthening activities often mean a less hands-on, more facilitating role for humanitarian agencies such as the Making Markets Work for the Poor (M4P) approach (ACF, 2008; DFID and SDC, 2008). In this model humanitarian or development agencies act as facilitators, linking target groups such as small farmers to other critical value chain actors to improve their participation in and income from dairy or textile sectors. Other market strengthening activities may include micro-enterprise development and vocational training or apprenticeships for individuals and groups or support for financial inclusion at a local or national level. Market strengthening activities are integral to an early recovery approach to humanitarian response, meaning that development approaches and best practices are applied in humanitarian settings. These approaches typically fall under one or more of the MERS technical standards (SEEP Network, 2010).

Case studies: Haiti earthquake response and Philippines flood response, 2010–2013

The following two case studies explore the use of markets and cash-based programming following two disasters.

Market-based programming in the 2010 Haiti earthquake response

In Haiti[6] following the 2010 earthquake emergency response organizations from the Cash Working Group (which later became the Livelihoods Working Group, to accentuate the overlap between response and recovery) carried out EMMAs and other market assessments and designed a number of market-based interventions that aimed to meet immediate basic needs including food, water and shelter (rent) for the most affected and most vulnerable households while supporting the restoration of markets.

Humanitarian agencies carried out a range of interventions to support both demand and supply for basic goods and services and to contribute to economic recovery. To meet immediate needs, humanitarian agencies provided cash grants and vouchers to the most affected vulnerable households to purchase basic goods such as food, water and household items and services such as school fees and healthcare. In one example of combined market-integrated relief and market support programming, the NGO Oxfam GB supported local restaurants with grants to restock their ingredients and coaching on how to offer nutritionally balanced meals, while vulnerable households and individuals received meal vouchers for these restaurants in the weeks immediately following the earthquake. On the supply side humanitarian agencies also engaged in market support by providing rebuilding and restocking grants to local grocery, household and hardware store owners and to local water kiosks (the main source of potable water for households in Port-au-Prince) and grants and business training to service providers such as masons, plumbers, bakers and street food stall owners who offered critical supplies and services to affected households.

One example of a key market intervention focused on rice supply. The major markets of Port-au-Prince were physically destroyed and approximately 80 percent of small wholesalers of mainly imported rice, a staple food, were killed or lost their storage facilities (IRC et al., 2010). EMMA showed that small rice wholesalers, retailers and a network of 10,000 intermediaries of both locally produced rice from the countryside and imported rice were key to the recovery of the rice market (IRC et al., 2010). By supporting these actors with temporary cash grants, humanitarian agencies could help improve the supply of rice to disaster-affected households.

Humanitarian and development actors also worked to facilitate access to microfinance (and particularly microloans, insurance and savings) for small business owners as part of an early recovery strategy. They made efforts to continue work that had been ongoing prior to the earthquake, including strengthening local financial service providers, and looking more closely at how financial products and services could extend to the poorest and most crisis-affected households – particularly relevant in an urban area where many people relied on micro-enterprise activities, at least in part, for their livelihoods.

These activities boosted income and employment opportunities, increased access to goods and services, and engaged local financial institutions in the delivery of grants and vouchers. The majority of beneficiaries who received restocking grants restarted their businesses, and nearly half of them acquired replacement assets or repaid onerous debts accrued just after the earthquake (Young and Henderson, 2010).[7]

The humanitarian community also leveraged new technologies by partnering with the private sector in response efforts, identifying an opportunity to strengthen mobile money services as a way to reach poorer segments of the population with relief and recovery grants. The Bill and Melinda Gates Foundation and the United States Agency for International Development (USAID) launched the Haiti Mobile Money Initiative (HMMI), a US$10 million incentive fund in June 2010 to facilitate the rapid deployment of mobile money services at large scale after the earthquake, while contributing to the development of longer-term access to financial services. Two major mobile network operators were jointly awarded US$3.2 million for being the first to market with 5 million mobile transactions (USAID, nd).

Working with electronic payment providers to respond to disasters in the Philippines, 2011–2013

Urban contexts have served as flagship areas for leveraging and scaling up new technologies in collaboration with the private sector. Humanitarian agencies are increasingly using electronic and mobile transfers to facilitate access to cash, goods and services for crisis-affected populations. These mechanisms can increase the efficiency and scale of response and improve transparency and accountability. In its response to floods in urban Cagayan de Oro, Mindanao, Philippines in 2011 the NGO Action Against Hunger (ACF) piloted the use of debit cards as part of a larger distribution of paper vouchers for use in local grocery stores. While the debit cards had a higher start-up cost than paper vouchers, they could be loaded electronically, used on multiple occasions so that households did not have to purchase all their items at once, facilitated easier digital record-keeping and were less subject to fraud and theft (Navarro et al., 2011). Research by the Cash Learning Partnership has shown that electronic transfers generally require more time and cost more than paper vouchers in the set-up phase, but save time and money per disbursement as they are scaled up (O'Brien et al., 2013).

In 2013 ACF conducted a study on the use of electronic transfers as part of systematic, large-scale emergency preparedness in the Philippines. ACF interviewed different private sector service providers with a presence in Manila as well as regional cities including card issuers, mobile companies and platforms for the redemption of electronic vouchers. The study found that three pre-paid card issuers (banks) and two remittance companies were most suitable for emergency response. The main advantages of these service providers entailed their amount of past experience working with NGOs, the flexibility and adaptability of their services to different clients and areas, their customer identification requirements and their coverage, costs, support services and set-up lead time (Smith, 2013). As debit cards, mobile money and other electronic transfers depend on a certain level of infrastructure including network signal and electricity, the presence of ATMs or the liquidity of mobile agents, this and other electronic transfer pilots typically begin in urban areas, though rural pilots do exist as well (Smith, 2013).[8]

The study found that there was scope to increase the scale and effectiveness of response in the Philippines if humanitarian agencies partnered and collectively approached service providers and government to raise awareness, improve infrastructure and address barriers in the enabling environment for electronic transfers, particularly before a major emergency as part of contingency planning and preparedness (Smith, 2013). This recommendation applies more broadly: urban areas are home to an array of public and private actors, whose social, technical and marketing expertise can be harnessed to improve response and recovery. Regular stock-taking or mapping of service providers, establishment of agreements and collective humanitarian private-public response planning would contribute to better response and allow for continuity with ongoing initiatives, improving both recovery and resilience options.

Working with governments to aid recovery and resilience: social protection including safety nets

The United Nations Food and Agriculture Organization (FAO) outlines three key approaches to strengthening the resilience of populations, namely strengthening livelihoods and market access, improving social services and setting up safety nets (FAO, 2014). Safety nets offer cash or in-kind transfers to poor and vulnerable people, with no requirement of contribution from recipients, which fall within the rubric of social protection. Safety nets may also include school feeding, regular cash transfers, social insurance and minimum standards for the workplace (FAO, 2014). Social protection is defined as actions carried out by the state or privately, to help people address risk, vulnerability to crises and changes in circumstances, and chronic poverty (DFID, 2006).

In Kenya, the NGOs Oxfam GB and Concern Worldwide began a three-phase program in 2009 to address food insecurity in the informal settlements of Nairobi following the food crisis of 2008 (Beesley, 2011). Phase one addressed immediate food needs directly through cash transfers to 5,000 poor households for eight months, phase two added a skills development and business training component for the same households, to improve their income earning potential, and phase three focused on longer-term monitoring of emergency triggers and advocacy towards the government to establish social protection programs. The Kenyan government adopted the program's cash transfer model and began a pilot for 10,000 households in informal settlements in Mombasa (Harvey, 2012). Rural safety net programs have also been successful in Kenya, but poor infrastructure, particularly in terms of transport and communications, have posed challenges in their roll-out (Beesley, 2011).

According to the World Bank, three major recent sets of global crises – the food price crisis, quick-onset natural disasters such as floods and cyclones, and the global financial crisis – demonstrated the importance of safety nets in particular for urban areas. The urban poor were hit hard due to their dependency on food purchase and wage labor, and their sub-standard housing, and safety net programs that covered only the poorest rural areas did not take into account vulnerable urban households (World Bank, 2012). The targeting approach, scale and other characteristics of social protection programs, including safety net programs, will have to be tailored to urban, rather than rural, environments. Social protection programs have great potential to allow urban populations to better prepare for and respond to crises, and to become more resilient to recurrent disasters and conflict. Cash-based social safety nets would provide regular, predictable complementary income; unemployment insurance would protect livelihoods and help households fill in gaps in employment; and support to labor systems would help to ensure regular income. Humanitarian agencies might be out of their comfort zone in advocating for these initiatives, but they may voice their advocacy in partnership with development organizations and civil society for the analysis and design, in close coordination with government agencies or private actors that could ultimately take over the administration of social protection activities in the long term.

Market analysis, particularly with predictions about how poor and vulnerable populations might capitalize upon social protection to mitigate the impact of crises, and social protection pilot programs could feed into advocacy in front of government in support of regular or permanent social protection activities. Humanitarian agencies could lead the identification of most crisis-affected and vulnerable people, which is complicated by the diversity and number of groups in urban areas. Humanitarian agencies have tools and practices from recent urban emergencies[9] and are accustomed to working in coordination with local civil protection representatives and local communities. By combining strong local-level targeting with sound market analysis, humanitarian agencies can develop convincing arguments for public social protection initiatives in urban areas.

Pre-existing transfer systems such as remittances and savings and credit schemes can also provide systems from which urban social protection systems can draw inspiration. In 2012 studies in Guinea, Zimbabwe and Guatemala, ACF found that rural-urban migration and related transfers represented efforts by households to create their own safety nets, which government policymakers could capitalize upon and strengthen as part of emergency preparedness and their poverty reduction strategy (Action Against Hunger, 2012). Rotating savings and credit associations (ROSCAs, also known as savings groups, merry-go-rounds or tontines) are another local mechanism used in both urban and rural areas to facilitate access to savings and credit, particularly amongst those who may not be able to access the formal financial services sector. These forms of locally initiated financial services could serve as models in terms of transfer frequency, value and delivery mechanisms for humanitarian agencies and governments looking to support poor and vulnerable households in a way that builds upon and strengthens the local market.

Urban market analysis and programming: where are we now?

The majority of market analysis toolkits were designed for immediate post-crisis analysis and humanitarian actors are now looking at how to integrate market analysis into the whole project cycle, including emergency preparedness and recovery involving regular monitoring and evaluation of markets in post-crisis or high-risk contexts. Market monitoring, and particularly price monitoring, is one way that agencies gauge market dysfunction and the effects of crisis and when these changes may have deleterious effects on livelihoods, as opposed to typical seasonal price changes. In 2014 a consortium of humanitarian NGOs developed and used an adapted EMMA to produce baseline market information that may be used to inform analysis during sporadic or chronic crises.[10] In 2013, Oxfam GB conducted an EMMA in informal settlements in Nairobi, where 50 percent of households are chronically poor. The informal settlements, where the vast majority of residents depend on the market for food and other basic needs, were affected by high food prices linked to Kenya's severe 2011 drought. Recommendations included advocacy to the government to establish safety nets for poor households, lobbying with government and communities for identity card registration to enable poor and very poor wealth groups to have access to wider sources of credit, promotion of group saving and lending for the poor and very poor, and in the case of a slow onset emergency, cash transfers to poor households and traders (Brady and Mohanty, 2013). One interesting finding was the stratification of wealth groups in the informal settlements, and the dependency of very poor households on in-kind credit and gifts from those slightly better off, that is, the poor and middle poor. Market awareness would dictate that response options include support across these groups to ensure impact on the target group, the poorest households (Oxfam GB and WFP, 2013).

Conclusion

Across both urban and rural areas, gaps and challenges remain for humanitarian actors in terms of market analysis and market-based programming. Market support and strengthening programs have not yet been conducted at the scale of market-based relief programs, nor is there a strong body of evidence showing their impact on recovery and resilience. Market analysis must be institutionalized in terms of inclusion in the entire project cycle and across sectors of humanitarian action, such as in shelter and education, and through improved staff capacity to conduct market assessment and response programs (Oxfam GB and WFP, 2013). Examples from the Syrian crisis, including market analyses focusing on water and shelter, serve as good examples of this potential institutionalization (IRC et al., 2013; Wildman, 2013).

Coordination of market analysis and standards for market-based programming has led to promising new initiatives and the sharing of lessons and best practices. Market learning events have brought together a variety of practitioners from the humanitarian, academic and private sectors to share experiences and lessons from market engagement in humanitarian and development settings, to build consensus around the role of markets in humanitarian programming, and to promote better quality market-based programming. Participants agreed that the findings and recommendations of market analysis must be systematically translated into response analysis and programming. The humanitarian community is getting better at conducting market analysis, but data must be used to inform response analysis, program design, monitoring and evaluation and other phases of the market-based project cycle.

Information sharing, and particularly the integration of community, government and private sector data on market systems, is critical for better emergency preparedness, recovery and response (Jowett, 2014). Humanitarian agencies can work with other actors to monitor trends, develop crisis triggers and leading indicators for market systems that are critical to the poor and vulnerable segments of the population, and carry out baselines and pre-crisis mapping. This is germane to urban environments where government and private sector data is typically accessible, even if quality checks are necessary. Across conflict and disaster areas, with rapid and slow onset crises, humanitarian agencies must devote more energy to exploring urban-rural linkages and idiosyncrasies, and how they impact markets in emergencies. Finally, the study of power relationships and governance is important to all market analysis, but particularly relevant to urban markets with their diversity of groups and power structures.

As they increase in number, scale and frequency, market support and strengthening programs will need to be well documented, with learning shared across the wider response community. These levels of market intervention in humanitarian response and recovery would benefit from collaboration with development actors and the private and public sectors, all of which may have existing information on vulnerable populations. Planners, policymakers and civil society representatives in particular can contribute important information to market baseline studies, pre-crisis market analysis and scenario planning. Ultimately, a merging of complementary humanitarian and development approaches will strengthen linkages to social protection and access to public and private services for poor and vulnerable populations, which will help to build resilience and chip away at the root causes of poverty and marginalization.

Notes

1 In 2013 the Zaatari Refugee Camp became the second largest refugee camp in the world and the fourth largest city in Jordan.
2 See, among others: http://emma-toolkit.org/category/emma-reports-tmp/.
3 Save the Children conducted a meta-analysis of Household Economy Analysis (HEA) data from 316 livelihood zones, or contexts, across 26 countries in Africa and Asia as well as Colombia and Haiti, including 12 urban contexts.
4 The MERS lays out five core standards as well as standards for assessment and analysis and four technical areas of intervention (productive assets, financial services, employment and enterprise development) that are key to economic recovery.
5 Based on definitions in Oxfam GB and WFP (2013) and SEEP Network (2010).
6 For more information see Young and Henderson (2010) and Hartberg et al. (2011).
7 As well as the reference this is also based on the author's own experience.

8 See also the partnership between Mercy Corps and MasterCard in Kathmandu, Nepal: MasterCard Worldwide & Mercy Corps: ELEVATE Phase I Report, Mercy Corps, July 2013. For an example of a rural pilot, see Cash for Assets: World Food Programme's Exploration of the In-Kind to E-Payments Shift for Food Assistance in Kenya, Bankable Frontier Associates for the Consultative Group to Assist the Poor (CGAP)/World Bank, 2013.
9 See, among others, Levron (2010).
10 See *Market Analysis for Preparedness and Development: Piloting Innovation in Guatemala* available at: www.cashlearning.org; also Juillard (2014).

References

Action Against Hunger (2012). *Rural-Urban Linkages, Household Food Security and Child Nutrition*. Available at: www.actionagainsthunger.org.uk.

ACF International Network (2008).*'The Market for the Poor' Approach: A New Methodology to Integrate Poor People in Market System*. Available at: www.actioncontrelafaim.org/sites/default/files/publications/fichiers/acf_market_for_the_poor.pdf (accessed June 1, 2014).

Beesley, J. (2011). *The Hunger Safety Nets Programme, Kenya: A Social Protection Case Study*. Oxford: Oxfam GB.

Boudreau, T. (2013). *Food Security in a Changing World*. London: Food Economy Group and Save the Children. Available at: www.savethechildren.org.uk/sites/default/files/images/Food_Security_in_a_Changing_World.pdf.

Brady, C. and Mohanty, S. (2013). *Market Analysis for Preparedness: The Urban Informal Settlements of Nairobi*. Oxford: Oxfam GB. Available at: http://policy-practice.oxfam.org.uk/publications/market-analysis-for-preparedness-the-urban-informal-settlements-of-nairobi-315687.

CaLP (2011). *New Technology Enhancing Humanitarian Cash and Voucher Programming*. Oxford: The Cash Learning Partnership (CaLP).

Concern (nd). *Kenya: Government Asks Concern to Pilot First-Ever Social Welfare Program for Urban Poor*. Available at: www.concernusa.org (accessed October 2014).

Cross, T. and Johnston, A. (2011). *Cash Transfer Programming in Urban Emergencies: A Toolkit for Practitioners*. Oxford: The Cash Learning Partnership (CaLP).

DFID (2006). *Social Protection Briefing Note Series*, Number 1. Available at: www.gsdrc.org/docs/open/SP17.pdf (accessed October 2014).

DFID and SDC (2008). *A Synthesis of the Making Markets Work for the Poor (M4P) Approach*. Available at: www.value-chains.org/dyn/bds/docs/681/Synthesis_2008.pdf (accessed October 2014).

FAO (2014). *Nutrition and Resilience: Strengthening the Links Between Resilience and Nutrition in Food and Agriculture*. Rome: Food and Agriculture Organization of the United Nations. Available at: www.fao.org/3/a-i3777e.pdf.

Hartberg, M. with support from Proust, A., Bailey, M. et al. (2011). *From Relief to Recovery: Supporting Good Governance in Post-Earthquake Haiti*. Oxford: Oxfam GB.

Harvey, C. (2012). *Cash Transfers in Nairobi's Slums: Improving Food Security and Gender Dynamics*. Oxford: Oxfam GB. Available at: http://policy-practice.oxfam.org.uk/publications/cash-transfers-in-nairobis-slums-improving-food-security-and-gender-dynamics-247193.

IRC, American Red Cross, Haitian Red Cross, International Federation of the Red Cross, Save the Children, Mercy Corps, Oxfam GB, ACDI/VOCA, World Food Programme and FEWS/NET (2010). *Emergency Market Mapping & Analysis (EMMA) Report: The Market System for Rice in Haiti*. Available at: http://emma-toolkit.org/wp-content/uploads/2010/08/EMMA-Haiti-report-Rice-Market.pdf.

IRC, Save the Children, DRC and Oxfam (2013). *Lebanon Emergency Market Mapping and Analysis (EMMA): Executive Briefing for Analyses of the Construction, Service Sector and Agricultural Labor Systems*. International Rescue Committee. Available at: http://reliefweb.int/report/lebanon/

lebanon-emergency-market-mapping-and-analysis-emma-executive-briefing-analyses (accessed September 2014).

Jowett, E. (2014). *Markets in Crises, Learning 2, IRC.* Available at: http://emma-toolkit.org/wp-content/uploads/Markets-in-Crises-Learning-Event-2-Final-Report.pdf.

Juillard, H. (2014). *Pre-Crisis Market Mapping and Analysis: Step-By-Step Guidance for Practitioners.* International Rescue Committee and Oxfam GB. Available at: https://rescue.app.box.com/s/u3i5yajmrt9gyt16wffv.

Ledwith, A. (2014). *Zaatari: The Instant City.* Boston, MA: Affordable Housing Institute.

Lehmann, C. and Masterson, D. (2014). *Emergency Economies: The Impact of Cash Assistance in Lebanon.* International Rescue Committee. Available at: www.rescue.org/sites/default/files/resource-file/Emergency%20Economies%20Evaluation%20Report%20FINAL%2009.09.14%20%282%29.pdf (accessed September 2014).

Levron, E. (2010). *Identification of Vulnerable People in Urban Environments.* Paris: ACF.

Navarro, I.S., Militante, D.D. and Hughbanks, K. (2011). *CaLP Case Study Vouchers for Flood Relief in Cotobato City and Sultan Kudarat, ARMM, the Philippines, ACF.* Available at: www.cashlearning.org/resources/library/254-vouchers-for-flood-relief-in-cotobato-city-and-sultan-kudarat-armm-mindanao-the-philippines.

O'Brien, C., Hove, F. and Smith, G. (2013). *Factors Affecting the Cost-efficiency of Electronic Transfers in Humanitarian Programmes.* Oxford: CaLP.

Oxfam GB (2013). *Market Learning Event Communique.* Available at: www.logcluster.org/document/oxfam-markets-learning-event-communique-2013.

Oxfam GB and WFP (2013). *Executive Brief: Engaging with Markets in Humanitarian Responses.* Available at: http://policy-practice.oxfam.org.uk/publications/executive-brief-engaging-with-markets-in-humanitarian-responses-302197.

Pantuliano, S., Metcalfe-Hough, V., Haysom, S. and Davey, E. (2012). Urban vulnerability and displacement: a review of current issues. *Disasters,* Overseas Development Institute, London. Available at: www.cmamforum.org/Pool/Resources/Urban-vulnerabiity-and-displacement-Disasters-Pantuliano-et-al-012.pdf (accessed October 2014).

Sanderson, D. and Knox-Clarke, P. (2012). *Responding to Urban Disasters: Learning from Previous Relief and Recovery Operations,* ALNAP Lessons Paper. London: ODI.

SEEP Network (2010). *Minimum Economic Recovery Standards.* Available at: www.sphereproject.org/handbook/handbook-companions/the-mers-handbook/.

Smith, G. (2013). *Electronic Transfers Scoping Study and Preparedness Plan: ACF Philippines.* New York: ACF.

Sphere (2011). *The Sphere Project: Humanitarian Charter and Minimum Standards in Humanitarian Response.* Available at: www.sphereproject.org/handbook/.

UNHCR (2014). *Syria Regional Response Plan: Jordan.* Available at: www.unhcr.org/syriarrp6/docs/syria-rrp6-jordan-response-plan.pdf.

UNDP (2008). *Guidance Note on Early Recovery, Cluster Working Group on Early Recovery.* UNDP

USAID (nd). *Haiti Mobile Money Initiative Reaches the Five Million Transaction Milestone and Awards Final Prize in Incentive Program.* Available at: www.usaid.gov/news-information/press-releases/haiti-mobile-money-initiative-reaches-five-million-transaction.

Wildman, T. (2013). *Water Market System in Balqa, Zarqa, and Informal Settlements of Amman & the Jordan Valley – Jordan.* Oxford: Oxfam GB.

World Bank (2012). *Safety Nets Work – During Crisis and Prosperity.* Washington, DC: World Bank.

World Bank (2013). *Technical Assessment of the Kenya National Safety Net Program for Results.* Washington, DC: World Bank.

Young, P. and Henderson, E. (2010). *The Haiti Earthquake: An Urban Solution.* Oxford: Oxfam GB.

Chapter 10

Petty trade and the private sector in urban reconstruction

Learning from Haiti's post-earthquake Iron Market

David Smith

Introduction

Following the devastating 2010 earthquake that affected Haiti and in particular its urban areas, the recovery has been very challenging for stakeholders involved in the reconstruction. Despite large investments and good intentions of many actors, the fact that several years later many displacement camps remain open with large numbers of people still unable to return home serves as a reminder of the complexities of urban recovery.

Building on experiences in Haiti and elsewhere, such as in the Philippines following 2013's Typhoon Haiyan, the humanitarian community largely acknowledges that approaches to post-disaster reconstruction need to be rethought in order to address the complexity of urban environments (Knox Clarke and Ramalingam, 2012); for example, statements emerging from consultation platforms of the 2016 World Humanitarian Summit (WHS) address this issue. They relate to the urban context of intervention stating, for instance, that 'the humanitarian response needs to … build on coping and support mechanisms of communities … (and) take into account local economic mechanisms' (WHS, 2015b). Other statements refer to improving technical and logistical levels of intervention that such urban context requires by supporting and developing the involvement of the private sector's 'experience, skills and resources … (and) explor(ing) ways of channelling their expertise, resources and innovative approaches' (WHS, 2015a).

In Haiti, specialist reports following the earthquake have also suggested taking advantage of the way urban citizens have accessed resources and developed their livelihoods (Clermont et al., 2011; Kyazze et al., 2012; Fan, 2012; see also Schaeffer Brown, 2015). Spatially, this primarily applies to the numerous street markets, public markets and small shops that give character and vibrancy to the urban spaces of Haitian cities (Sanderson and Knox Clarke, 2012; Sokpoh et al., 2014; Kyazze et al., 2012). Such places for many constitute the most popular and useful livelihood spaces of the city, in short, places where livings can be made.

Public markets involve more than petty trade transactions. They are important urban places. The Declaration of the 9th International Public Markets Conference in 2015 asserts that 'unlike other forms of commercial enterprise, public markets … add great value to the economic, social, physical, and environmental health of the communities they serve' (PPS, 2015). They constitute unique and appropriate spaces of intervention as 'the daily commercial exchange that forms the heart of public market systems … offers powerful opportunities for transforming cities and regions across the globe into thriving, sustainable, and socially cohesive places' (PPS, 2015).

The reconstruction of the Iron Market (see Figure 10.1) after the earthquake received widespread attention. Of particular interest is how the reconstruction related to both

Figure 10.1 On the central place of the Market
Source: Smith (2011)

global discussions about urban humanitarian contexts and the involvement of the private sector in post-disaster reconstruction. The international press, built environment journals and a few expert reports often refer to the Iron Market project – called 'Marché en fer, marché Hyppolite or marché Vallière' in French – as a successful project (Ryan, 2011; Forbes, 2011; Galilee, 2011; Davis, 2012; Mone, 2011). Their appreciation generally comes from the appropriateness of a project that both uses and promotes economic, social and cultural elements, a post-disaster approach that embraces the urban context.

The reopening ceremony of the Market, which took place on January 11, 2011, the eve of the first anniversary of the earthquake, received extensive coverage locally and globally (see for example Forbes, 2011; Mone, 2011; Duval, 2011). In contrast with many projects around the city, its reconstruction was not financed and managed by international aid but rather privately financed by the owner of Digicel, a large mobile phone company in Haiti. To these ends the project has also been promoted as an example of what private enterprises are capable of achieving in urban post-disaster recovery.

A short history of the Iron Market

Since Haiti's independence from France in 1804 the present site of the Iron Market, occupying a central location in the 'Bord-de-mer' neighborhood, the historical commercial heart of the capital city of Port-au-Prince, has been occupied by a vibrant market (ISPAN, 2010b). The neighborhood was filled with traders and merchants, along with their warehouses and outlets (ISPAN, 2010a). The informal markets on covered sidewalks (known as galleries-trottoirs) have developed and expanded considerably in the last decades, building links of dependency between the area's formal and informal traders and transforming the area into one of the most dynamic commercial locations of the city.

Petty trade on this particular site was formalized in 1890 by the Hyppolite government, which instigated the construction of a cast iron structure fabricated in Paris (see Figure 10.2). The Market is organized into the South Hall, dedicated to food trade, and the North Hall, reserved for commerce of arts and crafts and voodoo objects (see Plate 28). These two sections stand on either side of a central public place (see Figure 10.3), enhanced by a grand entrance with minarets that gives the Market both charm and monumentality. The

Figure 10.2 The Iron Market in 1907
Source: Léger (1907: 248)

popularity of the Iron Market reached its peak in the decades of the 1940–1960s benefiting from the development of tourism at that time (ISPAN, 2010b). Its distinct architecture and cultural and economic significance has made the Iron Market a 'city emblem' (ISPAN, 2011); the Market is also represented on local currency, appearing on the 1000-gourde note since 1999.

A fire in 2008 destroyed the North Hall and therefore terminated the trade of cultural items at the Market. All but completely destroyed by the 2010 earthquake, the Market was rebuilt (see Figure 10.4) due to the personal US$12 million contribution and determination

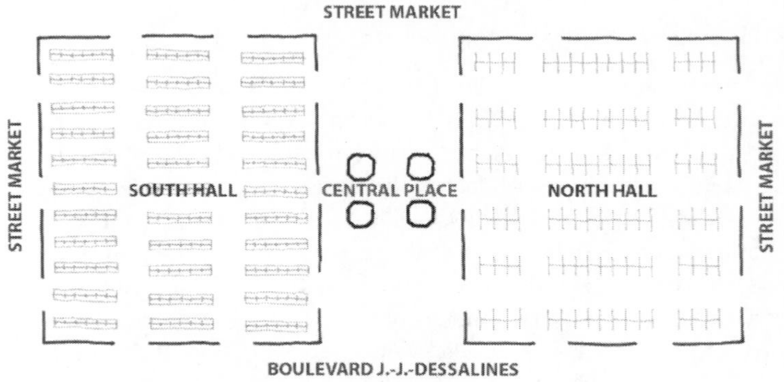

STREET MARKET
STREET MARKET
SOUTH HALL
CENTRAL PLACE
NORTH HALL
STREET MARKET
BOULEVARD J.-J.-DESSALINES

Figure 10.3 Sketch of the Iron Market's floor plan
Source: the author

Figure 10.4 In front of the Iron Market a few months after its reconstruction
Source: Smith (2011)

of Denis O'Brien, the owner and chief of Digicel, the dominant mobile phone network provider in Haiti (Reitman, 2011). The reconstruction being assured, a presidential decree confirmed the Iron Market as a National Heritage Building in May 2010 (Dieudonné, 2010).

Prioritizing the rebuilding of commerce

The reconstruction of the Iron Market has been seen as one of a few projects that focuses on the economy (da Silva cited in Davis, 2012; Forbes, 2011) with the intention of responding to the high demand for employment (Vulliamy, 2011). Rebuilding infrastructure dedicated to commerce makes economic sense: Haitian city dwellers rely on local markets (distinguished here as commercial activity rather than the physical structure) to access goods and services and meet their basic needs (Sanderson and Knox Clarke, 2012; Sokpoh et al., 2014), underlining that 'cash and markets are essential to urban livelihoods' (Kyazze et al., 2012: 25). This view is illustrated by one vendor from the arts and crafts hall, who in an interview said, 'When you build a market, I like that. You build jobs. I lost my job when it burnt' (Smith, 2011: 56).

Commerce of course is not new: while city dwellers take part in the complex, vibrant and fragmented Haitian economy seeking formal jobs or offering goods and services in local markets (Bailey, 2014; Fan, 2012), statistics show how challenging it is to successfully make a living in Haiti's local economy. Eighty percent of Haitians live in poverty, more than 40 percent are unemployed and more than two-thirds rely on the informal economy (Clermont et al., 2011; CIA, 2014). Every need has a price and thus it is not surprising that earning cash through petty trade or employment is a primary activity among Haitian city dwellers.

Another way to understand the importance of access to livelihoods and local markets is the urban poor's prioritization of proximity to livelihood opportunities even if that means worse housing conditions and neighborhood services (Fan, 2012) and lack of access to credit due to an absence of land title (Sherwood et al., 2014).

Of course, rebuilding a single commercial place after disaster does not necessarily mean successfully rebuilding commerce. In the case of the Iron Market the short-term impact on the local economy seems limited. Merchants face constant and important economic difficulties (St Juste, 2013). Two years after the earthquake, working at the Iron Market was not yet profitable for all vendors. The most obvious reason may be that customers remained scarce. This might be related to the type and variety of products vendors are (to a certain extent) limited to sell, which might not match with what buyers demand or can afford. To illustrate, arts and crafts products may essentially be dedicated to the tourism industry, which still has a long way to go before being vibrant (Nagle Myers, 2015; Thomson, 2014; Nelson, 2014). This precarious situation beyond the physical structure itself has inevitably had an impact on vendors' livelihoods, leading to reduced household income.

While the majority of the interviewees[1] appreciate the practical advantages of renting a stall at the Market such as adequately protecting the merchandise from weather conditions and thieves, being able to store goods in-place during the night and accessing water and waste services, they consider the renting price too high for the little profit they make. 'I'm satisfied but it's too expensive,' said a female vendor in the botanica section. In other words the price may be seen as fair for the services they get, but vendors struggle to pay the rent. 'We are afraid of being expelled' stated a female vendor in the food section, scared of the long-term consequence this might imply.

As a result many vendors rely on informal or formal support such as micro-credit schemes and, more importantly according to them, on social solidarity (i.e. lending and borrowing) to be able to pay weekly rents. These friendships based on proximity in the Market are a vital source of help. For many, solidarity appears to be more important than competition among vendors as a means of survival. One group of women in the market's food section said that they were constantly helping each other financially. Even this may, however, not be enough in the long term; as one interviewee stated, 'Everyone is on the verge of bankruptcy. We can no longer help each other here.'

In order to improve the economic situation of the Market, the city center (the former economic hub of the country) needs other economically focused projects to tackle root causes of its economic decline. The city center of Port-au-Prince used to be an important place for business but had started to deteriorate before the earthquake struck (Noel, 2013), which then damaged the city center to such an extent that the vast majority of remaining formal vendors – known as 'les grands magasins et entrepôts' – moved to the suburbs, reshaping the economic map of the capital city (Sherwood et al., 2014; Noel, 2013). With the loss of formal and bigger businesses, the center of Port-au-Prince is (for now at least) deprived of its economic power of attraction that informal vendors capitalize upon.

To this day, the development prospects of the city center are unclear. While urban planners, entrepreneurs and politicians agree on the importance of regenerating the city center, formal reconstruction there is slower than in other parts of the city. Formal merchants wishing to rebuild the commercial city say their initiatives are 'repressed' by land title issues, mortgage loan problems and lack of security needed to protect their investment (Alphonse, 2014; Noel, 2013). Additionally, plans to rebuild this part of the city are tied to political agendas: expropriation and urban plans significantly change over the years in terms of size and content due to pressure of different groups of interests, different political visions and previous irregularities being revealed and addressed (Noel, 2013). Notwithstanding these challenges, demolition of remaining buildings within a selected dedicated zone is underway and investments are expected to take place in the near future if the political will remains stable (SL/Haiti Libre, 2014). It is hoped that in the long term the return of public administration will create a 'critical mass' to lead to the recovery of the city center (Dumas, 2014).

Improving work environments

Surprisingly perhaps, while vendors at the Iron Market make a low income, they stay to benefit from the relatively good working conditions. This contrasts with the surrounding crowded streets, perceived to yield more profit but where vendors work in very difficult and unsecure environments (see Plate 29): 'people sell more on the streets but here we feel secure,' said a female vendor in the food section. The Iron Market vendors benefit from a safe, spacious, clean and comfortable working environment which also offers access to water and to controversial but much needed pay-per-use restroom facilities. The environment reduces health and violence threats but provides limited financial benefits. More than a decent communal space, the reconstructed Iron Market also provides an improvement through defining vendors' personal space (see Plate 30). Under the Market's roofs, retail space is equally and clearly divided between vendors which improves subsequently the quality of relationships within the vendor community, 'We have more space; so less problems. We are not stuck. Everyone has his own space,' confirmed a vendor working in the North Hall. While the competition for commercial space had caused conflicting situations in the past, an equal distribution of the space now has helped vendors maintain good relations with their colleagues and thus improved their useful social assets. A crucial level of solidarity takes place and helps vendors to sustain themselves throughout constant difficult economic times, for instance as noted earlier securing rental payments by redistributing individual earnings. The social atmosphere is thus much better now than it used to be. As one vendor noted, 'All the vendors, we are a family.' Venders in the Market on the whole liked the new environment, 'It is very pleasant here. We are well,' noted a female vendor in the food section. 'Look at this! It's a palace! I own a palace!' said an arts and crafts male vendor.

Informal markets next to the Iron Market

It is important to note that the working conditions and the strong sense of belonging is limited to the users of the Iron Market, mostly the market venders themselves, and does not appear to extend to the neighboring street community. The difficult working conditions in the streets, described as 'inhuman' by many street vendors, persist. The neighboring street vendors feel they have not really benefited from the Market's reconstruction. 'It's not for us, it's for them,' expressed a neighboring female vendor. Nevertheless she and her neighboring counterparts working in the street markets insisted on the significance of and the aspiration for such an exemplary environment.

While much of the aid community focus internationally for post-disaster urban reconstruction tends to be on domestic living conditions, the Iron Market project highlights the importance of considering working conditions and their potential for recovery. Indeed, the scope of urban recovery should be enlarged to consider a more complete and realistic urban way of living, moving from a rural or suburban vision of living conditions towards including more central or strategic working spaces. Most of the cash-based livelihood activities occur outside the homes, at street markets or more formal places. Too often unconsidered within the Haitian recovery discourse – informal markets have been rarely mentioned in recent reports – these urban spaces (see Plate 31) form a vital part of urban life that have a 'particularly large bearing on living conditions' (Gehl, 2010: 217). Considering work environments is also a way of understanding the need to address various urban forms of living, a need highlighted in one specialist report drawing lessons from urban post-disaster relief and recovery operations (Sanderson and Knox Clarke, 2012). The Iron Market is a powerful example of the centrality of working conditions not only to achieve a dignified and healthy life but also to develop personal and community assets.

Learning from the private sector in urban disaster recovery

In addition to the urban physical and economic work context, the case of the Iron Market also demonstrates the crucial role the private sector can play as a driver of post-disaster reconstruction projects that offer much needed jobs and adequate working environments. While the slow pace of the reconstruction in Haiti has been criticized in local and international press and in independent expert reports (Reitman, 2011; Granitz, 2014; Olivier, 2014; Clermont et al., 2011), there may be additional lessons to learn from the private sector's engagement in Haiti.

The business sector has been seen as a significant player given its contribution to constructing structures that enhance economic development (Reitman, 2011; William J. Clinton Foundation, 2011). The Iron Market project shows the private sector can bring considerable financial investments into reconstruction and recovery as well as management and technical expertise. In this way, entrepreneurs can and should be seen as important actors in providing jobs and work environments, especially in urban environments. Without Digicel's financial contribution, it is unlikely that the Iron Market would have been rebuilt.

The private sector brings more than just money to the table, offering technical expertise of critical importance given the complexity of post-disaster urban environments. The private sector can use its expertise in subcontracting work to planning, architecture and engineering professionals and using experienced entrepreneurs (Sanderson and Knox Clarke, 2012). In the case of the Iron Market, although the strategy raises other questions, the development company outsourced many of the most significant construction tasks to external international companies such as hiring professionals and building the new prefabricated structure, preferring a high level of efficiency of the construction process over investing more (in the short term at least) in the local economy. While the project used locally available expertise (for example masonry, restoration work and supervision), the strict schedule imposed by the donor may have limited much needed long-term development and financial support of a local construction industry.

Large successful private companies could also be helpful in implementing human resource and management structures that could strengthen the Market in the long term. With the Iron Market, Digicel committed to finance, manage and maintain the Market for the immediate future (Duval, 2011). While some might critique the corporate model of private sector actors engaging in philanthropic 'do-gooding' (for instance see Sontag, 2012 and Lazare, 2013) the Iron Market indicates that there can be some positive outcomes.

The Market's governance structure has directly and positively impacted vendors. The efforts to clarify and formalize the spatial distribution of commercial space have also been reflected in the implementation of a new management structure (see Figure 10.5). On the one hand it gives vendors an opportunity to be represented by elected members who address relevant issues with the Market managers (perceived as Digicel) and on the other hand allows the managers to efficiently govern the Market, for example to collect rent payments. This structure has significantly increased workers' levels of influence on decisions that affect them such that the apparent privatization of the Iron Market has not necessarily reduced the power of the vendors. Indeed this is even more evident when contrasted with the level of influence the neighboring street vendors have on improving their working conditions. Democratic representation alongside an equal distribution of commercial space has helped prevent unfair arrangements and potential conflicts that could have darkened the image of the Market.

The Market vendors' sense of belonging is strongly associated with the work and social environment they enjoy from renting a stall at the Market. They use the physical and managerial structures in their best interests and improve their assets. More precisely, however, the involvement of the vendor community is in fact restricted to the commercial space (see Figure 10.6). It is important not to overstate the level of participation. The management structure does not seem to provide involvement in other 'meaningful' activities other than the 'necessary' ones, such as cultural events and social gatherings for passers-by and local vendors (see Gehl, 1996 in Carmona et al., 2010).

The central part of the Iron Market, which is also the most architecturally significant section, is occasionally used for special occasions. Such events, some visible in national and international media, that have taken place at the Market (for example the

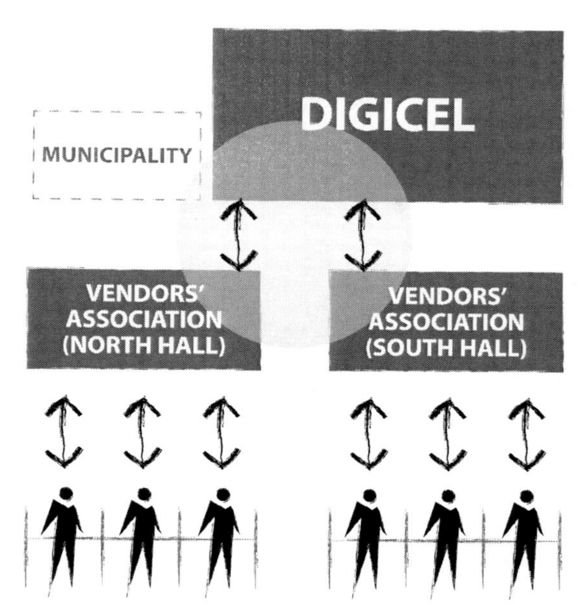

Figure 10.5 The governance structure as perceived
Source: Smith (2011)

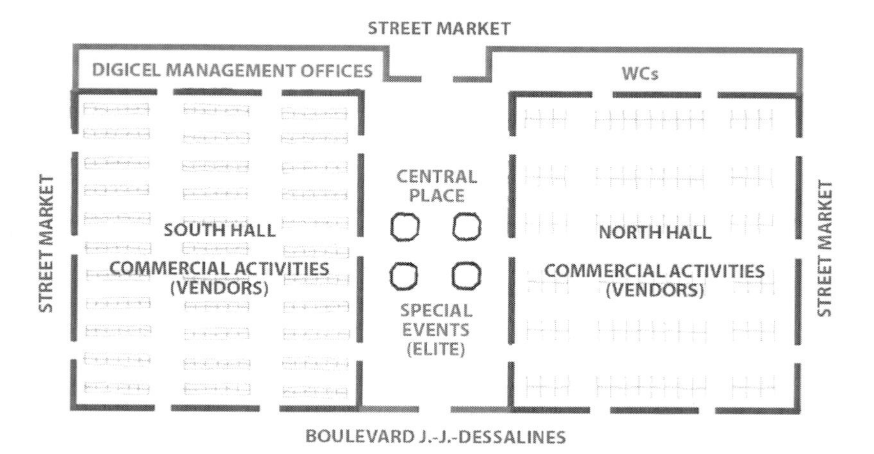

Figure 10.6 A socio-spatial segregation
Source: the author

opening ceremony and the president's tribute to Haitian artists, see Figure 10.7) have been organized for dignitaries, politicians and philanthropists without really involving the local working community. Many vendors from the Iron Market and the neighboring workers were prevented from attending. Remembering the event, one vendor stated, 'All the gates were closed,' while another lamented she was 'not invited.' Those who were selected and present at the events were kept aside, 'It wasn't fair; it was a party for Haitian artists and guests. It was for the honour of the president. It was not for us,' expressed another vendor from the North Hall.

Figure 10.7 The physical setting of one special event in 2011, at the central place
Source: Smith (2011)

This situation consequently creates a division between the commercial space designated for local vendors and the symbolic space that serves the political or marketing purposes of the elite, showing a problematic side to the philanthropic implications of private businesses in rebuilding previously collective infrastructures, 'Are you talking about the marché Digicel (Digicel Market)?' asked one vendor in the neighboring streets, literally making the link. The symbolic image of the Market's reconstruction has thus been implicitly claimed by those who contributed to its reconstruction, transforming people's image of the place (see Plate 32). This effect illustrates a potentially negative aspect when state-owned infrastructures are rebuilt by and in the interests of the investors. It suggests that greater attention should be paid to how vendors themselves might be included professionally and symbolically in such public events that could further improve their sense of belonging to the Market (Gehl, 2010).

Towards new approaches in urban reconstruction and recovery

The reconstruction of the Iron Market by Digicel demonstrates that a private sector company can be a powerful actor in reconstruction, with the potential to strengthen the economy and to impact working environments. Increasing collaboration between the private sector, humanitarian organizations and governments in order to scale up and better tackle the urban post-disaster recovery offers opportunities for more effective responses for the next urban disaster. To be sure, as discussed above, the dangers of privatization need to be understood, specified and addressed lest the benefits be lessened.

Notwithstanding potential benefits, the local private sector, and especially that part of it dealing with non-housing concerns, continues to be largely ignored by aid responses in urban disaster recovery. The private economic sector is rarely mentioned in humanitarian reports (see for instance IFRC, 2014; Sokpoh et al., 2014). After the Haiti earthquake only 0.1 percent of the approximately US$2.4 billion donor funding was directed towards Haitian businesses and NGOs, while the overwhelming amount went to international organizations (such as UN agencies and international NGOs), international enterprises and donors' civil and military entities (Office of the Special Envoy for Haiti, 2012, in Bailey, 2014: 7). While these statistics do not tell the whole story (cash grants and vouchers for instance given by agencies contributed to the saving and recovery of Haitian small businesses), the relative lack of private sector involvement in such large influxes of funds has probably led to missed opportunities for using humanitarian aid as investments in recovery.

How then can this be improved? One way to increase private investments in the local economy is to build more collaboration between international agencies and local enterprises. Sarah Bailey, independent consultant and research associate at the UK's Overseas Development Institute (ODI), highlights this point in her report on the role of the private sector in Haiti,

> The role of the private sector in humanitarian response tends to be a divisive topic amongst international humanitarian actors. On the one hand, the private sector is held up as offering a way of improving efficiency and promoting innovation; on the other, it is seen as a bastion of profiteering that runs counter to the humanitarian mission. International humanitarian actors often view the private sector only in its role as a supplier of goods and services and as a source of donations through philanthropy and corporate social responsibility initiatives. Moving beyond stereotypes and developing a more nuanced understanding of the possibilities and limitations of engagement between businesses and humanitarian agencies is necessary in order to take advantage of potential opportunities, and to support the markets and businesses people rely on for their livelihoods.
>
> (Bailey, 2014: 3)

Even though such collaborations are more the exception than the rule in Haiti, some have been successfully implemented. An example is cash transfer programming, involving NGOs, banks and telecommunications companies. These enterprises had 'strong commercial incentive' in implementing these channels while the NGOs needed 'safe, accountable and wide-reaching' distribution systems (Bailey, 2014). The cash directed toward people in need has then been spent in local markets. This example does not involve supporting local economic markets directly and building back better infrastructure, but it is nonetheless a partnership that has been reported successful in improving livelihoods and shelter conditions (Bailey, 2014; Sokpoh et al., 2014; Condor et al., 2013; Clermont et al., 2011). Furthermore several NGOs such as Oxfam International have started to develop and increase their engagement with the local private sector (Bailey, 2014).

It is important to acknowledge that working with the private sector and within Haiti's economic environment is complex. A few formal players control almost half of the economy and numerous informal enterprises participate in this vibrant but under-regulated sector, where corruption is endemic (Sokpoh et al., 2014). While increasing collaboration between the private sector, NGOs and local government might be an innovative way to address 'how' post-disaster urban recovery could be improved, petty trade and marketplaces in particular should also be part of 'what' to support and rebuild. These markets in Haiti, as in many poorer countries, house one of the main existing livelihood activities of urban citizens. In fact, markets seem extremely resilient in the aftermath of a disaster: Port-au-Prince's street markets were operational a few days after the earthquake despite extensive loss and damage (Clermont et al., 2011). Existing markets could form a strong economic basis upon which to build.

For now, the Iron Market stands as a unique case of an economic infrastructure being rebuilt, physically and symbolically standing alone in the devastated neighborhood. Despite its positive social and well-being impact on the vendor community, the new Iron Market does not at least for now play its past role of an economic hub. More research is therefore needed to fully understand how to support local petty trade and to rebuild economic infrastructures for strong local impact. As the Declaration of the 9th International Public Markets Conference adopted in March 2015 states,

> Today, despite their long history and numerous benefits, public markets face serious challenges due to insufficient recognition in policy, research, and funding. Many cities do not have appropriate policies or resources to invest in basic maintenance and sanitation, to expand or create new markets, or to manage public spaces effectively to integrate market activity.
>
> (PPS, 2015)

Conclusion

The case of the Iron Market should be seen as a learning ground for those involved in post-disaster urban recovery to build back better. Approaches to reconstruction by diverse agencies and organizations in these particular contexts should move towards a better consideration of the local economy that actually rules day-to-day the lives of urban citizens. The Market's inclusion of workers in governance is an important further lesson in thinking through how private aims can be partially harmonized with worker aims.

Numerous issues associated with post-disaster reconstruction have not been considered in this chapter, but four main lessons may be gleaned from this particular project. The first is the directing of reconstruction efforts towards rebuilding the local economy and developing employment as a top priority. The second is that work environments and conditions should also be considered in actions aiming to improve living conditions. Third, aid spending should be seen as an investment to be made in collaboration with the local private sector (Sanderson and Knox Clarke, 2012). Finally, merging humanitarian and entrepreneurial approaches to reconstruction provides better opportunities for urban recovery, especially if each actor's interests are recognized and respected, and if local working communities have the opportunity to grow and remain part of their city's destiny. Perhaps markets are truly good places to start rebuilding after urban disaster.

Note

1 Twenty-eight women and three men were interviewed in the Iron Market and one man and eight women in the street markets nearby.

References

Alphonse, R. (2014). *Port-au-Prince attend le retour de ses magasins.* Port-au-Prince: Le Nouvelliste. Available at: http://lenouvelliste.com/lenouvelliste/articleprint/126085.html (accessed October 15, 2014).

Bailey, S. (2014). *Humanitarian Crises, Emergency Preparedness and Response: The Role of Business and the Private Sector: A Strategy and Options Analysis of Haiti.* London: Overseas Development Institute.

Carmona, M., Tiesdell, S., Heath, T. and Oc, T. (2010). *Public Places, Urban Spaces: The Dimensions of Urban Design.* Oxford: Elsevier.

CIA (2014). *The World Factbook: Central America and Caribbean, Haiti.* Available at: www.cia.gov/library/publications/the-world-factbook/geos/ha.html (accessed October 10, 2014).

Clermont, C., Sanderson, D., Sharma, A. and Spraos, H. (2011). *Urban Disasters – Lessons from Haiti: Study of Member Agencies' Responses to the Earthquake in Port au Prince, Haiti, January 2010.* Disasters Emergency Committee (DEC).

Condor, J., Juhn, C. and Rana, R. (2013). *External Evaluation of the Rental Support Cash Grant Approach Applied to Return and Relocation Programs in Haiti.* The Wolfgroup Performance Consultants.

Davis, I. (2012). *What is the Vision for Sheltering and Housing in Haiti?: Summary Observations of Reconstruction Progress following the Haiti Earthquake of January 12th, 2010.* Available at: www.alnap.org/pool/files/1379.pdf.

Dieudonné, J. (2010). *La rénovation du Marché en fer progresse.* Port-au-Prince: Le Nouvelliste. Available at: http://lenouvelliste.com/lenouvelliste/article/81566/La-renovation-du-Marche-en-fer-progresse (accessed August 1, 2011).

Dumas, P.-R. (2014). *La cité administrative de Port-au-Prince, la cité de la reconstruction.* Port-au-Prince: Le Nouvelliste. Available at: http://lenouvelliste.com/lenouvelliste/article/134703/La-cite-administrative-de-Port-au-Prince-la-cite-de-la-reconstruction (accessed October 10, 2014).

Duval, F. (2011). *Haïti: Le Marché en fer rouvre ses portes ce lundi, la Digicel a déjà d'autres projets au centre-ville.* Port-au-Prince: Le Nouvelliste. Available at: http://www.lenouvelliste.com/article.php?PubID=1&ArticleID=88452 (accessed August 10, 2011).

Fan, L. (2012). Shelter strategies, humanitarian praxis and critical urban theory post-crisis reconstruction. *Disasters* 36: S64–S86.

Forbes, P. (2011). *From Haiti's Ashes.* BBC2.

Galilee, B. (2011). Haiti Iron Market: one year after the eathquake, the first large-scale building of the city has been restored with a project by John McAslan + Partners. *Domus.* Available at: www.domusweb.it/en/architecture/haiti-iron-market/ (accessed May 5, 2011).

Gehl, J. (2010). *Cities for People.* Washington, DC: Island Press.

Granitz, P. (2014). Four years after earthquake, many in Haiti remain displaced. *NPR.* Available at: www.npr.org/2014/01/12/261723409/four-years-after-earthquake-many-in-haiti-remain-displaced (accessed October 15, 2014).

IFRC (2014). *Haiti Earthquake: Four-Year Progress Report.* Geneva: International Federation of Red Cross and Red Crescent Societies.

ISPAN (2010a). Centre historique de Port-au-Prince, l'image révélée. *Bulletin de l'ISPAN*, 17.

ISPAN (2010b) La restauration du Marché Hyppolite a débuté. *Bulletin de l'ISPAN*, 13.

ISPAN (2011). Le Marché Hyppolite renait de ses cendres. *Bulletin de l'ISPAN*, 20.

Knox Clarke, P. and Ramalingam, B. (2012). *Meeting the Urban Challenge: Adapting Humanitarian Efforts to an Urban World*. ALNAP meeting paper. London: ALNAP/ODI.

Kyazze, A.B., Baizan, P. and Carpenter, S. (2012). *Learning from the City: British Red Cross Learning Project Scoping Study*. London: British Red Cross.

Lazare, S. (2013). *Clintons' Pet Project for Privatized 'Aid' to Haiti Stealing Workers' Wages: Report*. Common Dreams. Available at: commondreams.org/news/2013/10/16/clintons-pet-project-privatized-aid-haiti-stealing-workerswages-report (accessed October 10, 2014).

Léger, J.N. (1907). *Haiti: Her History and Her Detractors*. New York: The Neale.

Mone, J. (2011). *Haiti's Iron Market Reopens*. Associated Press.

Nagle Myers, G. (2015). Post-earthquake efforts improving Haiti's tourism prospects. *Travel Weekly*. Available at: www.travelweekly.com/Caribbean-Travel/Post-earthquake-efforts-improving-Haiti-tourism-prospects (accessed April 1, 2015).

Nelson, D. (2014). In Haiti, beauty that plays hard to get (to). *The New York Times*. Available at: www.nytimes.com/2014/02/16/travel/in-haiti-beauty-that-plays-hard-to-get-to.html (accessed April 1, 2015).

Noel, R. (2013). *Les défis de la reconstruction du centre-ville de Port-au-Prince*. Groupe URD. Available at: www.urd.org/Les-defis-de-la-reconstruction-du (accessed March 25, 2015).

Olivier, L.-J. (2014). *L'Etat absent du centre-ville de Port-au-Prince*. Port-au-Prince: Le Nouvelliste. Available at: http://lenouvelliste.com/lenouvelliste/article/129341/LEtat-absent-du-centre-ville-de-Port-au-Prince.html (accessed October 10, 2014).

PPS (2015). *Declaration of the 9th International Public Markets Conference – Barcelona, Spain*. Project for Public Spaces. Available at: www.pps.org/blog/sign-the-declaration-promote-healthy-public-markets-for-all/ (accessed April 1, 2015).

Reitman, J. (2011). Beyond relief: how the world failed Haiti. *Rolling Stone*. Available at: www.rollingstone.com/politics/news/how-the-world-failed-haiti-20110804 (accessed August 10, 2011).

Ryan, R. (2011). The rebirth of Port-au-Prince's historic Iron Market. *The Architectural Review*. Available at: www.architectural-review.com/essays/the-rebirth-of-port-au-princes-historic-iron-market/8614230.article (accessed October 10, 2014).

Sanderson, D. and Knox Clarke, P. (2012). Responding to urban disasters: Learning from previous relief and recovery operations. ALNAP Lessons Paper. London: ALNAP/ODI.

Schaeffer Brown, E. (2015). Haiti: The locals attacked us because they thought we were the doctors who'd promised to return. *The Guardian*. Available at: www.theguardian.com/sustainable-business/2015/jan/12/haiti-earthquake-business-charity-social-enterprise (accessed April 1, 2015).

Sherwood, A., Bradley, M., Rossi, L., Gitau, R. and Mellicker, B. (2014). *Supporting Durable Solutions to Urban, Post-Disaster Displacement: Challenges and Opportunities in Haiti*. Brookings Institution and International Organization for Migration.

SL/Haiti Libre. (2014). Haiti – Reconstruction: the demolition of the area of public utility, began in Port-au-Prince. *Haiti Libre*. Available at: www.haitilibre.com/en/news-11287-haiti-reconstruction-the-demolition-of-the-area-of-public-utility-began-in-port-au-prince.html (accessed October 19, 2014).

Smith, D. (2011). *Learning from the Marche Hyppolite, Port-au-Prince, Haiti: An Assessment of the Philanthropic Reconstruction of an Urban Place*. Master of Arts in Development and Emergency Practice Dissertation. Oxford Brookes University.

Sokpoh, B., Groupe URD and Carpenter, S. (2014). *Urban Livelihoods Recovery: Lessons from Port-au-Prince, Haiti*. London: British Red Cross.

Sontag, D. (2012). Earthquake relief where Haiti wasn't broken. *The New York Times*. Available at: www.nytimes.com/2012/07/06/world/americas/earthquake-relief-where-haiti-wasnt-broken.html?_r=0 (accessed March 25, 2015).

St Juste, E. (2013). *Une fin d'année malheureuse pour les petits commerçants*. Port-au-Prince: Le Nouvelliste. Available at: http://lenouvelliste.com/lenouvelliste/article/125616/Une-fin-dannee-malheureuse-pour-les-petits (accessed October 10, 2014).

Thomson, I. (2014). Haiti returns to the tourist map. *The Telegraph*. Available at: www.telegraph.co.uk/travel/destinations/centralamericaandcaribbean/10988666/Haiti-returns-to-the-tourist-map.html (accessed October 10, 2014).

Vulliamy, E. (2011). How an Irish telecoms tycoon became Haiti's only hope of salvation. *The Guardian*. Available at: www.theguardian.com/world/2011/jan/09/haiti-anniversary-denis-obrien-vulliamy (accessed August 10, 2011).

WHS (2015a). *The Power of Business in Emergencies*. World Humanitarian Summit. Available at: www.worldhumanitariansummit.org/whs_business (accessed March 25, 2015).

WHS (2015b). *Urban Discussions*. World Humanitarian Summit. Available at: www.worldhumanitariansummit.org/whs_urban# (accessed March 25, 2015).

William J. Clinton Foundation. (2011). *Haiti Relief and Recovery*. Available at: www.clintonfoundation.org/haiti_longstanding/haiti_earthquakerecovery.php (accessed August 10, 2011).

Chapter 11

Using disaster insurance to build urban resilience

Lessons from micro-enterprise in India

Mihir Bhatt and Ronak Patel

Introduction

Due to the combination of high exposure to natural hazards and a rapidly developing economy, leading to quick urban growth with high vulnerability, India experiences significant economic losses caused by disasters. While disaster insurance for large business enterprises is available and utilized, a vast majority of micro-enterprises – a significant sector of urban economies – lacks information and access to such products. India's Finance Minister said in his 2014–2015 budget speech that 'a large proportion of India's population is without insurance of any kind – health, accidental or life' (Jaitely, 2015). According to the Insurance Regulatory and Development Authority (IRDA) of India, insurance penetration (the premium collected by Indian insurers) was only 3.96 percent of GDP in the financial year 2012–2013 and per capita premium underwritten (insurance density) in India during FY 2012–2013 was US$53.2 (IRDA, 2013–2014). Indeed, 'insurance penetration has grown from 2.3 percent (1.8 percent life and 0.7 percent non-life) in 2000 to 3.9 percent (3.1 percent life and 0.8 percent non-life) in 2013 (Economic Survey of India, 2015: 48). This progress is relatively small in terms of the available opportunities and need in the country.

A study in 2007 by the United Nations Development Programme (UNDP) on micro-insurance demand in the country estimated that the market size could include up to 70 percent of those earning US$1–2 a day (UNDP, 2007: 2). Progressive insurance regulation in India also mandates that insurers enter the low-income market and carry such clients on their portfolio. The insurance regulatory authority guides insurance companies to address the needs of what is called the 'weaker section' of society, that is, the poor and vulnerable. Despite such huge market potential and supportive regulations, coverage of insurable losses in India remains low. Although disaster insurance facilities are made available to the agricultural sector of India, mainstreaming risk transfer mechanisms for housing and other businesses remains a challenge (GOI, 2010: 22) for the government and private sector.

Urban risk

In India 85 percent of the land is vulnerable to one or multiple hazards and most cities are located on hazardous terrains. For example, about 60 cities with populations exceeding half a million are located within India's risk designated zones III, IV and V where severe impact of an earthquake is possible (NIDM, 2013: 42–43). Moreover, 53 Indian cities have a population of more than a million (2011 Census) and 25 of these cities are in the coastal states (TERI, 2014: 5) which make them extremely susceptible to climate risk. In a global list of cities facing the highest climate change risk in the coming decades the Indian metropolis Kolkata is ranked seventh, Mumbai eighth and Delhi twentieth (Indian Express, 2012). Cities such as Chennai, Ahmedabad and Bangalore with substantial public-private investments and population growth are also expected to suffer from adverse impacts from naturally induced disasters and climate extremes in the future.

The intensity of disasters and damage is usually very high in urban areas; of late, there has been an alarming increase in such disasters (Ministry of Home Affairs, 2009: 18). According to the National Institute of Urban Affairs (NIUA), the substantial increase in extreme precipitation (similar to Mumbai in 2005 and the 2005 and 2006 Gujarat flood events) expected over a large area of the west coast and central India will require a significant revision of urban planning practices across city and neighborhood scales to integrate flood, climate change mitigation and adaptation measures into day-to-day urban development and service delivery activities (NIUA, 2013).

Exposure and sensitivity to hazards in urban India is aggravated by high population density, concentration of economic activities, poor living conditions, unsafe housing, inadequate infrastructure and the lack of essential services in key areas of health, water and sanitation. The world's growing population is concentrating in urban centers (Brown, 2012). Global risk is increasing due to people moving to earthquake, storm and flood prone areas in cities that cannot safely accommodate such growth, leaving their populations highly vulnerable (The Press Office, 2013). Two distinct but intertwined trends in the twenty-first century – urbanization and the increasing severity of disasters with greater numbers of people affected – are leading to increasing economic losses as well.

At present, about 31 percent of India's population (around 380 million people) live in urban areas and this will increase to about 600 million by 2030 (Planning Commission, 2013: 34). There is an emerging concern about several Indian cities becoming more vulnerable to disasters on account of unsafe construction to meet this demand (Planning Commission, 2011: 72). High concentrations of people in cities also make urban areas more vulnerable to terrorism as well as industrial hazards. Because urban areas in India contribute to 60 percent of the Gross Domestic Product (GDP) of the country and this contribution is expected to grow to 75–80 percent by 2030 (TERI, 2014: 2), it is imperative for India to protect urban development from disaster risk.

Economic impact of disasters

Each year, India suffers disaster losses totaling just under US$1 billion, according to a World Bank study (Lester and Gurenko, 2003). On average, direct disaster losses amount to 2 percent of India's GDP and up to 12 percent of central government revenues. These estimates do not fully include losses incurred by informal sector businesses and workers, which constitute a major proportion of the growing urban economy in India. The Calamity Relief Fund (CRF) of the government of India on average spends US$286 million annually towards providing relief for those affected by disasters. Over the past 35 years, India has suffered direct losses of US$30 billion, and the pace of losses is increasing: US$9 billion in direct losses were suffered between 1996 and 2000 alone (Lester and Gurenko, 2003: 5).

Naturally induced disasters and climate extremes pose a serious threat to the socio-economic gains of developing and least-developed countries. It is estimated that a warming of the world's climate by two degrees Celsius could lead to a global economic loss of between 1 and 2 percent of GDP, but in Asia's middle- and low-income countries these losses could be as high as 6 percent of GDP (ADB, 2013: xi). Extreme weather events with likely links to climate change are leading to direct losses of jobs and incomes (ILO, 2013: xii), not just in the agriculture sector but other areas of economic activity as well. With limited capacity to cope with natural hazard-induced disasters and climate extremes, micro-enterprises – which play an important role in providing services and employment to the urban poor – tend to be disproportionately affected by disasters by way of damage or loss of assets, infrastructure, service capacity, and eventually, client base.

Risk governance

The government of India has designed various legal policy frameworks for mitigation and preparedness during and after naturally induced disasters (Save the Children, 2006). In 2005 a legal institutional framework was developed based on the provision of the 2005 Disaster Management Act across the country which provides for an elaborate system of disaster risk management at the national, state and city levels.

In this structure, the National Disaster Management Authority (NDMA) is responsible for formulating policy and guidelines for all disaster management work in the country. The state authorities further lay down the guidelines for departments of the state and the districts falling in their respective jurisdictions. Similarly, district authorities direct the civil administration, departments and local authorities such as the municipalities, police department and civil administration. Typical city level disaster risk reduction activities include preparation of city/district disaster management and resilience plans and the implementation of various projects funded by national and state governments.

However, not much emphasis has been put on promoting risk transfer mechanisms. A number of obstacles impede making risk transfer mechanisms available to the most vulnerable and poor. Current risk transfer mechanisms in India have two major funding approaches for disaster relief and rehabilitation efforts; one, the CRF, managed by India's states; and two, the National Calamity Contingency Fund (NCCF), in which the central government supports states in case of calamities that exceed the capacity of the state government to manage financially. While the government of India has put much emphasis on promotion of life, health and agriculture insurance, disaster insurance coverage for meeting catastrophic losses from natural hazards and climate extremes is not yet promoted at a scale that makes a difference. A lack of data and feasibility studies comes across as one of the major hindrances in promoting risk transfer approaches in India. Even the 13th Finance Commission recognized the importance of risk transfer mechanisms for funding disaster-related expenditures in India, but refrained from making any recommendations on account of the prevailing low insurance penetration and operational issues (Singh, 2013).

Case study: the All India Disaster Mitigation Institute's (AIDMI) experiences of implementing the Afat Vimo (disaster insurance) scheme

AIDMI is a registered non-governmental organization based in Ahmedabad in the state of Gujarat. It is a community-based action planning, action research and advocacy organization, working towards bridging the gap between policy, practice and research related to disaster mitigation. Established after the 1987–1989 Gujarat droughts, AIDMI has expanded its work over the years to cover nine types of disasters in 12 areas of India and beyond to eight countries in Asia. AIDMI strives to link local communities to national and international levels of risk reduction, relief and long-term recovery policies and programs. As an operational and learning organization, AIDMI works towards promoting disaster risk mitigation and adaptation to climate change risk by supporting, capturing, processing and disseminating disaster-related information, lessons and innovative ideas as well as conducting stakeholder roundtables, trainings of trainers, reviews, evaluations and pilot projects. Since its establishment AIDMI has worked in different areas of disaster mitigation including risk reduction, knowledge management, innovations in disaster response and recovery and policy advocacy, covering 37 cities and 52 districts.

Following the 2001 Gujarat earthquake, AIDMI found that a majority of relief beneficiaries were still exposed to significant disaster-induced financial losses. The 2001 Gujarat earthquake, measuring 6.9 on the Richter scale, was the third largest and second most destructive earthquake in India over the last two centuries (GSDMA, nd). According to the government of India the earthquake killed 19,727, injured 166,000 and left 600,000 people homeless, with 348,000 homes destroyed and 844,000 damaged (Sinha, 2001). In terms of economic impact, of the estimated Rs 9,900 crore (US$2.1 billion) total asset losses, Rs 7,400 crore (US$1.6 billion) were private assets (World Bank et al., 2001: viii). While the districts of Kutch, Surendranagar and Radhanpur were the most severely affected, widespread damage was also reported from the cities of Rajkot, Jamnagar, Surendranagar, Patan and Ahmedabad districts. The cities of Bjuj, Anjar, Bhachau and Raper were worst affected by the earthquake in the Kutch region.

A 2002 survey in Gujarat revealed that access to insurance was correlated with sustainable economic recovery among those affected by the earthquake. The survey was conducted in September 2003 within 14 earthquake-affected slum communities in Bhuj, Gujarat. The survey provided information on what percentage of the population already had insurance (only 2 percent) and how many respondents were interested in taking out a policy in the future (7 percent) (AIDMI, 2006: 8). Based on this finding, AIDMI designed a micro-insurance scheme to augment its ongoing livelihood relief activities. The resultant scheme was the product of discussions and negotiations with insurance providers who were interested in supplying low-premium insurance policies to poor clients. Two regulated Indian insurers were invited to underwrite the *Afat Vimo* (Gujarati for disaster insurance) scheme. The Life Insurance Corporation of India covered life and the United India Insurance Company provided coverage for the non-life assets of the plan.

In 2004, AIDMI became the first agency in India to design such a combination of life and non-life disaster insurance product for disaster victims through public insurance companies with support from the global network the ProVention Consortium.[1] The *Afat Vimo* scheme covering 19 types of disasters was first piloted in Gujarat in 2004 and was later extended to the 2004 Indian Ocean tsunami victims in Tamil Nadu, 2005 earthquake victims in Jammu and Kashmir and 2007–2008 Koshi floods victims in Bihar. In 2011, the pilot scheme was extended to the flood and cyclone victims in Odisha through the Society for Women Action Development (SWAD) with support from the European Union in partnership with the NGO Concern Worldwide India. The pilot projects implemented were linked with recovery and disaster preparedness, especially in climatic hotspots where climatic hazards occur frequently, for example 2013's Cyclone Phailin and 2014's Cyclone Hudhud in Odisha. The need and demand increased in urban areas due to extreme events which, although not widespread, severely impacted local urban areas. In the town of Puri in coastal Odisha and the city of Bhubaneswar near the coast insurance benefits were available and when payments were received, money was used to restock businesses and to rebuild shops or buy new assets.

The *Afat Vimo* scheme protects its clients (micro-enterprises) from the impacts of hazards on their livelihoods and assets by providing pre-determined cash payouts after a disaster. This is carried out in return for monthly premiums, which are paid to the insurance companies through AIDMI. By bundling several hazards in one contract, premiums paid for better understood hazards such as floods and cyclones further help to reduce the effective premium rates for less predictable and lower frequency ones such as earthquakes. The scheme covers damages or losses on a very wide range of natural hazards including but not limited to earthquakes, floods and cyclones, being struck by lightning and landslides (19 types of hazard in total). The most recent *Afat Vimo* package offered in the Indian state of Odisha has the risk coverage shown in Figure 11.1.

Current purchasers of the scheme include small business owners (for example those with small grocery, confectionary or snack stalls), small vendors (such as those with hand carts selling vegetables, fruits and plastic utensils), home-based workers (such as those operating sewing machines, preparing ready-made clothes and weaving products) and landless laborers (for example construction workers and small-scale plumbers, carpenters and barbers).

Vulnerable families are underserved by mainstream insurance, especially laborers and micro-enterprise owners. *Afat Vimo* makes some progress in bringing together insurance providers and livelihood recovery support in times of disaster. *Afat Vimo* is a partner-agent micro-insurance model, where poor communities and commercial and public insurance companies cooperate. The role of AIDMI in the *Afat Vimo* scheme is that of both facilitator and intermediary. At present AIDMI does not serve as an agent or collect a commission. The scheme is promoted in areas where AIDMI or its partner NGO or community-based organization has ongoing community development work. This uniquely designed operational feature allows this product to reach the most vulnerable and poor, making it effective in urban areas with marginalized populations.

The *Afat Vimo* team compiles a list of potential candidates for the scheme based on their registered demands. Once the insurance companies have designed their insurance policies and premiums have been set, AIDMI or the partner reconfirms the beneficiaries on the list and ensures that all of the requisite information has been collected, organized and passed on to the insurance companies. Details of policyholders are stored in a database and premiums are paid to the insurance companies on behalf of the beneficiaries, ensuring immediate coverage. Subsequently the Afat Vimo team or partners begin to collect the premiums from the beneficiaries. The process is effective but time consuming and costly,

Figure 11.1 Risk coverage from *Afat Vimo* offered in the state of Odisha

Scheme components	*Amount*
Maximum liability for lost life	Rs. 35,000 (US$560)
Maximum liability for damage to house	Rs. 30,000 (US$480)
Maximum liability for damage to house contents	Rs. 30,000 (US$480)
Maximum liability for stock-in-trade	Rs. 15,000 (US$240)
Maximum liability for personal accident	Rs. 25,000 (US$400)
Total coverage	Rs. 135,000 (US$2160)
Total premium (non-life) yearly	Rs. 135 (US$2.16)
Total premium (life)[2]	Varies based on the age

especially when renewal is optional. If and when disaster strikes, the beneficiary immediately informs the *Afat Vimo* team or partners of the occurrence and the team responds quickly to assist beneficiaries in processing the claim.

Following the 2013 cyclone Phailin in Odisha, 165 clients were affected, facing loss and damage. The claims were registered to the relevant insurance company. An AIDMI study showed that people affected by Cyclone Phailin who received a claim settlement amount due to their enrolment with *Afat Vimo* recovered faster, while other non-clients had to cope with the economic loss and damage by using parts of their savings, borrowing money from self-help groups, private money lenders and relatives and from relief aid (AIDMI, 2014: 4). The study utilized a qualitative approach and collected data in the form of 150 semi-structured interviews with clients and non-clients in 13 villages in the Puri district of Odisha.

Discussion: building resilience through insurance

There is plenty of empirical evidence that risk transfer mechanisms can help build resilience. Both the Hyogo Framework for Action (HFA) 2005–2015 as well as the Sendai Framework for Disaster Risk Reduction, adopted in 2015, have identified risk transfer as one of the key priorities for governments and civil society. AIDMI's work has been instrumental in capturing such empirical evidence from the ground. A participatory review of AIDMI's work on *Afat Vimo* in January 2007 found that it was clearly welcomed by clients and there was demand to extend it (AIDMI, 2007). Schemes such as *Afat Vimo*, a financial tool for risk sharing, reduces the policyholders' underlying risks and offers financial protection. Moreover they can build resilience to future shocks when policyholders are supported with micro-mitigation measures such as fire safety, seismic-safe construction practices and business development support.

Another recent client impact evaluation of disaster insurance schemes led by AIDMI with support from the ProVention Consortium and the International Institute for Applied Systems Analysis (IIASA) in 2010 covering Bangladesh, India and Sri Lanka showed interest in and willingness to pay for disaster micro-insurance programs.[3] The study found that products are now beginning to reach poor clients, many of whom live below the poverty line, are highly indebted and employ limited and problematic coping mechanisms after disasters. The study signaled high demand for disaster micro-insurance after non-insured clients had been given information showing the relevance and pricing of such products as well as the power of organizations to reach more clients simply through outreach. An overwhelming majority (80 percent) of clients felt that disaster micro-insurance should be promoted to others while only a minority (2.3 percent) thought it should not. The study concluded that the key to an effective program lies in better awareness and information: even non-insured clients showed interest after receiving information on the product, benefits and pricing.

Like many forms of social security measures, including micro-insurance, *Afat Vimo* offers several advantages. Micro-insurance can be a transparent means of providing compensation against damage. Additionally, micro-insurance offers those affected by disaster a more dignified means to cope with disasters than relying on the generosity of donors after disaster strikes (Mechler et al., 2006). Experience shows that the growth of a micro-insurance scheme such as Afat Vimo can be attributed to its affordable premium and simple administrative arrangements. Such arrangements put insurance within the reach of those who otherwise would not be able to access conventional insurance. Similarly the program has had a great deal of success in the prompt settlement of claims which has translated into client satisfaction and a good relationship with the insurance companies. Observing prompt payouts and the satisfaction of clients is the chief driver of demand among those that do not possess insurance.

The AIDMI experience suggests that the convergence of micro-mitigation measures with micro-insurance and micro-credit is important for the sustainability and success of such schemes on the ground. 'Efforts to establish discounts in insurance premiums as incentives for risk reduction have not been viably demonstrated in ways that preserve the base affordability of the microinsurance' (O'Donnell, 2009: 12). Mitigation measures such as interest free loans for livelihoods following the first infusion of livelihood relief, retrofitting support for housing (both financial and technical), installation of fire extinguishers (especially in communities residing in thatched roof or wooden houses), use of cash transfers for creating vital community infrastructure and capacity building for insurance clients with regard to key risk reduction concepts such as drought proofing, disaster resistance construction, early warning and first aid have all been extremely well received at the community levels, but have not been entirely successful in convincing insurance providers to offer differentiations in premium amounts. To allow this to happen at a larger scale more effort needs to be made to bring together disaster risk reduction authorities and insurance regulators. A further concern exists: 'Because *Afat Vimo* does not adjust premiums to reward risk-reducing behaviour, this may introduce a moral hazard in the sense that clients may not take cost effective preventive measures' (Microinsurance Network, 2010). Some incidents of this moral hazard, such as not taking preventive measures before cyclones or floods to protect weakened housing or to protect food grains from flood waters, have been reported. Involvement of beneficiaries, however, and appropriate training and certification requirements from local authorities have proved very useful in minimizing such behaviour.

Next steps

In late 2014 AIDMI, along with Stanford University, and a grant from the Enhanced Learning and Research for Humanitarian Assistance (ELRHA) Humanitarian Innovation Fund (HIF) began a randomized controlled trial entitled 'Innovating Disaster Micro-Insurance for Local Market Recovery' in India. The core challenge being addressed by this project is promoting local recovery after a crisis rather than engendering dependence on international aid.

The project highlights local markets as an advantageous feature of urban crises to deliver goods and services for affected populations. Increasingly, humanitarian aid employs cash assistance as a means to allow beneficiaries to drive local demand and thus recover markets. These cash infusions alone, however, may not be enough to support the markets that themselves have been affected by the disaster and can possibly lead to inflation if the suppliers of the goods and services are unable to maintain adequate supply. In the absence of any type of insurance coverage, most micro and small businesses employ traditional coping mechanisms following a disaster, involving dramatic increases in high-interest debt and sales of personal and business assets. Those micro and small businesses that cannot bear the losses shut down for long periods of time and many never reopen. This initiative intends to complement cash programs to address the supply side of the recovery equation so that community resilience is established by enabling markets to recover more quickly. The objective of the project is to create a rigorous evidence base for humanitarian and development agencies, urban authorities, global financial institutions and insurance providers to take up risk transfer issues in their policies and practice and scale-up risk transfer approaches for this rapidly growing and important segment of urbanizing economies.

Most urban poor populations obtain many of their basic needs from local small businesses, which remain untargeted and unreached by traditional financial institutions. These businesses also provide important livelihoods that have multiplicative effects on creating and sustaining employment. While the vast majority of the micro-enterprises in urban settings lack access to traditional disaster insurance, there is evidence that when access is available, there is an uptake of this type of insurance. While uptake may be incremental, change could be radical. If taken to scale, growing urban populations that represent a challenge for humanitarian operations would have an internal mechanism to allow rapid recovery, limiting the need for high-cost and inefficient outside aid. As this innovation can be implemented in the pre-disaster phase and through private markets, the growth potential or scalability is immense.

Conclusions

Small enterprises in urban areas play an important role in local market, community and livelihood recovery following a disaster. They cannot, however, play this role effectively when they themselves are affected. Access to micro-insurance products can help these enterprises recover faster. The growing insurance market in India is certainly capable of covering these enterprises with well-designed products. AIDMI's experience of working in disaster-affected urban areas showed a high demand and willingness to pay for such products. These enterprises are also willing to address disaster risk by adopting risk reduction actions.

The low level of insurance coverage is an opportunity for the authorities, private sector and aid agencies to promote risk reduction approaches through convergence of micro-insurance with mitigation and micro-credit facilities in India. Most urban authorities in India have yet to explore this possibility. State and donor support for combining microfinance and disaster risk reduction during recovery (between two disasters) could make a huge difference in reducing losses and mitigating the slowdown of vital economic activity in India's cities.

> The insurance sector can lend its expertise in risk assessment and evaluation and promote the widespread use of risk transfer tools, including micro insurance/insurance pools to enable faster recovery and reconstruction, as well as provide fast liquidity in times of crisis.
>
> (SAARC, 2014)

Municipal corporations from cities must demand coverage of disaster losses in their cities from the State Disaster Response Fund for meeting relief and reconstruction expenditure both at individual levels for small enterprises as well as the city level for public assets.

Similarly, the National Disaster Management Authority with support from India's Insurance Regulatory and Development Authority (IRDA) must facilitate the coverage of low-frequency but high-impact disaster events such as earthquakes and cyclones. The IRDA also has an important role to play in providing incentives for insurance providers to increase their risk coverage and for policyholders to take up risk reduction in urban areas. Catastrophic events and covariate risk, the risk that the entire pool of clients requires assistance beyond an insurer's capacity, must be hedged against with re-insurance mechanisms from private actors or development agencies.

Finally, more investment needs to be made in studying and scaling up innovations such as Afat Vimo in Indian cities by donors, authorities and others with the purpose of designing and launching similar innovations at national and state levels for covering high-risk urban areas. Micro-enterprise disaster insurance can improve the recovery of local markets that play a critical role in providing goods and services and livelihoods to vulnerable disaster-affected populations in urban settings. Programs that aim to enhance resilience among these small enterprises are vital for economic recovery as well as the recovery of affected communities.

Notes

1 The ProVention Consortium operated between September 2000 and January 2010, and 'was a global coalition of governments, international organizations, academic institutions, the private sector, and civil society organizations aimed at reducing disaster impacts in developing countries' (www.preventionweb.net/english/professional/contacts/v.php?id=177_).
2 Linked with a money back policy based on the demand from the clients.
3 Report is available at: www.iiasa.ac.at/Publications/Documents/XO-11-059.pdf.

References

ADB (2013). *Low-Carbon Green Growth in Asia: Policies and Practices.* Hong Kong: Asian Development Bank Institute. Available at: www.adbi.org/files/2013.06.28.book.low.carbon.green.growth.asia.pdf (accessed October 24, 2013).

AIDMI (2006). *Community Risk Transfer: Through Microinsurance.* Available at: www.southasiadisasters.net (accessed May 26, 2006).

AIDMI (2007). *Risk Transfer Initiative.* Available at: www.aidmi.org/risk-transfer-initiative.asp.

AIDMI (2014). *Reducing Underlying Risk Factors: Assessing the Effectiveness of Risk Insurance Post-Cyclone Phailin in Odisha, India, A Case of 2013 Cyclone Phailin from Odisha.* Briefing Note, April 2014. Available at: http://cdkn.org/wp-content/uploads/2014/05/briefing-note1.pdf.

Brown, C. (2012). *The 21st Century Urban Disaster.* Available at: www.globalcommunities.org/publications/21st_century_urban_disaster-global-communities.pdf.

Economic Survey of India (2015). *Volume II. 2014–2015.* Ministry of Finance, Government of India. Available at: http://indiabudget.nic.in/es2014-15/echapter-vol2.pdf (accessed March 26, 2015).

GOI (2010). *National Progress Report on the Implementation of the Hyogo Framework for Action (2009–2011) – Interim.* New Delhi: GOI (Government of India), Disaster Management Division, Ministry of Home Affairs.

GSDMA (Gujarat State Disaster Management Authority) (nd). *Earthquake, India: Gandhinagar.* Available at: www.gsdma.org/hazards/earthquake.aspx.

ILO (2013). *Sustainable Development, Decent Work and Green Jobs.* Geneva: ILO. Available at: www.ilo.org/wcmsp5/groups/public/---ed_norm/---relconf/documents/meetingdocument/wcms_207370.pdf (accessed November 2, 2013).

Indian Express (2012). *Kolkata, Mumbai in Top 10 Climate Change Risk Cities.* Bangladesh: Dhaka, November 16. Available at: http://archive.indianexpress.com/news/kolkata-mumbai-in-top-10-climate-change-risk-cities/1032090/.

Insurance Regulatory and Development Authority (IRDA) (2013–2014) *Annual Report (2013–2014). Indian Insurance Market.* Available at: www.policyholder.gov.in/indian_insurance_market.aspx (accessed March 25, 2015).

Jaitely, A. (2015). *Budget Speech by Honorable Finance Minister.* New Delhi: GOI. Available at: http://indiabudget.nic.in/bspeecha.asp (accessed March 26, 2015).

Lester, R. and Gurenko, E. (2003). *India: Financing Rapid Onset Natural Disasters in India: A Risk Management Approach*. World Bank Report, No. 26844-IN. New York: World Bank.

Mechler, R., Linnerooth-Bayer, J. and Peppiatt, D. (2006). *Microinsurance for Natural Disaster Risks in Developing Countries: Benefits, Limitations and Viability*. Geneva: ProVention Consortium and IIASA.

Microinsurance Network (2010). *The Microinsurance Trilogy*, Newsletter Winter 2010. Available at: www.google.co.in/url?sa=t&rct=j&q=&esrc=s&source=web&cd=5&cad=rja&uact=8&ved=0CDUQFjAE&url=http%3A%2F%2Fwww.microinsurancecentre.org%2Fresources%2Fdocuments%2Fnewsletter-no-20-the-microinsurance-trilogy%2Fdownload.html&ei=AUwcVdS-JdOhugS97oCwBg&usg=AFQjCNGPnRNjtFjqLoV0WVnX67KhnnxB5g&bvm=bv.89744112,d.c2E.

Ministry of Home Affairs (2009). *National Policy on Disaster Management*. New Delhi: GOI. Available at: www.preventionweb.net/files/12733_NationaDisasterManagementPolicy2009.pdf.

NIDM (2013). *Training Module on Urban Risk Mitigation*. New Delhi: NIDM. Available at: http://nidm.gov.in/PDF/modules/urban.pdf.

NIUA (2013). *Urban Climate Change Resilience Policy Brief*. Available at: file:///C:/Users/Sony/Desktop/Policy%20Brief%201%20NIUA_Policy%20and%20Regulatory%20Frameworks.pdf.

O'Donnell, I. (2009). *Global Assessment Report – Practice Review on Innovations in Finance for Disaster Risk Management*. Geneva: ProVention Consortium. Available at: www.preventionweb.net/english/hyogo/gar/background-papers/documents/Chap6/ProVention-Risk-financing-practice-review.pdf.

Planning Commission (2011) *Report of the Working Group on Disaster Management. For the Twelfth Five Year Plan (2012–2017)*. New Delhi: GOI. Available at: http://ndma.gov.in/images/pdf/Working%20Group%20Report%20on%20Disaster%20Management%20for%2012th%20FYP.pdf.

Planning Commission (2013). *Twelfth Five Year Plan (2012/2017). Faster, More Inclusive and Sustainable Growth*, Volume I. Available at: http://planningcommission.gov.in/plans/planrel/12thplan/pdf/12fyp_vol1.pdf.

SAARC (2014). *Conference Report: SAARC Regional Conference on Business Continuity Planning & Disaster Risk Reduction in South Asia*. 15–16 December, New Delhi, India. Available at: http://saarc-sdmc.nic.in/pdf/bcp-2014.pdf (accessed December, 2014).

Save the Children (2006). *Child Rights Perspective in Response to Natural Disasters in South Asia: A Retrospective Study*. Kathmandu: Save the Children Regional Office for South and Central Asia. Available at: www.preventionweb.net/files/15091_Childrightsprespectivesinresponseto.pdf.

Singh, P.K. (2013). *NDMA First Session on National Platform for Disaster Risk Reduction, Thematic Session-3, Risk Financing Mechanisms, Changing Dimension in Disaster Risk Transfer*. Available at: http://nidm.gov.in/npdrr/pres/ses3/pres5.pdf.

Sinha, A. (2001). *The Gujarat Earthquake 2001*. Asian Disaster Reduction Centre. Available at www.adrc.asia/publications/recovery_reports/pdf/Gujarat.pdf.

The Energy and Resources Institute (TERI) (2011). *Mainstreaming Urban Resilience Planning in Indian Cities: A Policy Perspective*. A Report prepared for the Asian Cities Climate Change Resilience Network (ACCCRN) in India. New Delhi, India. Available at: www.acccrn.org/sites/default/files/documents/Final_Mainstreaming%20Urban%20Resilience%20Planning%20copy.pdf (accessed March 3, 2014).

TERI (2014). *Climate Proofing Indian Cities: A Policy Perspective*. New Delhi, India. Available at: www.teriin.org/policybrief/docs/Urban.pdf.

The Press Office (2013). *New Report: World Population Shift to Urban Areas Is Increasing Risk of Natural Disasters*. Available at: www.imeche.org/news/institution/New_report_world_population_shift_to_urban_areas_is_increasing_risk_of_natural_disasters.

UNDP (2007). *Building Security for the Poor: Potential and Prospects for Microinsurance in India*. Colombo, Sri Lanka: UNDP.

World Bank, Asian Development Bank and Government of Gujarat (2001). *Gujarat Earthquake Recovery Programme Assessment Report*. Available at: www.preventionweb.net/files/2608_fullreport.pdf.

Chapter 12

'Humanitarian hybrids'

New technologies and humanitarian resilience

Marianne F. Potvin

Introduction

In recent years there has been increasing interest around new technologies that claim to improve humanitarian assistance. Crisis mapping, crowdsourcing and crowdseeding, to name a few, are at the forefront of all discussions about humanitarian innovations. The 2013 World Disasters Report, published by the International Federation of the Red Cross and Red Crescent Societies (IFRC), explores how technology will influence the future of humanitarian action; it '(examines) the profound impact of technological innovations on humanitarian action, how humanitarians employ technology in new and creative ways, and what risks and opportunities may emerge as a result of technological innovations' (Vinck, 2013). Also in 2013 the United Nations Office for the Coordination of Humanitarian Affairs (OCHA) released a report entitled 'Humanitarianism in the network age' where it offered its own reflections on the use of new technologies in the context of humanitarian interventions (Chandran and Thow, 2013). Meanwhile other endeavors such as the Harvard Humanitarian Initiative (HHI) have been dedicating considerable resources to developing tools for representing disasters, as well as various standards for measuring the impact of interventions and evaluating response effectiveness. Because these technological developments are such recent additions to the humanitarian toolkit, little if any research exists as to their actual impact on improving performance of disaster response.

It is important to contextualize this trend with regards to the general state of the humanitarian enterprise today. Humanitarian thinkers and critics argue that the neutrality and impartiality of humanitarian action is more contested today than ever before (though this may not be such a dramatic statement, considering that the emergence of humanitarian action is still relatively recent in Western history). Observers have pointed for example to the securitization and privatization of humanitarian aid, and to how humanitarian principles are being co-opted for political purposes deeply incompatible with humanitarian values. Since the 1970s, humanitarianism has become a variegated landscape of international NGOs, civil society actors and donor agencies, claimed to be more openly partisan and politically less neutral (Donini, 2010). In addition, 'governments around the world [have begun] recasting their own political projects and military adventures as humanitarian ones' (Weizman, 2011) and the humanitarian project has become one of interventionism. Under the ever-encompassing human rights and human security umbrellas, humanitarianism has been alleged to be recasting its mandate and shifting its focus from traditional assistance to exporting peace, democracy and economic development. Spatially, humanitarian efforts have robustly entered active conflict zones, thus generating overlaps between the once-restricted humanitarian space – the allegedly neutral space contained within the protected boundaries of humanitarian camps – and the state space, that is, the territory onto which norms of national sovereignty apply.

There may not appear, at least initially, to be any connection between the changing roles of humanitarian actors and the enthusiastic adoption of technological innovation. Perhaps the importance of technology is merely hype, but even if this were the case, the following questions nevertheless remain. Why are humanitarian actors suddenly feeling this need for technological 'upgrading'? Are they just following a trend? Is technology being used by humanitarian actors with the aim to professionalize their discipline? Is it used to legitimize (or solidify, or establish) their place in contemporary power or global governance networks, in other words, to assert their own position as powerful actors?

Applying a science, technology and society studies (STS) lens to the discussion could productively shed light on interrogations about humanitarian resilience. Following a brief descriptive account of the two recent reports cited above, which arguably are indicators of a broader trend in the humanitarian discipline, the bulk of this chapter is articulated around two main axes, each drawing from themes central to STS.

The first axis, entitled 'seeing like an aid agency,' explores how humanitarian information and communication technologies (HICT) perform a role of stabilization in the realm of humanitarianism. This discussion addresses themes of simplification and normalization by analyzing processes of categorization and classification of disasters and victims, which underpin any attempt at data genesis. It also explores how humanitarian data is used to make order out of the chaos of disasters; among other things, it asks what images of crisis emerge from humanitarian mapping, what reality is created through these representation techniques and how that relates to an understanding of distant human suffering. A final part of this discussion focuses on how numbers and scientific models strengthen the power of humanitarian actors, allowing them to display objectivity, especially measured against a backdrop where the integrity of humanitarian principles, namely those of neutrality, impartiality and independence, are challenged.

The second axis focuses on the constitution and the distortion of the humanitarian polity. Drawing from the co-productionist idiom, this section examines the ways in which the infusion of new technologies destabilizes the humanitarian ethos. It does so by tracing the emergence of what I call 'humanitarian hybrids' – those practices or instruments that associate values and principles which are humanitarian in essence with techniques borrowed from other (often quite distant) fields in ways that defy conventional, or easy, categorization.[1] Weaving technical objects with agency and human politics, these hybrids, in turn, alter the humanitarian polity. In this section, attention is thus given to the ways in which the claims of power decentralization, conveyed by the HICT proponents, obfuscate other power plays. Finally, questions are asked as to whether refined modes of measuring serve the interests of affected populations or the technocratic customs of the donor entities (states or private actors).

Description of sources

The two humanitarian institutions that produced the two key reports discussed in this chapter are important, mature, humanitarian players that possess an undeniable authority in the humanitarian community. These two institutions, however, have distinct traditions and diverging histories and founding principles, and these differences are revealed in how each report approaches issues of convergence between the humanitarian and technological ethos.

The first report analyzed is the 2013 World Disasters Report *Focus on Technology and the Future of Humanitarian Action*, which is part of a series of annual reports produced by the IFRC (Vinck, 2013). The IFRC describes itself as the world's largest volunteer-based humanitarian organization; its members are the national Red Cross and Red Crescent societies of 189 countries. Given its creation as a component of the Red Cross movement founded by Henri Dunant in 1864, it should be no surprise that its culture is characterized by the fundamental principles of the Red Cross, namely humanity, impartiality, neutrality, independence, unity, universality and voluntary service. The IFRC's report focuses on HICT, which it views as 'rapidly becoming a major field of the humanitarian practice (Vinck, 2013: 13). It embeds its discussion about HICT in its inherited framework of fundamental principles, which are used as a basis for analysis for evaluating the outcomes of technological innovation on humanitarian action. In other words, and this will be discussed in more detail later, the report examines the successes and risks of technological elements in relation to an overarching humanitarian mandate to 'save lives, alleviate suffering and maintain and protect human dignity during and in the aftermath of emergencies' (Vinck, 2013: 13).

Produced by OCHA as part of its policy and study series, 'Humanitarianism in the Network Age,' the second document examined discusses the same topic from an intergovernmental organization's standpoint. In contrast to the IFRC, which attributes authorship to individual researchers and authors, the OCHA report is presented as the product of one single institutional voice; references to supporting evidence are fewer. Echoing the agency's own motto, 'coordination saves lives,' OCHA's report contends, rather boldly, that 'data saves lives' (Chandran and Thow, 2013: 27). Indeed, with much less nuance than the IFRC report, it propounds that the time has come for humanitarianism 'to adapt' to the 'network age':

> The network age, with its increased reach of communications networks and the growing groups of people willing and able to help those in need, is here today. The ways in which the people interact will change, with or without the sanction of international humanitarian organizations. Either those organizations adapt to the network age, or they grow increasingly out of touch with the people they were established to serve.
>
> (Chandran and Thow, 2013: 5)

When it comes to technology, humanitarians are warned that resistance is futile.

In tying the technological discussion of the first two reports to this book's focus on resilience, and with the aim of presenting views of a multilateral governmental organization (as opposed to intergovernmental or non-governmental) involved in humanitarian aid, this chapter also introduces a third source, the United Kingdom Department for International Development's (DFID) publication *Promoting Innovation and Evidence-Based Approaches to Building Resilience and Responding to Humanitarian Crises* (DFID, 2012). Framing its role in the humanitarian enterprise in terms of 'ending the need for aid'[2] (a variant to the more common humanitarian goal of 'ending human suffering'), DFID discusses the role of humanitarian data-making in reference to important themes that are also recurrent in the two previous sources – notions of the use of evidence, cost-effectiveness and resilience.

Seeing like an aid agency

In the face of sudden disasters or the seemingly inexplicable evils of war, it seems that humanitarians are finding relief in the genesis and display of scientific facts and scientifically generated data. The statistics, categories, images and maps that are populating the humanitarian databases are presented as objective ways of making sense of the horrors of disasters. They validate what humanitarians know and what they have to say. In the 'network age,' it would appear that this authoritative scientific view is replacing what would otherwise be a moral or emotional, or even visceral, way of experiencing and understanding tragedies.

Normalization

Generating data about humanitarian crises and the ensuing humanitarian responses requires first and foremost the normalization of the terrain; categories related to what constitutes a disaster, and which disasters trigger or warrant the mobilization of humanitarian aid must first be established. However, disaster scenes are by nature chaotic, highly complex, barely readable, scenes. Parallels can be drawn between the simplification processes that humanitarians deploy on such terrains and those that the utilitarian foresters practiced on the German forest, as described by James C. Scott in *Seeing Like a State*, 'The fact is that forest science and geometry, backed by state power, had the capacity to transform the real, diverse, and chaotic old-growth forest into a new, more uniform forest that closely resembled the administrative grid of its techniques' (Scott, 1998: 15). Sheila Jasanoff further qualifies the power that simplification processes hold in terms of their role 'in constituting political power.' In reference to the work of both James C. Scott and Benedict Anderson, she writes,

> for these authors, however, the power of representation lies not so much in the resources invested in creating them (though these are not irrelevant) as in the resources used to disseminate them, so that they alter the behavior or command the belief of masses of sentient human actors.
>
> (Jasanoff, 2004: 25)

The IFRC report classifies disasters[3] as either 'natural disasters,' which include biological, geophysical, climatological (droughts), hydrological (floods and wet mass movements) and meteorological (storms) disasters, or 'technological disasters,' which include industrial, transport and miscellaneous accidents. These categories enable the creation of boundaries along which aid organizations then define their respective mandates. This is the case within, for instance, the Red Cross Movement's tradition, where responsibilities have been divided along the rubrics of natural disasters, under IFRC's mandate, and armed conflicts, under the ICRC's mandate. Thus, through a seemingly objective and rational classification exercise, what is actually an ideological agenda is presented as a purely technical exercise. The image of 'order' produced through such categorization, whereby a given calamity neatly fits one definition, obfuscates many realities, where different types of disasters occur simultaneously and have compounding effects on one another.

Surprisingly enough, however, technological disasters – disasters that are arguably very much man-made – are often placed in the same category as, or in a category adjacent to, natural events such as landslides, tsunamis, droughts and tropical storms. The Centre for Research on the Epidemiology of Disasters (CRED) qualifies technological disasters as 'unforeseen and often sudden' (Vinck, 2013: 222–227). Putting technological disasters in the accident category is particularly interesting as an object of STS deconstruction. The remarks that Jasanoff makes about the alleged unpredictability of technological disasters are highly relevant; in reference to the Bhopal disaster, she writes,

> If they seem to strike without notice, it is because we have drawn an artificial boundary between the technological and the social, imputing to the former a false infallibility, and have accepted a temporarily stable working relationship among machines, people, and their environment as the only imaginable state of affairs. Seeing technologies as heterogeneous systems, combining technical and social elements in a fragile equilibrium, provides the antidote to these comfortable assumptions. By putting technological artifacts back into their social contexts, we uncover pathological patterns that hold the clues to both past and future disasters.
>
> (Jasanoff, 1994: 4)

Today, given the increasing awareness of climate change, this remark could very well be extended to characterize current conceptualizations of climatological, meteorological and hydrological disasters as well. Interestingly enough, it should also be noted that while the evils of industrialization are accounted for as technological disasters in CRED's specialized disaster database, the evils of people, displayed in war and armed conflicts, receive very little attention, suggesting that perhaps it is easier to make sense of seemingly accidental occurrences. In wars, evil intentions complicate the picture.

Categories of disasters also define categories of persons. Put bluntly, the disaster creates the victim. Another observation by Jasanoff, which, although written in reference to victims of the Bhopal technological disaster, informs a wider discussion about other disaster-struck communities, is relevant here. She writes,

> victims of technological disaster do not constitute a clearly demarcated social group until they are struck by tragedy. They possess no common identity, and hence no political voice or force that would allow them to declare in advance which hazards they are prepared to accept ... the tragic event demolishes not just the physical but the psychological foundations of preexisting communities, making recovery arduous. Reconstructing communities under such circumstances involves a very special and chancy kind of politics: the gradual accretion of power around a community of the dispossessed, whose only significant resource is the symbolic status engendered by their extraordinary suffering.
>
> (Jasanoff, 1994: 9)

While 'victims' are granted a certain symbolic status in the eyes of the aid agencies, the disaster obfuscates the (sum of) individual suffering. In traditional humanitarian parlance, victims are more often than not referred to as 'beneficiaries' – they are 'recipients' of aid. Increasingly, in profit-driven brands of humanitarianism, they are referred to as 'clients' or 'customers' in an arguably clumsy attempt to present them as empowered persons. However, in OCHA's vision of data-driven humanitarianism victims may also be seen as data providers. As information gets generated by or extracted from the victims, two shifts occur in parallel. First, the humanitarian institutions lose their exclusive position (in times of strife that is) of being (as some may see it) the only ones with the right to see, and the right to speak, for others. Second, the victims become the witnesses and the data collectors.

With regard to the processes of normalization of individuals, a link with G.C. Bowker and S.L. Star's work on classification and reclassification under South African Apartheid may be drawn. Their essay describes how 'in the process of making people and categories converge, there can be tremendous torque of individual biographies.' They explain that while for powerful groups 'the infrastructures that together support or construct their identities operate particularly smoothly' (Bowker and Star, 2000: 224–225), for the less advantaged groups the reverse happens. Within the humanitarian apparatus the politics of normalization aims at differentiating the deserving victims from the non-deserving individuals. Classifications change with the categorization of threats and the changing political or economic regimes. To mention one example, think of Afghan nationals who have known a succession of disasters: in a single lifetime, they have been called citizens, refugees, displaced persons and sometimes insurgents; their status has oscillated between that of deserving victims to that of undeserving poor.

Stabilization

The data that is mobilized and disseminated through HICT encompasses a multitude of sources including social media, text messaging, censuses, tax information, public health indicators, banking transactions, satellite imagery and geo-spatial referencing. These sources are both private and public. The underlying assumption is that the combination and analysis of all this data allows the constitution of a clearer picture of the situation, as numbers and statistics reduce cognitive uncertainty. It is just as easy to think of the use of crisis mapping and geo-spatial referencing as instruments of performativity. By displaying their mastery of these particular technologies, it may be said that humanitarian actors can show the world that they are getting things right, and that they are grasping, if only in geographical terms, the extent of the situation. They are also able to prove that they can see what others do not.

The Satellite Sentinel Project (SSP), described in the IFRC report, is a good example of a humanitarian hybrid. In this case, the hybridity comes from the fact that SSP relies on satellite imagery as assuming the role of a technological super-witness of war crimes: it combines high-tech objects (satellite imagery), intelligence expertise (data analysis) and humanitarian agency (witnessing, responding). The SSP was launched in 2010 in collaboration with researchers at the HHI with the aim of foreseeing the risks of violence breaking out between Sudan and South Sudan. If the conflict did erupt, the SSP was intended both to predict threats to populations and to anticipate the quantity, type of humanitarian assistance and the locations where aid would need to be deployed. The analysts borrowed surveillance tools and methods from the intelligence industry to carry out their objectives. As opposed to conventional photography already used to document war crimes, the satellite could see real things that the human eye can only imagine or visualize through deductive processes – it enlarged the vision of aid agencies so to speak. And yet, this kind of satellite or aerial photography, like many other techno-humanitarian initiatives, conveys too little about the suffering, loss of dignity and dispossession that is occurring at ground level.

Here, the use of spatial data does not put space back into 'humanitarian space.' That is to say that while 'spatial' data may precisely geo-locate the witnessing of crime or a humanitarian violation in tridimensional space, it fails to accurately convey an embodied, material experience of the humanitarian crisis: the humanitarian viewer is still dislocated from the pain. Despite the technological prowess, the distance and the lack of consideration for the physicality of 'humanitarian space'[4] remain.

To further interrogate the role of the humanitarian hybrid (in this case, the SSP), it can be productive here to refer to Bruno Latour's concept of 'centers of calculation.' Latour conceives centers of calculation in relation to immutable mobiles, 'objects which have the properties of being mobile but also immutable, presentable, readable and combinable with one another' (Latour, 1990: 26); immutable mobiles '[become] useful when … combined with all the other inscription devices; then, the different points of the world become really transported in a manageable form to a single place which then becomes a centre' (Latour, 1990: 59). He further argues that:

> by working on papers alone [or, in our context, by working through the mathematical medium alone], on fragile inscriptions that are immensely less than the things from which they are extracted, it is still possible to dominate all things and all people.
>
> (Latour, 1990: 60)

Analyzing the SSP project described above as a center of calculation – one that combines military techniques (in this case remote surveillance) with humanitarian motives – gives us insight into the evolving nature of humanitarian action. As disquieting as it may be to conceive of humanitarian action as being closely associated with military means, such hybridity is not unprecedented: historically, the evolution of warfare and humanitarian practices has always been tightly intertwined.

Display of power

The framing of humanitarian action in scientific terms stabilizes a field that has yet to become fully professionalized. In addition to conferring more authority to humanitarian institutions, the mobilization and the display of new technologies reinforce humanitarian actors in their positions as experts. This enhances their credibility as it redirects the discussion away from the irrational humanitarian impulse (the subjective feeling of compassion for the suffering of a fellow human being) towards more quantifiable, tractable, concerns of efficiency and cause-to-effect reasoning. This bestows on humanitarian actors a more prominent role in broader political arenas and legitimizes their existence in networks of powerful global governance actors. From this place of strength humanitarian institutions may be better positioned to counter public or political inertia, or resist the co-optation of their principles by private interests, although these are hardly guarantees. In parallel, within the internal humanitarian hierarchy, specialized data experts also gain rank, since 'using new forms of data may also require empowering technical experts to overrule the decisions of their less informed superiors' (Chandran and Thow, 2013: 4). This signals the advent of the technician in playing a key role, if not fully orchestrating the humanitarian response. Paradoxically, the spread of HICT also presents the potential to weaken the sovereignty of humanitarian experts by making the creation and manipulation of data banal. Both the IFRC and OCHA consistently characterize crowdsourcing as a decentralization of power from the humanitarian institutions to the disaster victims.

Furthermore, seemingly objective data and numbers provide the sought-after evidence for justifying decision-making. The idea that humanitarian calculations and data aggregation constitute evidence may itself be critiqued, but what is perhaps more interesting is examining how this notion of evidence participates in building an image of disasters as being preventable events; events that can be scientifically anticipated and for which humanitarian solutions can be accurately tested. Furthermore the scientific models, which permit simulations and the testing of potential solutions, not only broaden the constitutive vision of humanitarian institutions, but also participate in creating the fiction that humanitarians can truly control risks. While efforts at anticipation are clearly beneficial, in many cases (for instance, in the use of early warning systems or with the dissemination of building codes regulations) it needs to be understood that the evidence on which anticipation can be built does not rely on numbers alone, and that prevention requires societal mobilization that goes well beyond the reach of humanitarian actors.

It is important to understand why this emphasis on evidence-based decision-making, admittedly something of a 'flavor of the day' in the management of humanitarian interventions as well as in medical care and many other fields, raises concerns. Values of transparency are of particular significance in a context where the integrity of key humanitarian principles, such as neutrality and impartiality, remains so contested. The objectivity of neutral data can render broader, more fundamental, debates more invisible. To give one, although rather extreme, example, the OCHA report reduces the 2011 famine in the Horn of Africa and the 2010 Floods in Pakistan to 'technological,' and not political, humanitarian shortcomings (Chandran and Thow, 2013: 4). It suggests that these disasters were not prevented or sufficiently addressed owing to a lack of information, implying that with better information, the humanitarian crisis would have been avoided. This reductionist view is misleading, and the absence of any recognition of the lack of political will as being one reason for the lack of action is perplexing.

(Re)constitution of a humanitarian polity

After having explored in the previous section how new humanitarian hybrids are stabilizing, if not buttressing the humanitarian field, the focus of this section now concerns how they change, or destabilize, it, concerning in particular how the co-productionist idiom can be used to understand better the workings of the new socio-technological formations that emerge from the convergence of scientific and humanitarian practices. The concept of co-production, introduced by Jasanoff, stems from the dual acknowledgment that 'the dynamics of politics and power, like those of culture, seem impossible to tease apart from the broad currents of scientific and technological change,' and that 'most theoretical explorations of how social worlds evolve only imperfectly reflect the complicated interplay of the cognitive, the institutional, the material and the normative dimensions of society.' Seeking to fill the 'gap between frames of analysis,' co-production therefore suggests avenues for grasping how 'increasingly, the realities of human experience emerge as the joint achievements of scientific, technical and social enterprise' and how 'science and society ... are co-produced, each underwriting the other's existence' (Jasanoff, 2004: 16–17).

Co-production

A first indication that co-production is going on can be found in the following claim set forth by OCHA. Its report states, as the first of its four primary objectives, that information ought to be recognized as a basic need in humanitarian response, 'information in itself is a life saving need for people in crisis. It is as important as water, food and shelter' (Chandran and Thow, 2013: 4–5). The affirmation is rather bold; it nevertheless echoes similar claims dotting the reports, for instance, 'my mobile, my life' or better yet, 'data saves lives' (Vinck,

2013: 126–127 and Chandran and Thow, 2013: 27), both plays on words resonating with the core, most basic purpose of humanitarian interventions, which is to save lives. And yet, the idea that information is vital raises important questions. A prisoner of war – which incidentally, in the history of the constitution of humanitarianism, is among the first categories of individuals protected by International Humanitarian Law[5] – might not equate the need for information with the need for water or food. OCHA's report further specifies,

> understanding information as a basic need requires a reassessment of what information is for. Instead of seeing it primarily as a tool for agencies to decide how to help people, it must be understood as a product, or service, to help affected communities determine their own priorities.
>
> (Chandran and Thow, 2013: 4)

Ignoring for a moment that this statement casts humanitarians into makers of products, the notion that information deserves to be elevated to the ranks of a universal and vital need (a right almost) profoundly reshapes the basic understanding of the scope of humanitarian action and responsibility, and thus demands more reflection. After all, in addition to questioning the claim of its vital nature, one could also argue that the need for information is a culturally specific concept, rather than a universal one.

Understanding disasters and designing appropriate responses through information technologies also poses an epistemological shift within the humanitarian field which constitutes a second indication of co-production between technology and humanitarianism. The very idea of knowing through data, propounded in both the IFRC and OCHA reports, challenges the centrality if not validity of knowing through compassion. It also suggests that knowing through calculation is better than knowing through action. In other words, the celebration of data as better and improved humanitarian devices somehow implies that what is not measurable, quantifiable or transposable in maps or databases ought not to be addressed (or at least not prioritized) in humanitarian response. Put differently still, describing a disaster in terms of the intensity of trauma, the acuteness of suffering or the extent of dispossession thus appears as an irrational, therefore, illegitimate way of making sense of the reality. And yet it could be argued that notions of dignity and suffering – subjective and not objective notions – have been crucial to the constitution of humanitarian intentionality. The technological turn steers humanitarianism away for a principle-based logic that had governed its place in the world until now.

Fictional power in the 'network age'

Historically humanitarian action has been undemocratic in many regards. The practicalities involved in saving lives and protecting and assisting victims have not always been compatible with listening to political voices of these victims. The 'traditional' temporalities of emergencies, which implied that humanitarian action lasted a rather short amount of time, have not necessarily involved a democratic moment. Since the 1990s, critics have started questioning the governance role that humanitarian actors play, referring to the humanitarian polity as a 'humanitarian government' and characterizing humanitarian experts as 'relief sovereigns' (almost reaching the infamous 'Republic of NGOs' label given to Haiti). In his ethnographies of refugee camps, anthropologist Michel Agier denounces the role of humanitarian institutions as that of 'low-cost managers of exclusion on a planetary scale' (Agier, 2008: 60). He further describes humanitarian refugee camps – which allow for the simultaneous protection of and undemocratic control over populations – as 'government(s) without citizens' (Agier, 2011) and as the embodiment par excellence of the ambiguous and paradoxical nature of humanitarianism. It may be said as a result that technologies only further destabilize an already problematic polity.

Both the OCHA and IFRC reports cast the entry of communication technologies as

> the world has seen not simply a technological shift [but] also a process of rapid decentralization of power ... Many new entrants are appearing in the field of emergency and disaster response. They are ignoring the traditional hierarchies because (they) perceive that there is something they can do which benefits others.
>
> (Chandran and Thow, 2013: 16)

Access to social media, mobile communication and participation through crowdsourcing or crowdseeding are presented as ensuring representation of wider publics; 'Accessing new data sources may require listening to people who may previously have been ignored' (Chandran and Thow, 2013: 4), representing a path towards greater empowerment of affected populations. For the researchers at OCHA, the number of tweets, the rates of mobile phone subscribers or the statistics of digital humanitarian platforms or Facebook pages followers of, for example, the Global Disaster Relief page all become proxies and measures for talking about democratic participation in the polity.

Equating the use of social media with increased political power raises questions in any realm, but in the humanitarian realm, the assumption raises perhaps more acute ethical concerns. As has been alluded to in the previous section, claims that HICT are enabling victims to become more involved in the decision-making process imply a shift from the status or the category of victims to that of participants, (self) responders, and (self) aid-givers. The lines between who provides and receives humanitarian aid are thus blurred. Although empowerment should be a key consideration in all humanitarian endeavors, especially in situations of protracted emergencies, are there not risks that the burden of the responsibility gets transferred to the victims? This concern might be somewhat far-fetched, but in a climate where more and more of the proposed solutions seem to include self-help or resilience-building measures – a sort of do-it-yourself life-saving – the risk that the institutions mandated to ensure the respect for a minimum standard of humanity will eschew their responsibilities is not negligible.

Humanitarian hybrids and digital voluntarism

Building on this question of empowerment, it is worthwhile to ask to whom or to what do victims get empowered. Are victims demanding more accountability of the institutionalized humanitarian actors, which are viewed as imposing inadequate solutions on the dispossessed population? Of local governments, which are seen as disengaged from the disaster? Or of the world, which perhaps seems to have stopped caring?

This leads to the question of community, or more specifically, to the question of how humanitarian hybrids are enlarging the humanitarian polity. Again, the accepted view seems to be that technology, particularly social media, is building (new) humanitarian communities. The case of Google as assuming the role of a first responder, through its Google Crisis Response, provides a good example of a humanitarian hybrid. But is featuring a 'unit devoted to information access in disaster settings' (Vinck, 2013: 24) enough to grant Google a place in the humanitarian polity? Do disaster databases have purpose or agency? In the same vein, the OCHA report also emphasizes the potentialities of expanded partnerships between traditional humanitarian institutions and private sector actors; it describes, for instance, the role played by private mobile telecommunication providers who participate in disaster response by way of delivering services and lending their infrastructures for humanitarian purposes. Are these companies acting solely or primarily out of pure altruism or charitable impulses?

This raises the question of intentionality. The OCHA report casts the increase of volunteers as being a new phenomenon brought on by new technologies. In OCHA's narrative, the new volunteers are the crisis-mappers or data gatherers and analysts, who are often volunteering their time and digital skills, yet located very far from the crisis epicenter. While HICT permit an unprecedented number of such individuals to participate in humanitarian action (however remotely), the value in itself is nothing new. It is crucial to recall that historically humanitarianism possesses a tradition of being a volunteer-based endeavor, especially within the Red Cross brand of humanitarianism. The humanitarian ethos is therefore closely linked with the voluntarism ethos. There is a long-standing recognition that the bulk of humanitarian work is usually shouldered by dedicated members of the local community. Indeed, the IFRC rightly points out that 'by its very nature, humanitarian aid has always been crowdsourced – through family, friends, neighbors, tribesmen and fellow believers,' further noting that it is the institutionalization of crowdsourcing that becomes problematic (Vinck, 2013: 155). What is to be made of digital voluntarism, then?

Accountability

The promotion of HICT articulated in the OCHA and IFRC reports puts forward the idea that information will render humanitarian providers more accountable to the beneficiaries of aid. It suggests that more and more accurate data will improve the flow of information between humanitarian institutions and disaster victims; in other words, information will heroically level the unequal power relations between those who give and those who receive aid. This is another problematic assumption that obfuscates important challenges in terms of contextualization, interpretation and translation of data into reliable, actionable information. Another crucial obfuscation is that of the accountability of humanitarian institutions towards those who fund them, including the donors or the general public. This relationship between humanitarian institutions and money is perhaps more important for understanding why and to what extent data would constitute a solution of all of humanitarianism's ills.

Indeed to consider the promotion of cost-benefit analysis as an innovative approach to humanitarianism, as formulated in DFID's strategy of improved humanitarian action, may well be to infer that the technological turn is a way to comply with the technocratic standards of state or intergovernmental institutions. In fact the enthusiasm for data finds its root in a desire to rationalize aid expenses. Technology mediates in the interplay between the humanitarian ethos and the prevailing economic climate. Here it is worth recalling Scott, 'Some level of abstraction is necessary for virtually all forms of analysis, and it is not surprising that the abstractions of state officials should have reflected the paramount fiscal interests of their employers' (Scott, 1998: 13).

DFID declares rather clearly its goals to improve the cost-efficiency of humanitarian action. For some members of the humanitarian polity, the issue is thus more about savings than it is about saving lives. DFID formulates what the expected results of a more objective approach to humanitarian aid are,

> use of high quality data and evidence to inform decision-making at all levels ... will help ensure that resources are targeted more precisely and allow us to track the outcomes and impacts of our work, deepening accountability to disaster-prone communities and to British tax-payers.
>
> (DFID, 2012: 6)

Again, objective, quantifiable evidence is elevated over other types of evidence (such as suffering and trauma). Moreover it is not clear what happens when these simultaneous accountabilities, to both distant disaster-struck populations and a closer citizenry, are incompatible, or worse, irreconcilable.

The mobile cash transfer technology embraced by OCHA as an unquestionably progressive solution to ensure basic needs of individuals are met during emergencies is another indication of the extent to which the humanitarian enterprise is redefined by political-economic trends. The report describes how 'The Cash Learning Partnership, a group of five global NGOs and IFRC, supported by VISA and ECHO, has highlighted how electronic payment-and-registration systems can improve aid accountability by providing a clear data trail from funding to recipients' (Chandran and Thow, 2013: 34). With the promotion of mobile banking as a humanitarian technology, what is also implied is that assistance coming directly through the diaspora's remittances is not only becoming increasingly significant but is encouraged as a privileged way of providing/receiving assistance. Mobile cash becomes yet another humanitarian hybrid, reshuffling power relations in unprecedented ways.

Conclusion

This chapter has sought to examine claims that the network age is a new age in the history of humanitarianism and that innovative technologies and the globalization of data collection will increase humanitarian resilience, by saving a greater number of lives. By using the lens of STS it has been possible to observe how such claims both stabilize the humanitarian field, i.e. produce a form of humanitarian resilience, by legitimizing the humanitarian epistemology as an objective way of knowing the world, and profoundly destabilize the humanitarian ethos, by enlarging, complicating and at time distorting the humanitarian polity, i.e. making it less resilient. By exploring how data is generated and disseminated, the sub-politics of humanitarianism have been explored and the proclaimed apolitical essence of these humanitarian trends has been challenged.

While the humanitarian commitment to act in the public interest was not directly under review in the reports analyzed, an important shift was identified: doing good is no longer sufficient; humanitarians now need the data to prove that they are doing it. Even if the technological turn promises to advance humanitarian resilience, more scrutiny into humanitarian hybrids is necessary to predict what the future holds for the community of those who are committed to saving lives, protecting human dignity and imposing order on chaos.

Notes

1 The term 'hybrid' echoes the work of Bruno Latour and other scholars of science studies who focus on the concept of 'imbroglios' to explain 'strange situations that the intellectual culture in which we live does not know how to categorize.' More to the point, the analysis of hybrids helps

us to crisscross 'the divide that separates exact knowledge and the exercise of power'. (Latour 1993: 3–5). In this chapter, the goal is to keep in view the materiality of the humanitarian tools as well as the political and sociological context in which these tools are developed.

2 Department for International Development (DFID) webpage. Available at: www.gov.uk/government/organizations/department-for-international-development (accessed July 2015).

3 The IFRC report relies essentially on the Centre for Research on the Epidemiology of Disasters (CRED) disaster database, the EM-DAT, created in 1988 and now maintained in collaboration with the US aid agency, various United Nations agencies, etc.

4 Humanitarian space is a concept that is mostly used within the framework of International Humanitarian Law. It is conventionally construed as a normative tool that refers to neutrality, rather than as a material/physical space or place. There is a general lack of consideration for the physicality of humanitarian space, and a real need to develop new ways of thinking about it, especially vis-à-vis techno-humanitarian claims of reduced distance between crisis and humanitarian responders. For more on the tensions between the physical and the political dimensions of humanitarian space, see Weizman 2011. Weizman provides an interesting departure from what a conventional understanding of humanitarian space is by attributing to the built environment new functions as a witness of war, and by stressing the wider role that architecture (the actual buildings) plays in revealing war crimes and inscribing them in the collective experience. He also reflects productively on the physicality of the entire web of relief institutions and their attendant infrastructure.

5 Within the International Humanitarian Law (IHL) framework, humanitarianism is based on

> the idea of respect for the individual and for his dignity. Persons not directly taking part in hostilities and those put out of action through sickness, injury, captivity or other cause must be respected and protected against the effects of war; those who suffer must be aided and cared for without discrimination. The Additional Protocols extend this protection to any person affected by an armed conflict.
>
> (Prelude to the Geneva Conventions)

The first and second Geneva conventions cover the protection of the wounded and sick in the armed forces, the third Geneva convention covers the protection of prisoners of war. Only in the fourth convention are civilians protected.

References

Agier, M. (2008). *On the Margins of the World: The Refugee Experience Today* (English edn). Cambridge, UK; Malden, MA: Polity.

Agier, M. (2011). *Managing the Undesirables: Refugee Camps and Humanitarian Government.* Cambridge; Malden, MA: Polity.

Bowker, G.C. and Star, S.L. (2000) The case of race classification and reclassification under Apartheid. *Sorting Things Out: Classification and Its Consequences.* Cambridge, MA: MIT Press, pp. 195–225.

Chandran, R. and Thow, A. (eds) (2013) *Humanitarianism in the Network Age; Including World Humanitarian Data and Trends 2012.* Office for the Coordination of Humanitarian Affairs (OCHA) Policy and Studies Series.

Department for International Development (DFID) (2012). *Promoting Innovation and Evidence-Based Approaches to Building Resilience and Responding to Humanitarian Crises: A DFID Strategy Paper* (Policy Paper (www.gov.uk)) (p. 44). Available at: www.gov.uk/government/publications/promoting-innovation-and-evidence-based-approaches-to-building-resilience-and-responding-to-humanitarian-crises.

Donini, A. (2010) The far side: the meta functions of humanitarianism in a globalized world. *Disasters* 34(s2): 220–237.

Jasanoff, S. (1994) Chapter 1: Introduction. In Jasanoff, S. (ed.) *Learning from Disaster: Risk Management After Bhopal*. Philadelphia: University of Pennsylvania Press, pp. 1–21.

Jasanoff, S. (2004). Chapter 2: Ordering knowledge, ordering society. In Jasanoff, S. (ed.) *States of Knowledge: The Co-production of Science and Social Order*. London: Routledge, pp. 13–45.

Latour, B. (1990). Drawing things together. In Lynch, M. and Woolgar, S. (eds) *Representation in Scientific Practice*. Cambridge, MA: MIT Press, pp. 19–68.

Latour, B. (1993). *We Have Never Been Modern*. New York: Harvester Wheatsheaf.

Scott, J.C. (1998) *Seeing Like a State: How Certain Schemes to Improve the Human Condition Have Failed*. New Haven: Yale University Press.

Vinck, P. (ed.) (2013). *World Disasters Report 2013: Focus on Technology and the Future of Humanitarian Action*. Geneva: International Federation of the Red Cross and Red Crescent Societies.

Weizman, E. (2011). *The Least of All Possible Evils: Humanitarian Violence from Arendt to Gaza*. London; New York: Verso.

Epilogue

Reflections on the practice of disaster resilience

Julia Leis

Resilience at the city level

Following a natural onset disaster, the political, economic and geographic landscape can drastically shift. The number of actors responding to crises on the ground often multiplies, seemingly overnight. Leadership is trickily defined between who should be in charge versus who actually commands authority; information is often uncoordinated or lags a few days behind events on the ground, often rendering it less than helpful; assumptions about what people need and what they can actually do themselves may be inaccurate, even when self-reported.

The chapters in this book look critically at humanitarian response in the context of urban resilience. Resilience in cities 'depends not only on physical assets, but also policies, social capital and institutions' (Kete, 2014). A critical urban challenge right now – and one where this interpretation of resilience has particular resonance – relates to refugee movements and rapid growth of existing towns and cities, and the creation of new 'instant settlements.' As urban refugees find shelter in cities such as Nairobi, Amman and Kuala Lumpur, or even as refugee camps themselves become quasi-urban spaces such as Za'atari camp in Jordan or in Haiti's Canaan, agencies are innovating on different forms of shelter options that move beyond transitional or temporary shelter. Za'atari refugee camp, for example, is one of the fastest growing places in Jordan. It is now considered Jordan's fourth largest settlement (Weston, 2015). At one point the camp peaked at housing 120,000 refugees, in December 2013, and is now relatively stable at 80,000–85,000 residents, who reside on a 530-hectare piece of land (with a five-mile circumference) in northern Jordan. It has become clear that the term 'camp' no longer adequately describes the realities for those living there. In alignment with Killing and Boano's observations (2016), the language used between designers, humanitarians and urban planners is important in understanding how to conceptualize a place that is rapidly transforming into an urban center.

Za'atari could well become a permanent settlement, with 'self-governance, a proper electrical grid, proper water and sewage, hookups, paved streets, and green areas' (Ledwith, 2014: 12). If this is the case, then the humanitarian aid agency originators of Za'atari need to engage with those more expert at large-scale settlement design (urban planners and designers) if 'Za'atari and its leaders seek to transform the camp into a place of empowerment, dignity and reduced dependence on foreign aid' (Ledwith, 2014). However, for Za'atari, as for many refugee camps worldwide, any decision on permanence rests with the host government. The notion of 'permanent impermanence' and when a settlement becomes worthy of long-term investment (a conundrum not only here but among other long-term refugee camps) is a challenging one for both humanitarian and planning interventions alike.

As government and humanitarian actors may in time need to acknowledge and arrange for Za'atari becoming a permanent 'urban' fixture, other interesting practices are emerging in regards to closing urban Internally Displaced Persons (IDP) camps. In the case of the closure of Haiti's post-earthquake Camp Place Saint Pierre, grants of US$500 per household covering one year of rent for many IDP families proved to be a quick, inexpensive and transformative housing intervention on the path to longer-term housing solutions (Fitzgerald, 2012). Certain targeted programs allowed for camp dweller households to work with Haitian social workers to review options for their resettlement, in combination with life-skills training, including financial planning and prioritizing needs for the future (CRS, 2013). The 'Haiti experience' has already repeated itself in other urban contexts; as Fitzgerald (2012) describes: 'a disaster in an urban setting, poor levels of basic services even before the disaster, unclear land tenure status, delays in delivery of long-term reconstruction … and internally displaced population in urban centers.'

The urban landscape offers complexities that humanitarian agencies are struggling to adapt to as quickly as possible. Housing, land and property (HLP) rights are a prime example of the substantial obstacles that arise out of a naturally induced disaster such as Typhoon Haiyan, which devastated the city of Tacloban in Eastern Leyte in the Philippines. In this case, HLP issues dominated the response efforts, dealing with massive displacement of affected populations who due to their HLP status were unable to relocate to adequate housing in a safe and sustainable area (Stodart, 2016). As Stodart underlines, 'space is a premium in any urban area, leading to an increasing need for multiple-occupancy and multi-storey dwellings.' There are often complex, overlapping arrangements of land tenure that exist in urban spaces, in addition to informal settlements that have arisen out of a lack of systematic urban planning processes. In the case of Tacloban, the legal notion of 'no-build areas' (or 'no build zones' – NBZ) was not a new concept before Typhoon Haiyan hit the Philippines in November 2013. However, 'land is political and valuable' making NBZ incredibly challenging to enforce in a fair, judicious and transparent manner (Stodart, 2016). Even when NBZs were instituted after the typhoon, zone enforcement often resulted in forced evictions and further marginalized already vulnerable groups (Stodart, 2016). Despite the precariousness of being situated on high disaster-risk land, people would rather stay in the communities they know and are familiar with, rather than relocate to available land that is far away from local markets, employment and services in the urban center.

Preserving what has been lost, either due to conflict or naturally induced disaster, is part of what Almukhtar (2016) calls 'place-identity.' Place-identity refers to the representation of space, or the specific images or appearance that a city shows, and it is not often solely one place-identity that exists in an urban area. Preserving the historical urban form should also be a measure of resilience, Almukhtar argues, and disaster response stakeholders must take the multiple place-identities that exist into account when redesigning destroyed areas. Another reminder, as urban spaces are rebuilt after a disaster, as stated in Killing and Boano (2016), is that the language used within humanitarian practice as compared to that of architects, engineers and planners, is quite disparate. As a result, urban design and urban designers need to be more broadly integrated into humanitarian urban practice (Killing and Boano, 2016).

Challenges of disaster risk reduction (DRR)

One of the most glaring gaps in DRR, an essential component of resilience, relates to timing and investing in communities where only an eventual disaster can prove whether or not the previous DRR interventions were effective in saving lives. Even then this can be hard: as the adage goes, successful DRR results in a series of *non-events*. Humanitarian action is most often geared towards response, and efforts over the past several decades have sought to address this imbalance in the system. Climate change adaptation is slowly being fused within the frame of disaster risk reduction, as sea levels rise and communities closest to water are predicted to become the most adversely affected populations in the subsequent decades.

DRR funding is often related to capacity building, for example, supporting local government efforts to create disaster preparedness plans and early warning systems, and amending budgets to accommodate related contingency plans. Capacity building may involve organizing for disaster preparedness at the household level such as helping families identify safe places for family members to gather in the event of disaster. Attempting to achieve capacity building results in a one- to two-year timeframe often imposed by or on humanitarian agencies, however, can prove challenging if not unrealistic. Disaster preparedness has to become both 'vertical' (bottom to top) and 'horizontal' (between structures) across communities and levels of power. Local communities are often the best-placed first responders in the first 72 hours of disaster response, before most international humanitarian response actors arrive (Katz, 2015). Fragility itself introduces complexity. Fragile cities must cope with urban poverty and violence (de Boer, 2016). Asking such cities to prepare in advance introduces the double complexity of priorities beforehand and capacity post-disaster.

Even when DRR efforts have reasonable collaborations between national and international actors prior to a major event, they may not be enough to address the impact of a big disaster. In Nepal there was no doubt among experts that preparation for a large-scale earthquake was needed, especially as the Kathmandu Valley was considered an earthquake 'hotspot' (Goldberg, 2015; Achenbach, 2015). The focus, appropriately enough, was on what would happen if an earthquake struck Kathmandu, the urban center of Nepal, which was rated in 2014 as the most at-risk city in the world (GeoHazards International, 2015; ReliefWeb, 2014). The 7.8 Magnitude Nepal earthquake in April 2015, followed by a second 7.3 Magnitude earthquake on May 12, provides an example where DRR was understood as important and partially implemented yet, inevitably, there were gaps and failures in the aftermath (Sanderson et al., 2015). To be sure, the creation of a Government Central Disaster Relief Committee, the Nepal Risk Reduction Consortium (NRRC) and a Search and Rescue Technical Working Group, composed of government officials, Nepal Security Forces and the Nepal Red Cross, were landmark achievements in preparing for the next disaster in Nepal (Trusilo, 2015). Kathmandu bore, to some extent, similar urban characteristics to Haiti's Port-au-Prince and other high-risk, low-income urban areas with unrestricted population growth, high-density informal settlements and unregulated zoning and construction (Relief Web, 2014).

Recovery is inherently a political process. The chapters in this book focusing on the Chilean earthquake and Typhoon Haiyan (by Allarde and Arrasate, and Stodart respectively) underline the importance of cooperation between local and national government after disasters. Allard and Arrasate (2016) discuss how this cooperation is essential, particularly as programming needs local input, coordination and context to succeed. In both country contexts, decentralization processes had occurred prior to the disasters, yet the challenging complexity of the recovery partnerships demonstrated the 'urgency of participation and inclusion of all stakeholders in the recovery process' (Allard and Arrasate, 2016). When compared to other country housing recovery programs post-disaster, 'Chile's program stands out, combining both top-down strong government management and bottom-up citizens' participation' (Allard and Arrasate, 2016).

While it remains to be seen how the HLP process will conclude in the Philippines due to the (political and financial) value of land, it is undeniable that the slow delivery of government programs was in part due to a lack of communication between the national and local level (Stodart, 2016). With a country of over 7,000 islands, the scale of destruction caused by Typhoon Haiyan posed great urban challenges to the local governments to enforce national government recommendations that were often enacted with little input from the local level (Stodart, 2016).

While communication between local and national government is rarely smooth, there are also cases where communities make opportunities out of a crisis using a predominantly grassroots approach. In the United States, the town of Greensburg, Kansas, experienced a 1.7-mile wide tornado in May 2007, which destroyed 95 percent of its entire infrastructure. In the aftermath, the town of 1,400 people worked together to develop a Sustainable Community Comprehensive Plan for the next 20 years that would make Greensburg a 100 percent renewable energy city. The plan balances the 'economic, ecological and social impacts of development' for Greensburg, reflecting the values of the Greensburg community (Pless et al., 2010). The energy of this small Kansas town serves as another example of how grassroots, community-driven solutions can make towns and cities more sustainable moving into the future (Nguyen and Morris, 2009).

Participation

Valuing local knowledge and capacity, demonstrated in the example of the Bang Bua Canal after the 2011 Bangkok floods (Sitko, 2016), demonstrates that localized solutions for promoting resilience post-disaster are not only needed but foundational to recovery processes. Anderson et al.'s seminal work, 'Time to Listen' (wherein thousands of people caught up in disaster around the world were asked about their experiences of aid), which discusses the idea of smarter aid (instead of more aid), encourages agencies to listen to not only what people are saying on the ground, but to what they did not say (Anderson et al., 2012).

This serves as a reminder that during the rapid assessment phase of a disaster, taking into account the four different types of needs (expressed, comparative, normative and felt needs)[1] and taking stock of local power systems can be crucial in coordinating data and information, and ultimately in determining how best to assist communities. Informal networks are critical to the resilience of urban populations, which often must overcome repeated urban disruptions, such as annual monsoons or flooding (de Boer, 2016). These informal networks are 'rooted in trust,' which can allow communities to respond and bounce back faster after a disaster (de Boer, 2016).

Markets and local economies

Private sector involvement in reconstruction efforts, such as the case of the Marché Hyppolite (the Iron Market) in Haiti's capital city Port-au-Prince, demonstrates the importance of private sector actors as stakeholders, in collaboration with humanitarian organizations and governments (Smith, 2016). Digicel, a large phone provider in Haiti, quickly rebuilt the Market within a year of the earthquake, investing in the local economy, creating employment and boosting the local market (Smith, 2016). Of less tangible but probably equally important value was restoring civic pride. This experience underlines the importance – and potential – for 'traditional' aid actors to engage the private sector in recovery, particularly when urban markets serve as the life-blood of many fragile economies as in Haiti.

Similar to Marché Hyppolite, urban markets can provide efficient entry points for response and recovery (Friedman, 2016). Working with and not against market forces is a core lesson for urban disasters, contributing to the overarching humanitarian goals of 'survival, recovery and restoring dignity' (Friedman, 2016; Sanderson and Knox-Clarke, 2012). Direct and indirect cash transfers, vouchers, and grants in particular are showing promise as being effective mechanisms for response and recovery programming for disaster victims, as the idea of 'market-smart' humanitarian objectives takes hold across multiple agencies (Friedman, 2016). In Jordan for example, Syrian urban refugees were given debit cards for rental assistance, which provided more flexibility and autonomy in how they received aid (Gamer, 2015). Disaster risk mechanisms, such as disaster micro-insurance, hold promise to help reduce the impact of disaster-induced economic losses while building community resilience (Bhatt and Patel, 2016).

An approach that recognizes the importance of the local economy is business continuity planning (BCP) in fragile cities. BCP is composed of the processes necessary for ensuring that businesses can operate as quickly and efficiently as possible in the wake of a disaster. For larger ventures, private companies will often conduct extensive risk analysis to find how they can best position themselves post-disaster. Most small and medium size enterprises in more fragile urban contexts may recognize the need for business continuity planning but often do not have access to the expertise or funding to invest in such programs (Gütermann, 2015). Humanitarian and development actors and funders could invest more in BCP when considering the importance of cross-cutting DRR programs.

Scenario planning

First used in World War II and then by, among others, Royal/Dutch Shell in response to the 1970s oil crisis, scenario planning is a way for varied stakeholders to envision different futures. Scenario planning, when used as a participatory planning process, can inform public policy decisions and facilitate strategic thinking across private, government and community actors (World Vision, 2013; Leis, 2014). Scenario planning is largely considered a time-intensive and challenging process to implement. At the same time, humanitarian actors can use it within the framework of disaster risk reduction and could consider at least three ways of measuring its effectiveness. One method is to use 'backcasting,' as Butina Watson (2016) mentions in her chapter, as a way of looking backwards to predict the future. Furthermore, if scenarios are linked to a broader strategy, such as a city master plan, scenarios can elucidate how response plans could be put into action in the immediate aftermath of a disaster. Lastly, the proper communication of scenarios to the public can greatly improve overall support and boost political will towards expanding the adaptive capacities of cities to respond to shocks and stresses (Leis, 2014). Creating a disaster plan should therefore be considered a product and not the overall goal of disaster preparedness. Effective disaster preparedness relates more to the process of engaging government, the private sector and local communities in the production of such a plan than in the plan itself (Twigg, 2004).

By envisioning the city as a system, humanitarian practitioners can reflect on the overall spatial and morphological structure, as well as patterns of land use (Butina Watson, 2016). Techniques such as scenario planning or backcasting are innovations that could be further integrated into humanitarian practice, as ways of planning for future changes in urban environments, either from man-made or natural causes (Butina Watson, 2016). By envisioning different futures, key actors who have decision-making power could take disaster planning and preparedness to a new level.

Technology

Technological improvements include the use of information and communication technologies (ICT) such as crisis mapping and crowdsourcing (Potvin, 2016). The need for evidence-based and rapid decision-making fostered by technology is clear (Potvin, 2016). Creating technology solutions that have human-centered design, such as rapid assessment and monitoring tools, can improve aid accountability, while new methods of delivery such as mobile cash transfers can reduce transaction costs and provide greater choice among those receiving aid. However, while streamlined information can improve communication between humanitarian actors and affected populations on the ground, it is a problematic assumption that such information will 'heroically level the unequal power relations between those who give and those who receive aid' (Potvin, 2016).

Looking ahead

Urban humanitarian practice surely warrants further study and research. Business as usual, in the face of increasing naturally induced disasters, conflicts and the impact of climate change will be challenged in densely populated urban areas, but the urban condition also presents an opportunity for embracing resilience approaches.

Note

1 Felt needs are what an individual says he or she wants. Expressed needs refer to what are demonstrated through action. Comparative needs are based on what one group may have as compared to another that does not. Normative needs are based on what experts dictate those needs are, based on evidence.

References

Achenbach, J. (2015). Experts had warned for decades that Nepal was vulnerable to a killer quake. *The Washington Post*, 25 April. Available at: www.washingtonpost.com/national/health-science/experts-had-warned-for-decades-that-nepal-was-vulnerable-to-a-killer-quake/2015/04/25/0275959e-eb78-11e4-9a6a-c1ab95a0600b_story.html (accessed July 30, 2015).

Allard, P. and Arrasate, M. (2016). Fables from the reconstruction: lessons from Chile's recovery after the 2010 earthquake and tsunami. In Sanderson, D., Kayden, J. and Leis, J. (2016), *Urban Disaster Resilience: New Dimensions from International Practice in the Built Environment*. New York: Routledge.

Almukhtar, A. (2016). Conflict and urban displacement: the impact on Kurdish place-identity in Erbil, Iraq. In Sanderson, D., Kayden, J. and Leis, J. (2016), *Urban Disaster Resilience: New Dimensions from International Practice in the Built Environment*. New York: Routledge.

Anderson, M., Brown, D., and Jean, I. (2012). *Time to Listen: Hearing People on the Receiving End of International Aid.* Cambridge, MA: CDA Collaborative Learning Projects. Available at: http://cdacollaborative.org/media/60478/Time-to-Listen-Book.pdf.

Bhatt, M. and Patel, R. (2016). Using disaster insurance to build urban resilience: lessons from micro-enterprise in India. In Sanderson, D., Kayden, J. and Leis, J. (2016), *Urban Disaster Resilience: New Dimensions from International Practice in the Built Environment.* New York: Routledge.

Butina Watson, G. (2016). Designing resilient cities and neighborhoods. In Sanderson, D., Kayden, J. and Leis, J. (2016), *Urban Disaster Resilience: New Dimensions from International Practice in the Built Environment.* New York: Routledge.

Catholic Relief Services (CRS) (2013). *Camp Closures through Market-Based Cash Transfers for Rental Subsidies: The Case from Haiti, 2010.* Available at: http://static1.1.sqspcdn.com/static/f/752898/23513484/1379342273683/haiti-camp-closures-market-based-cash-transfers.pdf?token=AX9qli63YdZhWQUZ558nNHwc2mo%3D (accessed August 15, 2015).

De Boer, J. (2016). Risk, resilience and the fragile city. In Sanderson, D., Kayden, J. and Leis, J. (2016), *Urban Disaster Resilience: New Dimensions from International Practice in the Built Environment.* New York: Routledge.

Fitzgerald, E. (2012). *Helping Families, Closing Camp.* E-Shelter & CCCM Cluster Returns Working Group. Available at: www.eshelter-cccmhaiti.info/jl/pdf/Helping_Families_Closing_Camps2.pdf (accessed September 5, 2015).

Friedman, J. (2016). Linking response, recovery and resilience to markets in humanitarian action. In Sanderson, D., Kayden, J. and Leis, J. (2016), *Urban Disaster Resilience: New Dimensions from International Practice in the Built Environment.* New York: Routledge.

Gamer, N. (2015). *Syrian Refugees Test Debit Card Aid.* Catholic Relief Services, May 20. Available at: www.crs.org/stories/syrian-refugees-test-debit-card-aid (accessed July 30, 2015).

GeoHazards International (2015). *Nepal Earthquake.* Available at: http://geohaz.org/nepal-earthquake (accessed September 5, 2015).

Goldberg, M. (2015). Aid groups knew a Nepal earthquake would be a disaster. But they couldn't raise enough money to help. *The Washington Post*, April 27. Available at: www.washingtonpost.com/posteverything/wp/2015/04/27/aid-groups-knew-an-earthquake-in-nepal-would-be-a-disaster-they-also-knew-they-could-never-raise-enough-money-to-help/ (accessed July 30, 2015).

Gütermann, N. (2015). The chance to make a difference. *Continuity.* Available at: www.bcifiles.com/Q32015.pdf#page=10 (accessed September 5, 2015).

Katz, J. (2015). How not to report an earthquake. *The New York Times Magazine*, April 28. Available at: www.nytimes.com/2015/04/28/magazine/how-not-to-report-on-an-earthquake.html?_r=1 (accessed September 5, 2015).

Kete, N. (2014). *A Framework for Articulating City Resilience.* The Rockefeller Foundation, April 10. Available at: www.rockefellerfoundation.org/blog/framework-articulating-city-resilience/ (accessed July 27, 2015).

Killing, A. and Boano, C. (2016). Reconstructing the city: the potential gains of using urban planning and design practices in recovery and why they are so difficult to achieve. In Sanderson, D., Kayden, J. and Leis, J. (2016), *Urban Disaster Resilience: New Dimensions from International Practice in the Built Environment.* New York: Routledge.

Ledwith, A. (2014). *Zaatari: The Instant City.* Boston: Affordable Housing Institute. Available at: www.affordablehousinginstitute.org/storage/images/AHI-Publication-Zaatari-The-Instant-City-Low-Res-PDF-141120.pdf (accessed September 4, 2015).

Leis, J. (2014). *Scenario Planning: Implications for Improving Urban Disaster Risk Reduction in Africa.* Master Thesis, The Fletcher School of Law and Diplomacy at Tufts University, Medford, MA.

Nguyen, B. and Morris, J. (2009). After tornado, town rebuilds by echoing green. CNN, 4 May. Available at: www.cnn.com/2009/TECH/science/04/29/green.kansas.town/index.html?eref=ib_us (accessed July 30, 2015).

Pless, S., Billman, L. and Wallach, D. (2010). *From Tragedy To Triumph: Rebuilding Greensburg, Kansas, To Be a 100% Renewable Energy City.* Presented at ACEEE Summary Study, Pacific Grove, CA, August 15–20. Available at: http://energy.gov/sites/prod/files/2013/11/f5/48300.pdf (accessed July 25, 2014).

Potvin, M. (2016). 'Humanitarian hybrids': new technologies and humanitarian resilience. In Sanderson, D., Kayden, J. and Leis, J. (2016), *Urban Disaster Resilience: New Dimensions from International Practice in the Built Environment.* New York: Routledge.

Relief Web (2014). How to save those who survive the next mega-earthquake in Nepal. Available at: http://reliefweb.int/sites/reliefweb.int/files/resources/SAR%20Nepal%20Article%20small.pdf (accessed September 4, 2015).

Sanderson, D. and Knox-Clarke, P. (2012). *Responding to Urban Disasters: Learning from Previous Relief and Recovery Operations,* ALNAP Lessons Paper. London: ODI.

Sanderson, D., Rodericks, A. and Shresta, N. (2015). *Nepal Earthquake Appeal Response Review.* London and Ottawa: DEC and HC.

Sitko, P. (2016). Urban disaster resilience: learning from the 2011 Bangkok, Thailand, flood using morphology and complex adaptive systems. In Sanderson, D., Kayden, J. and Leis, J. (2016), *Urban Disaster Resilience: New Dimensions from International Practice in the Built Environment.* New York: Routledge.

Smith, D. (2016). Petty trade and the private sector in urban reconstruction: learning from Haiti's post-earthquake Iron Market. In Sanderson, D., Kayden, J. and Leis, J. (2016), *Urban Disaster Resilience: New Dimensions from International Practice in the Built Environment.* New York: Routledge.

Stodart, V. (2016). Regulatory barriers and the provision of shelter in post disaster situations: housing, land and property (HLP) issues in the recovery of Tacloban, the Philippines, after 2013 Typhoon Haiyan. In Sanderson, D., Kayden, J. and Leis, J. (2016), *Urban Disaster Resilience: New Dimensions from International Practice in the Built Environment.* New York: Routledge.

Trusilo, D. (2015). *Nepal: Strength Through Community.* Fulbright Student Program Blog. Available at: http://blog.fulbrightonline.org/from-west-point-to-kathmandu/ (accessed July 30, 2015).

Twigg, J. (2004). Disaster risk reduction: mitigation and preparedness in aid programming. *The Good Practice Review*, ODI. Available at: www.odihpn.org/hpn-resources/good-practice-reviews/disaster-risk-reduction-mitigation-and-preparedness-in-aid-programming (accessed September 3, 2015).

Weston, P. (2015). Inside Zaatari refugee camp: the fourth largest city in Jordan. *The Telegraph*, 5 August. Available at: www.telegraph.co.uk/news/worldnews/middleeast/jordan/11782770/What-is-life-like-inside-the-largest-Syrian-refugee-camp-Zaatari-in-Jordan.html (accessed September 3, 2015).

World Vision UK (2013). *Participatory Scenario Planning for Community Resilience.* September. Available at: http://9bb63f6dda0f744fa444-9471a7fca5768cc513a2e3c4a260910b.r43.cf3.rackcdn.com/files/9813/7871/8703/Planning_For_Community_Resilience.pdf (accessed October 2013).

Index

Note: Page numbers followed by 'f' refer to figures.